HOUSING AND LIFE COURSE DYNAMICS

Changing Lives, Places and Inequalities

Rory Coulter

D1612598

First published in Great Britain in 2023 by

Policy Press, an imprint of
Bristol University Press
University of Bristol
1–9 Old Park Hill
Bristol
BS2 8BB
UK
t: +44 (0)117 374 6645
e: bup-info@bristol.ac.uk

Details of international sales and distribution partners are available at
policy.bristoluniversitypress.co.uk

British Library Cataloguing in Publication Data
A catalogue record for this book is available from the British Library

ISBN 978-1-4473-5766-7 hardcover
ISBN 978-1-4473-5767-4 paperback
ISBN 978-1-4473-5768-1 ePub
ISBN 978-1-4473-5769-8 ePdf

Cover design: Robin Hawes
Front cover image: iStock/kev303
Bristol University Press and Policy Press use environmentally responsible print partners.
Printed and bound in Great Britain by CPI Group (UK) Ltd, Croydon, CR0 4YY

FSC
www.fsc.org
MIX
Paper | Supporting
responsible forestry
FSC® C013604

To Jennifer, for everything.

Contents

List of figures and tables

List of abbreviations

APS	Annual Population Survey
BHPS	British Household Panel Survey
CDRC	Consumer Data Research Centre
DCLG	Department for Communities and Local Government (now DLUHC)
DfE	Department for Education
DLUHC	Department for Levelling Up, Housing and Communities (formerly MHCLG)
DWP	Department for Work and Pensions
ER	Escalator region
FCA	Financial Conduct Authority
GDP	Gross domestic product
GFC	Global Financial Crisis
HE	Higher education
HEI	Higher education institution
HESA	Higher Education Statistics Agency
HOP	Housing as opportunity
ICTs	Information and communication technologies
IFS	Institute for Fiscal Studies
LAT	Living apart together
LFS	Labour Force Survey
MHCLG	Ministry of Housing, Communities and Local Government (now DLUHC)
OECD	Organisation for Economic Co-operation and Development
ONS	Office for National Statistics
PRS	Private rented sector
SAR	Shared Accommodation Rate
SDT	Second Demographic Transition
UKHLS	United Kingdom Household Longitudinal Study (Understanding Society)

Notes on the author

Rory Coulter is Associate Professor of human geography at University College London where his teaching spans population, urban and economic geography as well as quantitative methods. His research examines population mobility, housing dynamics and neighbourhood change. This is his first book.

Acknowledgements

This book contains secondary analysis of microdata accessed through the UK Data Service. Neither the UK Data Service nor the following data collectors bear any responsibility for the analysis or interpretations presented in this book.

Annual Population Survey

The Annual Population Survey (APS) is produced by the Office for National Statistics (ONS). The research data are distributed by the UK Data Service. Crown copyright material is reproduced with the permission of the Controller of HMSO and the Queen's Printer for Scotland.

British Household Panel Survey and Understanding Society

The British Household Panel Survey (BHPS) is produced by the Institute for Social and Economic Research, University of Essex, with the support of the Economic and Social Research Council. The research data are distributed by the UK Data Service. Understanding Society is an initiative funded by the Economic and Social Research Council and various government departments, with scientific leadership by the Institute for Social and Economic Research, University of Essex, and survey delivery by NatCen Social Research and Kantar Public. The research data are distributed by the UK Data Service.

Labour Force Survey

The Labour Force Survey (LFS) is produced by the ONS and the Northern Ireland Statistics and Research Agency. The research data are distributed by the UK Data Service. Crown copyright material is reproduced with the permission of the Controller of HMSO and the Queen's Printer for Scotland.

Preface

Take a moment to conjure up some of your earliest childhood memories. Now spend a little time running through the whole sweep of your life in your mind's eye. Finally, try visualising what sort of life you expect, or hope, to be living a few years hence.

The chances are that while doing this, your mind has touched on images relating to what this book refers to as your housing career: in essence the succession of households, dwellings and places that each of us lives in through time. You may even have thought about how aspects of your housing career have related to things going on elsewhere in your life, such as your work or your relationships with others. This simple and highly personal exercise thus reminds us that housing is integral to the course of our lives and so people need to be placed centre-stage in both research and debates about housing issues. Yet frequently this is not the case as markets and government policies tend to dominate much of the intellectual and public conversation about the housing problems that today afflict much of the Global North.

This book aims to bring the dynamics of people's lives to the heart of how we think, study and talk about housing. It does this by exploring how who we are matters for our housing and how housing helps make us into who we are. The book develops a modern life course framework to explore how residential decisions are made, how housing shapes lives, and how these processes interact with changes in local populations and in the broader structure of societies. A core argument is that housing in the 21st century both reflects and helps amplify inequalities, not only of wealth and prosperity, but also across health, employment, education and in family life.

The catalyst for writing this book was my growing dissatisfaction with existing work on housing and the life course. These frustrations are neither about the quantity of research (there is an awful lot of it!) nor its quality. Rather, my main concern – exposed time and again while teaching – is that work in this area is far too fragmented. In one sense this is understandable. Not only is housing an interdisciplinary topic, but the competitive institutional pressures of today's universities strongly incentivise the rapid-fire production of short research papers. Yet while detailed empirical evidence on specific issues is undoubtedly essential for any field to progress, so too are wider-ranging overviews which integrate evidence and synthesise it into overarching frameworks that can inform how we think about a topic, guide the questions we ask and steer how we go about answering them. In writing this book, I have thus sought to integrate and synthesise what we know about housing and life course dynamics as the first quarter of the 21st century draws to a close. To help do this, the book outlines a toolbox of twelve life course concepts which can be applied to better understand housing issues. These tools are designed to be flexible and amenable to being used in diverse ways tailored to the needs of a wide variety of research and review projects. As with all toolboxes, there may be some missing or even some faulty tools in the toolbox I present; but hopefully my twelve will at the very least serve as a handy starter kit for others to test, alter and improve on as necessary.

The book's wide-ranging brief means that astute readers will no doubt spot gaps, simplifications and probably lapses of nuance. These are perhaps inevitable as my main objective is to provide a synthetic overview rather than a comprehensive review of everything that has ever been published on these topics. I have tried to honestly set out what the book does and does not cover in Chapter 1.

On a personal level, writing this book has been a rather more eventful life course process than I originally envisaged. In the three years it has taken to go from proposal to book I have become a parent, had a second child, moved home twice, bought one house and muddled through several COVID-19 lockdown spells of working from home. Taken together, these events have significantly impacted on the time and energy I have been able to devote to the book and they may also have shaped its contents. I have, however, tried to avoid writing much about the pandemic as I think it is still too early to assess anything more than its most immediate housing consequences.

Many people have improved my thinking on these topics by selflessly sharing their time and expertise over the years. Of these I'd particularly like to acknowledge Sait Bayrakdar, Bill Clark, Allan Findlay, Yang Hu, Paul Longley, Isabel Palomares-Linares, Karen Mak, Jackie Scott, Michael Thomas and Maarten van Ham. My thanks also go out to the book's anonymous reviewers for providing many valuable suggestions for improvement. Finally, I am grateful to UCL Geography for providing sabbatical time and, of course, to my students, whose probing questions and superb independent research have so often pushed my work in new directions. I hope this book will serve a useful resource for future generations of students interested in understanding housing's place in 21st-century societies.

I now leave it to readers to judge the final product, for which I alone am ultimately responsible.

1

Introduction

Over the last twenty years, housing has risen up the policy agenda to become a priority issue for Global North governments. This transformation has been driven by a growing consensus that housing systems are in crisis. This crisis is thought to have many interrelated components – ranging from physical problems of supply and dwelling quality through to social issues of housing access, affordability and security – the precise blend of which varies from place to place. In Britain, much of the contemporary housing debate focuses on the origins of an affordability crisis and how to get more homes built.

Yet housing is clearly not in a state of crisis for everyone. Many people are satisfied with their homes, have enough space, have few problems paying for housing and are able to move to somewhere they want to live at a time broadly of their choosing. Some have also made a lot of money from the housing market over the years. As a result, there is a growing public awareness that inequalities between generations, between people living in different places and along axes such as class and ethnicity are defining features of contemporary housing crises.

Understanding and addressing these inequalities requires thoroughly grasping how housing is embedded into the multifaceted dynamics of people's lives. Yet as Clapham (2005) argued nearly twenty years ago, the housing field's tendency to focus on systemic issues (such as planning and supply, state policy, housing finance, market dynamics and so forth) means that much analysis views people simply as passively responding to contextual stimuli. While such approaches clearly have heuristic value for describing how contexts influence very general patterns of behaviour, they leave little room for the agency, aspirations, preferences, life events and interwoven social relationships that we all know from our own experiences have a major bearing on residential decisions and experiences.

This book's objective is to bring the dynamics of people's lives to the heart of how we think about housing and inequality in the 21st century. It aims to show how who we are matters for our housing and how housing helps make us into who we are. In this context, 'who we are' refers both to the dynamic course of our individual lives and also to the characteristics of the collective social units we belong to, such as our families and local communities. To help understand these issues, the book develops a modern life course framework for integrating, synthesising and extending what we know about how people live in and move between dwellings, neighbourhoods and localities as their

Figure 1.1: Housing behaviour connects changing lives, places and societies

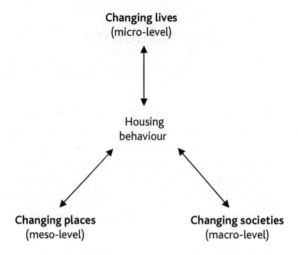

lives unfold. It argues that understanding these residential behaviours is important as the housing decisions people make as their lives change play important roles in local population dynamics and in reconfiguring the wider structure of society (Figure 1.1).

Although this is far from the first time that life course perspectives have been applied to housing issues, the book's framework is designed to address two weaknesses with previous literature. First, existing research is scattered across the social sciences and is often written as short empirical articles. Most of these examine either a specialised subtopic or instead concentrate on a particular life phase, such as young adulthood. This fragmentation means that we lack a synthetic overarching understanding of how people move through housing systems as their lives change in diverse ways across the entire life span.

Second, the most influential life course texts on housing such as Clark and Dieleman's *Households and Housing* (1996) or Beer and Faulkner's *Housing Transitions through the Life Course* (2011) are in urgent need of an update to take into account recent developments in societies, data resources, research methods and life course scholarship. In particular, neither these volumes nor many more recent contributions engage with some of the key concepts in modern life course thought such as the importance of considering how people's lives are 'linked' together by ties and bonds such as kinship (Coulter et al, 2016). This is perhaps unsurprising as housing is notable by its absence from recent overviews of life course sociology (for example Shanahan and colleagues' (2016) *Handbook of the Life Course: Volume II*).

At this point it is important to note that this book's life course framework is not intended to form a predictive model or grand explanatory theory. Instead, the framework is designed as a flexible approach or perspective which can be applied – in conjunction with middle-range theories of specific processes and sometimes other conceptual framings – to help understand how housing is embedded into the dynamics of people's lives and how these processes interact with broader social and spatial changes. The starting point for the book's approach are Glen Elder's five classic life course principles of life span development, timing, linked lives, agency, historical time and geographic place (Elder et al, 2003). These principles are used to derive twelve conceptual tools applicable to a huge range of housing-related topics. The overarching aim is for these twelve tools to create a shared life course conceptual framework which analysts can use to collect and integrate evidence, synthesise it and thus improve our understanding of how housing is unevenly embedded into 21st-century lives.

The rest of this chapter provides an introduction to the book. The next section summarises the principal ways in which housing matters for people's lives. The different functions of housing summarised here impinge on everyone's life in some way over the whole life span. Next, the chapter sketches how shifts in the macro-structure of societies alter aggregate patterns of residential behaviour by shaping housing-related aspirations and preferences, the events and transitions people experience, their resources and restrictions, and the opportunities and constraints they encounter (Mulder and Hooimeijer, 1999). This section is succinct as these issues are explored in much greater depth throughout the subsequent chapters. Thorough descriptions of the transformations of Global North housing systems as well as discussions of housing policy and supply are available elsewhere and so these topics are not covered here (Bowie, 2017; Lund, 2017; Clark, 2021).

The functions of housing

Housing has many functions that make it integral to human well-being. On a biophysical level, shelter lay towards the base of Maslow's hierarchy of needs and access to decent housing is essential for attaining the right to an adequate standard of living enshrined in Article 25 of the 1948 Universal Declaration of Human Rights. Yet the presence of homelessness in advanced economies indicates that even this most basic function of housing is not always fulfilled. For instance, in England official estimates suggest that over 4,000 people were sleeping rough on autumn nights from 2016 to 2019, while thousands of households with children were simultaneously living in temporary accommodation (MHCLG, 2021a).

Housing and prosperity

The functions of housing extend beyond the biophysical to the economic sphere. Housing costs in the form of rent or mortgage payments are typically one of the largest regular outgoings in household budgets and this means that how much people pay for housing helps determine the resources they expend and amass across the life span. Differences in the accumulated lifetime housing costs paid by people living in different places and divided *inter alia* by birth cohort, class, ethnicity and tenure can thus generate resource inequalities over the life course. For example, in 2019–20 English owner-occupiers devoted an average of 18 per cent of their household income to mortgage repayments, while social and private tenants on average spent 27 and 32 per cent of their respective incomes on rent (MHCLG, 2020a). These national figures mask much higher proportions in expensive locales such as Greater London. The economic advantages of mortgaged homeownership have generally increased since the 2008 Global Financial Crisis (GFC) as until recently central banks have maintained ultra-low interest rates while house prices and rents have risen and housing benefit support for tenants has been cut.

Understanding how housing costs affect patterns of prosperity requires examining who receives households' housing payments, particularly within the rental sector. In Britain this has changed dramatically in recent decades. In 1981, councils owned 69 per cent of rental dwellings and the large flows of rent within this sector were thus socialised for collective benefit (MHCLG, 2019a). However, the expansion of small-scale private renting since the late 1990s, combined with a steady decline in the stock of social housing to under 50 per cent of rental dwellings in 2017, means that much larger flows of rent and increased volumes of housing benefit are now channelled to private landlords. As many British landlords are older and drawn from relatively affluent social strata, this privatisation of rent has helped deepen economic inequality across birth cohorts and social groups (Ronald and Kadi, 2018). Indeed, the growth of small-scale private renting is perhaps the main way that millions of ordinary people are today participating in what Christophers (2019) terms the 'rentierization' of Britain's economy.

Housing is an investment commodity as well as a service and so plays a central role in wealth inequalities (Arundel, 2017). The expansion of homeownership and synchronised general trends of real house price inflation that have characterised many Global North countries through recent decades mean that housing is now most households' main asset (Lowe, 2011). Estimates by ONS (2022a) indicate that British households held £5.5 trillion of property wealth in 2018–20, up by around a fifth on 2014–16 figures. Although property wealth is more evenly distributed than financial assets or pension wealth, on average the least wealthy 30 per cent of British households have no property assets while those in the wealthiest 10 per cent hold more than £500,000 apiece in property (ONS, 2022a). Housing wealth also has a distinct geography with higher stocks in London and southern England than in northern areas.

Housing and access to opportunities

For most people, their residential location(s) act as spatially fixed node(s) around which daily mobility behaviours are organised. The location of one's dwelling(s) therefore structures access to the opportunities provided by workplaces, healthcare facilities, shops, schools and social and cultural facilities (Clark, 2021). In addition, residential location matters for exposure to amenities like green space, as well as environmental hazards such as air and noise pollution.

The spatial fixity of housing has important consequences for exposure to risks and access to opportunities. First, deciding where to live is often very complex, especially when the potentially competing access needs of multiple household members must be accommodated. People often try to circumvent this problem by engaging in mobility substitution. This involves using other physical and virtual mobility practices such as commutes or teleworking to access opportunities in other places without moving home (Green, 2018). However, factors like resource access and gendered divisions of household labour can limit who is able to engage in these types of substitution behaviours. As we have seen during the COVID-19 pandemic, disparities in, for example, who can work from home may ultimately deepen social inequalities.

Second, people's differential ability to exercise effective housing choice – defined as selecting a preferred option from among distinct alternatives (Brown and King, 2005) – influences their access to opportunities and exposure to risks. This can create local and sometimes self-reinforcing patterns of inequality. For example, high house prices in the catchment areas of high-performing schools may lead to pupil 'selection by mortgage' as children from less affluent backgrounds are priced out of attendance. In general, those with more resources have a greater capacity to exercise effective housing choice by buying access to more costly homes located in opportunity-rich locations.

Housing and social relations

Housing is a fundamentally social space that does more than just provide a site for social reproduction. Instead, housing plays an active role in social life by functioning as what Saunders and Williams (1988, p 83) termed a 'constitutive element' in social relations. Essentially this means that dwelling attributes (size, design, layout and so forth) as well as neighbourhood characteristics help configure people's relationships and interactions with others. This is a fundamentally relational process as social practices in turn influence how housing is experienced and imbued with meaning.

The socially constitutive function of housing is perhaps most obvious within the family practices shaping and sustaining kin relationships over the life course (Holdsworth, 2013). For example, the stress generated by falling into housing payment arrears has been shown to elevate the risk that couples separate, even after controlling for the confounding effects of financial hardship (Coulter and Thomas, 2019). Housing is also integral to vertical intergenerational relations across elongated 21st-century life courses. Three examples of this will suffice here. First, contemporary younger adults trying to overcome the monetary barriers to leaving home and entering homeownership often rely on financial transfers from parents or grandparents. Such support practices can reshape intergenerational relations in complex and ambiguous ways, for example if filial gratitude conflicts with feelings of indebtedness and unwanted dependence (Druta and Ronald, 2017). Second, people's ability to exchange (child)care and physical support with non-resident kin is shaped by their residential proximity to one another, which can influence migration behaviour (Mulder, 2018). Third, later-life care demands are influenced by current housing circumstances and the availability of suitable alternatives. For example, an older person ageing in a large rural home may need more everyday physical support than an otherwise identical peer who previously downsized to a supported flat with lift access. Access to housing wealth may further help determine the form (for example private or family provision) and quality of the later-life care people receive.

Housing, personal life and identity

On one level, housing functions as a highly visible site for the social construction of personal identities. Interior décor, furnishings, layout and so on, along with external features like design, upkeep and the style of gardens or yards, as well as the characteristics of the local area, are all important for the construction and display of identities and status (Saunders and Williams, 1988). Clapham (2005) has argued that the growing significance people attach to lifestyle preferences means that satisfying housing goals through these types of consumption practices has become a key life aim for many people. However, not everyone has the same inclination or capacity to do this. For instance, renters with little control over their dwelling and people with fewer resources are less able to use housing to satisfy lifestyle goals than affluent homeowners.

Housing and the places people live in are also deeply imbued with meanings and attachments which change over time (Clapham, 2005). Many qualitative studies have explored how people in different material circumstances become attached to places and use objects to turn their dwellings into homes that are imbued with emotional significance and act as repositories for memories (Atkinson and Jacobs, 2016). Social relationships are integral to these processes of homemaking as objects like photographs or displayed gifts write the presence of significant others into domestic space. Although, for some, home is a threatening space, for example those experiencing neglect or domestic abuse, for most the home is an intensely private place where people feel they are in control and not under surveillance (intriguingly, perhaps, despite the presence of virtual home assistants like Alexa). In Saunders' (1990) terms, home typically provides a space of comfort and ontological security where people can escape from an otherwise stressful social milieu. This makes access to secure, affordable and high-quality housing in a desirable location a very important precondition for psychological well-being.

The drivers of residential behaviour

These wide-ranging functions of housing mean that any attempt to understand contemporary inequalities needs to consider residential behaviour and the forces that impact on the types of dwellings and places people live in over the life course. Figure 1.2 identifies four constellations of macro-level forces which influence housing behaviours and the structure of longer-term housing careers – economic processes, demography, public policies and culture (all crosscut to varying degrees by technological change) – with the outer diamond highlighting their interconnections and overlaps. The figure shows that the effect that each of these drivers has on patterns of residential behaviour is mediated and filtered by the institutional characteristics that have evolved over time in a given society; for example its education and welfare systems, laws, political institutions and the composition and governance of its housing stock (Lowe, 2011). As we shall see in later chapters, this is not a one-way process, as changing residential behaviours in turn transform places and the structure of society.

Listed inside the outer diamond of Figure 1.2 are four mechanisms or pathways through which these macro-scale forces actually influence micro-level residential behaviours (see Mulder and Hooimeijer (1999) for an earlier formulation). These four mechanisms can be considered the *proximate determinants* of changing housing behaviours as it is through them that macro-scale forces impact on how people move through the housing system (Bernard et al, 2016). In essence, what this means is that changes in economic conditions, demography, policies and culture alter how people live in and move between dwellings by shaping their (1) residential preferences and aspirations, (2) household resources and restrictions, (3) the events and transitions they experience, and (4) the broader patterns of opportunity and constraint they encounter (Mulder and Hooimeijer, 1999). These four macro-level drivers and the four mechanisms through which they alter residential behaviours are now sketched briefly and explored further throughout the subsequent chapters.

Figure 1.2: Conceptualising the drivers of housing behaviour

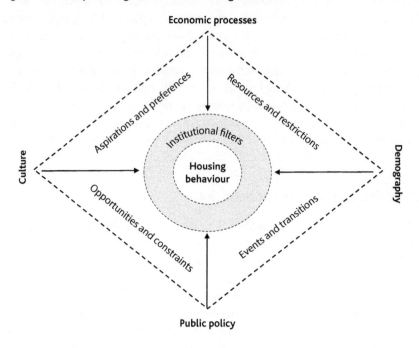

Economic processes

Residential behaviours are strongly influenced by economic forces and the ways these change over time and are governed by supranational organisations (for example the European Union), national governments and sub-national institutions (such as local governments). The economic processes which matter for housing behaviour can be broadly grouped into two interrelated clusters: those relating to labour markets, on the one hand, and to housing markets on the other.

Labour markets and the ways these vary geographically and change over the business cycle and across longer timescales shape residential behaviour in several ways. First, patterns of *participation in paid work* influence the resources people have to spend on housing as well as the degree of spatial constraint they face in deciding where to live. Across the Global North, employment trajectories and internal migration patterns have changed considerably in recent decades as young adults delay workforce entry to prolong their education. Rates of female employment have also risen sharply and in Britain the proportion of women aged 16 to 64 in paid employment rose from 53 per cent in 1971 to 72 per cent in 2021 (ONS, 2022b). This trend has greatly increased the proportion of dual-earner couples as the male breadwinner household becomes less common. Although having both partners in work boosts household income, the need to access two workplaces from one hub location means that the residential decisions of dual-earner couples (particularly highly skilled dual-career couples) are typically more spatially constrained than those of couples where only one partner does paid work (Green, 2018).

This indicates that the *sectoral and spatial distribution of jobs* is a second way in which the structure of labour markets shapes locational decisions and the local housing opportunities and constraints (for example available tenures or prices) people encounter when they look to move. These labour market structures have changed hugely over the last fifty years with the globalisation and deindustrialisation of Global North economies. For example, the growth of skilled professional work in the UK's enlarged service economy – particularly in the quaternary sector – has been concentrated in large cities (Champion et al, 2014) as well as around some university cities such as Cambridge and Oxford. By contrast, job opportunities for skilled knowledge workers are much scarcer in the ex-industrial and mining areas, port cities and coastal towns that have lost out during deindustrialisation.

The spatial concentration of highly skilled professional roles into agglomerative centres constrains the locational and housing options of people entering or working in these sectors to a greater extent than people working in more spatially ubiquitous sectors such as construction, health or teaching. Growth in the number of professional workers with higher educational qualifications could thus drive up overall rates of long-distance job-oriented migration (Green, 2018), although post-COVID-19 shifts towards homeworking may partially offset this trend. By contrast, reduced regional disparities in wages, sectoral specialisation and unemployment rates might be dampening the incentives for less qualified workers to migrate over longer distances (Judge, 2019).

Finally, labour markets influence housing behaviour through their effects on *incomes and economic security*. A large literature has shown that incomes and employment security influence housing demands and condition the size, type, quality, tenure and neighbourhood location of the dwelling choice set accessible to households (Clark and Dieleman, 1996). In part this is because lenders and landlords usually require applicants to demonstrate that they have a stable income before they can be considered for a mortgage or tenancy.

There have been major shifts in incomes and economic security across the Global North since the post-war Golden Age of Capitalism unravelled in the early 1970s. On one hand, real income growth for much of the population has slowed, stagnated or reversed while the distribution of economic resources has become much more unequal. According to Arundel and Doling (2017) and Christophers (2018), low levels of homeownership among the millennial cohort born 1980–2000 can be largely attributed to the way that globalisation and neoliberal policies (for instance curbs on labour bargaining power) have suppressed their earnings and job security.

At the same time, economic risks have intensified as states have cut public welfare provision and responded to globalisation by pushing 'flexible' labour markets characterised by the decline of structured occupational careers and new expectations that workers must retrain and change jobs throughout their working lives. Whereas unemployment during a downturn was the main economic risk facing 20th-century households, in recent years low UK unemployment rates have masked the growth of new forms of in-work precarity and working poverty.[1] These problems have developed alongside the 'hollowing out' of labour markets that has accompanied deindustrialisation (Arundel and Doling, 2017). This hollowing out has involved a decline of skilled clerical and manufacturing jobs and the growth of polarised forms of service sector work: well-paid and fairly secure professional occupations alongside precarious and poorly paid forms of less skilled employment, self-employment, part-time and casual 'gig' work. While the former group have a more favourable position in the housing system, the unstable employment and low incomes of the latter limit their residential options and could enforce dependence on local social networks (Preece, 2018). Policy efforts to create flexible labour markets may thus paradoxically have increased residential rootedness.

Looking beyond the world of work, the dynamics of housing markets and the decisions of the institutions that shape them (especially governments and central banks) have significant economic effects on residential behaviour. However, the relative importance of these forces varies internationally with (1) the relative size of a country's market and non-market housing sectors, (2) how strongly these sectors are integrated into global financial markets (sometimes termed the degree of housing financialisation) as well as (3) the extent of other state demand- and supply-side housing finance interventions (for example the level of benefit support or the provision of supply subsidies). In the UK, the common practice of labelling the housing system a singular housing market is something of a misnomer as around 17 per cent of dwellings are socially rented. Although the socially rented sector has shrunk and become more marketised since its heyday, rents are still pegged below market levels and housing is still allocated bureaucratically on the basis of needs.

Perhaps the most obvious path by which housing markets influence residential behaviour is the way that the *price and affordability of housing constrains locational, tenure and dwelling selection*. In addition, prospective movers require vacancies and so the volume of transactions and the rate of new construction – both of which usually track the business cycle – are important additional constraints. Figure 1.3 shows how average house prices have changed since 2000 across the UK's component countries. Price uplift has been especially pronounced in England (particularly in London and southern areas) while volatility has been exceptional in Northern Ireland.

Although prices fell in all countries through the GFC years, the crash was particularly extreme in Northern Ireland while Scottish and Welsh prices have recovered much more slowly since 2008 than prices in England. Similar trends of real house price inflation that is outstripping wage growth and being accompanied by rent inflation have been documented across the Global North and there is now a lively debate about the forces responsible for this synchronicity (Lowe, 2011).

Shifts in the price of housing in different tenures also affect residential behaviour by altering *household resources*. Meen (2013) argues that the rapid inflation of house prices shown in Figure 1.3 has created a 'financial accelerator' that enables existing owners – particularly those owning large dwellings in high-demand areas – to accumulate huge stocks of equity. This gives them insider advantages in the housing market as first-time buyers are increasingly squeezed out by mortgage lenders' deposit and income requirements. Equity stocks and the borrowing they enable also allow affluent owners to venture into buy-to-let, second home ownership and supporting their children's housing market entry through *inter vivos* transfers (Forrest and Hirayama, 2018). However, although housing prices have trended upwards through recent decades, history cautions that credit-fuelled homeownership is risky as it ties households into the movements of global finance and exposes them to interest rate fluctuations (Smith et al,

Figure 1.3: National trends in average nominal UK house prices, 2000–20

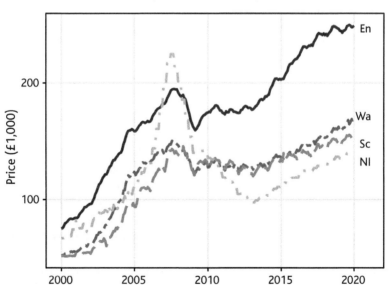

Source: Based on UK House Price Index data (HM Land Registry, 2021). Contains HM Land Registry data © Crown copyright and database right 2020. This data is licensed under the Open Government Licence v3.0.

2009). House prices often fall during a slump and this can have damaging consequences for overstretched households which may become trapped by negative equity (Hamnett, 1999).

Finally, housing market dynamics shape residential behaviour through their effects on *housing preferences and aspirations*. The strong past performance of property assets has fuelled the development of a conventional British wisdom that homeownership is a good investment. A combination of hopes and fears that house prices will inflate thus motivates younger households to prioritise entering homeownership and view long-term renting as a waste of money. These tenure perceptions are reinforced by reduced public welfare provision, encouraging people to become 'investor citizens' who need to accumulate private assets to buffer against the financial consequences of life course shocks (for example the onset of health problems), to offset meagre public pensions and to pay for later-life care (Smith et al, 2009). This may then legitimate further cuts to public welfare provision, illustrating the bidirectional links between housing behaviours and the political-economic system.

Demography

Shifts in the size, composition and distribution of population affect residential behaviours in the aggregate by changing housing demands and altering the timing and types of the demographic events people experience. Across Europe, the housing stock is relatively inelastic and typically responds slowly to these demand-side shifts (Mulder, 2006). This is largely because housing is a spatially fixed durable good that is capital intensive and time-consuming to produce. The high costs and slow pace of construction means that newly built units usually form only a small fraction of the total dwelling stock. For example, the 219,120 dwellings built in England in 2019–20 represent less than 1 per cent of the total March 2020 stock (DLUHC, 2021; MHCLG, 2021b).

This slow pace of change means that much of the housing people live in and select from was built using old techniques to accommodate past populations working in a vanished economy. Figure 1.4 illustrates this lag by showing the proportion of dwellings built over a century ago across England and Wales. High proportions of pre-1919 stock are found in northern England and Wales, in London, and in some peripheral rural areas such as the south west. Many of these places had thriving economies during the long 19th century and so have a lot of comparatively old housing, some of which has, of course, since been altered and adapted.

A number of ongoing shifts in the structure of populations have quantitative and qualitative implications for housing demand. The first is *ageing*, driven largely by rising life expectancies (although in Britain this trend has now stalled) coupled with low rates of completed fertility.

Figure 1.4: Percentage of dwellings built before 1919 across England and Wales

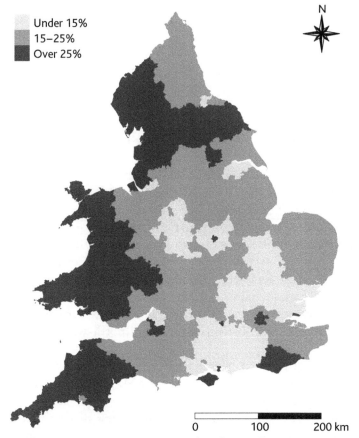

Source: Based on data from Valuations Office Agency (2020) and Office for National Statistics licensed under the Open Government Licence v3.0. Contains OS data © Crown copyright and database right [2022].

Ageing has several consequences for residential behaviour. In a crude sense, greater longevity alters the demand for different types of dwelling and neighbourhood (for example less demand for spacious homes with large gardens) while increasing the size of the population and in particular the number of households. This is because in recent years older adults have tended to live in smaller households than the young (Berrington and Simpson, 2016). Ageing also affects household restrictions as more people have no need to live near to workplaces and may instead prioritise amenities or living close to family.

Demographic impacts on housing behaviour are mediated by institutional filters. In many countries like Britain, the lack of financial incentives to downsize when household size falls – combined with an undersupply of small dwellings and a policy emphasis on ageing in place – has led to widespread overconsumption of space by older homeowners (Bowie, 2017). Going forward, Myers and Ryu (2008) argue that the large size and unprecedented affluence of the US baby boom cohort means that these types of ageing-induced housing pressures will become more acute over coming decades. Myers and Ryu posit that mass sales of boomer family homes around retirement, the onset of ill-health or at death might cause an 'epic transition' in the US housing market, characterised by falling house prices.

A second demographic driver of housing behaviour is the package of structural and aspirational changes forming what has been termed the *Second Demographic Transition* (SDT) (Lesthaeghe, 2010). The basic premise of the SDT model is that as societies become more affluent and secular, their populations increasingly adopt post-materialist values and attitudes by placing greater emphasis on individual autonomy, personal choice and satisfying lifestyle goals. According to Lesthaeghe (2010, p 211), this shift away from material concerns and following traditional normative life scripts brings 'sustained sub-replacement fertility, a multitude of living arrangements other than marriage, the disconnection between marriage and procreation, and no stationary population'. Different countries are currently at different points in the SDT, with Britain and much of north-west Europe towards the vanguard.

The greater diversity in household structures and greater dynamism in demographic behaviour that characterise the SDT have major implications for housing. This is partly because SDT processes create new types of housing preference and patterns of resource access. For example, people splitting up from a partnership are known to have an elevated risk of moving home, exiting homeownership and moving to cheaper dwellings and neighbourhoods (Feijten and van Ham, 2010). The increased prevalence of partnership dissolution accompanying the SDT therefore produces more of these sorts of residential move.

Immigration constitutes a third demographic influence on housing behaviours. In Britain, gross immigration and the net migration rate have generally been high since the mid-1990s and especially following the 2004 EU enlargement. The housing impacts of these migrant streams have been deepened by the above-average fertility of some arrival groups and the fact that many tend to settle in jobs-rich cities with established migrant populations where there is already often a shortage of affordable housing (Berrington and Simpson, 2016).[2] The demographic and socio-economic composition of recent migrants also fuels demand for specific housing submarkets, for example for rental dwellings and cheap shared housing in cities, or for upmarket student accommodation around smaller towns with expanding universities.

Public policy

A long tradition of housing research has documented how politics and ideology interact to produce public policies which influence housing behaviour. This does not happen in a contextual vacuum as local- and national-level institutions mediate the policy generation and implementation process (Lowe, 2011). For instance, Western Europe's tradition of social democracy and interventionist urban policy has created an institutional landscape of actors – ranging from political parties and civil service bureaucracies through to landlords, construction firms and local governments – who favour or at least accept some degree of direct government intervention in the housing system. This is not the case in more classically liberal contexts like the US where the institutional landscape favours leaving the market to provide and distribute housing.

Policies or their absence across almost the entire gamut of government areas have implications for residential behaviour. To make sense of this complexity, policy frameworks can be subdivided into three clusters according to how central changing housing-related behaviour is to their stated objectives. The most obvious cluster consists of policies *where the principal target is changing residential behaviours*. Although housing-focused, these types of policies are nonetheless often enacted as part of a broader political agenda. Examples include:

- Fiscal policies designed to adjust people's *preferences and resources* in order to incentivise or compel them to live in certain types of housing. Examples include adjusting the provision of housing vouchers or benefits to low-income households, changing how land and residential property are taxed or providing financial support for people to make particular types of housing transition (often into homeownership).
- Policies that generate specific housing *events and transitions*. In Europe, this has often occurred when estate redevelopment schemes alter the composition of the local population by displacing some residents while encouraging different sorts of people to move in.
- National housing policies that shape the *opportunities and constraints* people encounter in the housing system. Stark examples of this include the mass privatisation of public housing at particular historical moments – for instance through the UK's Right to Buy scheme or the 1990s restitution of housing after the collapse of communism in Eastern Europe – as well as the regulation of rental sectors. More generally, planning policy influences construction and thus housing opportunities and constraints.

A second cluster of policies seeks *to adjust housing behaviours as a means to some other end*. Often this consists of trying to improve the efficiency of labour markets by altering housing opportunities and constraints. For example, the direct provision or commandeering of cheap housing for key workers in expensive housing markets can be used to ease local labour shortages in important sectors such as healthcare, policing or education. Repeated calls to reform how UK social housing is allocated and managed have also frequently been motivated by an espoused desire to make it easier for tenants to move for work (Cho and Whitehead, 2013).

A final group of relevant policies are those *not focused on housing, but which nonetheless have consequences for residential behaviours*. These types of incidental impact can occur in many ways through all the four types of mechanism shown in Figure 1.2. Examples include:

- Policy interventions with side effects on residential *preferences and aspirations*. For example, education policies which shape the quality of schools or how they are rated impact on the residential priorities of (potential) parents. Similarly, the generosity of public pensions and social care arrangements (as well as interest rates and the taxation of different asset classes) influence how strongly people strive to enter homeownership.
- Public policies that can shape housing behaviour through their effects on household *resources and restrictions*. One example of this is the way that social policies on parental leave and childcare influence the need for households (particularly those with lower incomes) to live in close proximity to kin. Monetary policy is also relevant here as this influences the accessibility and costs of credit for house purchases.
- *Housing opportunities and constraints* that are shaped by policies regarding transportation and infrastructure. For instance, the provision of high-speed internet, greater acceptance of working from home developed during the COVID-19 pandemic and the forthcoming modal shift to electric and autonomous vehicles are likely to radically alter commuting patterns and thus residential constraints through the 2020s.
- Lastly, non-housing related policies can have major impacts on residential behaviour by altering the *events and transitions* people experience. For instance, the expansion of UK higher education has greatly altered when young adults leave home, their housing arrangements after leaving, and whether they subsequently 'boomerang' back to the parental residence (Berrington and Stone, 2014).

Culture

Housing preferences and the longer-term aspirations underpinning them are not formed in a cultural vacuum (Preece et al, 2020). On a broad level, shifts in social attitudes (for example regarding female employment, fertility, the environment or ageing) have significant implications for housing demands and behaviours (Beer and Faulkner, 2011). However, surprisingly little is known about how cultural norms, social attitudes and personal values influence residential behaviour. In part this is because culture is very difficult to capture with quantitative measures. Researchers also struggle with a more intractable challenge: how to separate the effects of cultural factors from the effects of the economic, institutional and policy systems that have arisen in particular socio-cultural contexts? The problem here is that a society's culture and institutions are mutually constitutive, with both developing interactively over the *longue durée* (Lowe, 2011). For example, the state policies that have evolved to support owner-occupation in Britain have both drawn on and simultaneously reinforced the UK's popular culture of homeownership (Ronald, 2008). Recognising the relational nature of these connections is probably the best way to understand how cultural factors shape residential behaviour not only by influencing preferences and aspirations, but also by configuring the opportunities and constraints people encounter in the housing system.

Clapham (2005) has argued that cultural factors have become more important drivers of residential behaviour in recent decades. In his view, the Global North's transition to post-modernity involves the spread of individualism and the decline of traditional collective values and the civic institutions that sustain them, such as religious communities. Globalisation has intensified this fragmentation process as the state's retreat from economic affairs and reduced public welfare provision leaves people exposed to greater levels of economic risk and uncertainty (Clapham, 2005).

One consequence of these trends is a dramatic shift in how people view and conduct their lives. Instead of following the fairly predictable types of life trajectory that characterised post-war societies, post-modern citizens have greater scope to construct their lives as unique lifestyle projects aimed at achieving personal fulfilment (Clapham, 2005). In essence, post-modern lives are improvised to achieve personal goals rather than being socially directed to follow a shared script. This dramatic analogy is helpful as it reminds us of post-modernity's ambiguity. While some groups – in particular the more skilled and capital rich – may be liberated by this freedom to improvise, for the less fortunate, the loss of a shared script and supportive direction often fuels insecurity and alienation.

Clapham (2005) contends that housing is a crucial aspect of destandardised post-modern lifestyles. This suggests that identity construction and the search for personal fulfilment shapes residential preferences, aspirations and behaviours. While people's idiosyncratic tastes obviously play a role here, shared cultural dimensions of desire and aspiration are evident too. For example, Savage and colleagues' (2010) work on 'elective belonging' indicates that middle-class Britons design their residential choices in order to stake symbolic claims to places and their heritage. Particular patterns of housing preference and behaviour are also part of the acquired *habitus* and lifestyles of other advantaged groups such as students and young gentrifiers (Smith and Holt, 2007).

By contrast, those from working-class families and ethnic minority backgrounds may have a more local *habitus*, in part because they have a greater material need to live in close proximity to kin support networks. Residential decisions can also be circumscribed by the religious segregation of space and ways this is used to safeguard and project group identity. Prominent UK examples of this include the division between Protestant and Catholic neighbourhoods in Belfast as well as the physical separation between Haredi and other Jewish communities across the north London neighbourhoods of Stamford Hill and Hendon/Golders Green.

The interplay between culture and institutions is thought to play a particularly strong role in shaping tenure demands. Although Saunders (1990) asserted that humans have an innate drive to seek the security of property ownership, the cultural attachment to homeownership has reached its apogee in the Anglophone world, where it has been absorbed deep into national self-imagery. British politicians have been portraying the country as a property-owning democracy for nearly a century while the acquisition of private property through rugged individual enterprise is integral to the frontier settler mythology of the US and Australia. In these countries, politicians have long used a range of policy levers to promote owner-occupation, thereby helping to reinforce and deepen its cultural appeal. Writing in 2008, Ronald proposed that this powerful ideology of homeownership had spread around the world from the 1980s. He argued that many governments have embraced the promotion of mortgaged homeownership as this contributes to their broader neoliberal agenda of economic deregulation, privatisation, shrinking the state and making citizens responsible for their own welfare (Ronald, 2008).

A positive cultural image of homeownership contributes to its popularity in the Anglophone world. Here, buying one's first dwelling is seen as a major life milestone which signifies independence, status and good citizenship while providing residential and financial security. Homeownership has also traditionally been viewed as the best context for family formation and childrearing (Lauster, 2010). These attitudes and moral judgements are sustained by a popular lexicon of terms like the 'housing ladder' as well as by political discourse, the mass media and the finance industry. By contrast, renting has traditionally been seen negatively as 'flawed consumption' and a waste of money (McKee et al, 2017a), with private renting considered appropriate only as a transitional step in early adulthood. This stigma contrasts with countries like Austria or Germany where renting is considered a normal long-term tenure, in part because homeownership has traditionally been hard to access and the state has sought to improve the affordability and quality of rental housing (Lennartz and Helbrecht, 2018). This example illustrates how cultural attitudes towards housing are heavily shaped by institutions and historic policy trajectories.

Looking forward, it is important to know more about whether changing patterns of housing opportunity and constraint are altering tenure preferences and aspirations across traditional homeowner societies. In Britain, qualitative evidence suggests that increased financial barriers to entering homeownership have not significantly dampened the tenure's appeal among younger cohorts (McKee et al, 2017a). Yet there are three reasons why this should not be read as evidence of cultural stasis:

1. The greater prevalence of prolonged renting and parental co-residence among younger cohorts could reduce the stigma which earlier studies reported was attached to these practices as people become accustomed to it taking longer to buy. Similarly, higher rates of family formation in rented housing are likely to breach the cultural assumption that owner-occupancy is normative for raising children.
2. Stable preferences may be accompanied by increased recognition that entering homeownership is a family and not an individual matter. This could reshape family relations as well as the traditional moral judgement that becoming a homeowner signifies independence.
3. Changes in cultural attitudes towards housing are always likely to lag behind changes in social contexts. This is because early life experiences, parental socialisation and thus the historic opportunity structure shape people's residential preferences and aspirations (Crawford and McKee, 2018). In essence, it seems plausible that it is cohort replacement and not the changing views of individuals that primarily drives shifts in societal attitudes towards housing over time. This issue is explored further in subsequent chapters.

The rest of this book

The subsequent chapters delve beneath this overview to consider precisely how housing is embedded into the dynamics of people's lives in ways that help change places, societies and patterns of inequality. The book focuses primarily on Britain but discusses other countries where this is illuminating. The UK focus is partly a pragmatic matter of space and expertise, but the British case is also unusually interesting because its housing system has changed so dramatically in recent years. Furthermore, devolution since the late 1990s has led to divergence in policy frameworks across the UK's component nations that may have pulled apart the course of British lives.

Chapter 2 starts by reviewing existing ways of thinking about housing behaviour before developing the book's life course perspective. It argues that this perspective provides a richer framework for understanding how housing behaviours tie changes in people's lives to changes in places and in the broader structure of society. The conceptual framework presented in Chapter 2 and in particular the twelve life course conceptual tools it outlines underpin the rest of the book.

Chapters 3–6 examine how housing and life course dynamics are intertwined in complex ways. Each of these chapters explores how housing behaviour is connected with the dynamics of one other life course domain. Chapter 3 concentrates on household and family, Chapter 4 examines education, Chapter 5 addresses employment and money and Chapter 6 considers health. This thematic structure is preferred over the more-commonly used life stage based subdivision as life course stages such as young adulthood are malleable constructs whose meaning and boundaries shift over time (Mortimer and Moen, 2016).[3] For example, what biological age is considered to mark later life has changed dramatically since 1945 as longevity has risen, new technologies have emerged and both culture and social institutions have been transformed (for instance through higher retirement ages). The meaning and categorisation of life course stages can also vary across the population, for instance as greater morbidity among the poor means they experience the onset of later-life issues (for example limiting illness or widowhood) at younger biological ages than their more advantaged peers (Mortimer and Moen, 2016). Greater diversity within contemporary populations thus produces less standardisation in age-graded experiences and this makes it more useful to focus on how housing interacts with other life course domains over the entire life span.

Chapter 7 moves beyond the micro-level focus of Chapters 3–6 to assess how residential behaviours are bound up with aggregate changes in local populations. This is an important chapter as it examines how the life course framework can be applied to better understand the mechanisms driving a wide range of geographical processes including segregation, gentrification and the studentification of parts of university towns. Chapter 7 thus shows how life course processes can have geographical outcomes and play important roles in the (re)production of spatial inequalities. Finally, Chapter 8 summarises the book's contents and offers some guidelines about how the life course perspective can enrich future research and debate.

2

Housing: a life course perspective

This chapter lays the book's conceptual foundations. After sketching three of the most influential disciplinary perspectives on residential behaviour, the chapter then reviews the specific conceptual approaches scholars have developed to understand how people move through housing systems as they pass through life. It contends that none of these approaches can fully describe or explain how housing is embedded into 21st-century lives. The chapter then moves on to outline a more modern life course framework which can provide new insights about contemporary residential processes and inequalities. The latter portion of the chapter develops this framework by revisiting five core principles of the life course perspective and using them to derive twelve conceptual tools which can be applied to better understand residential behaviours (Elder et al, 2003). These flexible tools are then used throughout the subsequent chapters to integrate and synthesise what we know about contemporary housing and life course dynamics.

Contrasting traditions

Three disciplinary traditions have most strongly shaped our understandings of residential behaviour. Of these, *the economic tradition* has been the most influential. Economic research has drawn heavily on neoclassical thought and its central assumption that people are rational actors who make utility optimising decisions after calculating the costs and benefits of different options. This rational choice framework has been applied to understand many demand-side housing processes, including:

- households matching themselves to suitable dwelling vacancies (Wheaton, 1990);
- residential adjustments around life events such as childbirth or unemployment (Rabe and Taylor, 2010);
- how variations in housing market conditions impact on household formation and residential mobility (Ermisch, 1999; Ferreira et al, 2010);
- the effects of income, house prices, housing supply and macroeconomic conditions on tenure and locational decisions (Andrew, 2012; Ermisch and Washbrook, 2012).

The hegemony of neoclassical models is now waning under the challenge of behavioural economics. Behavioural approaches use psychological evidence to explain why people systematically deviate from the predictions of neoclassical theory (Gibb, 2012). Although the psychological explanations for these deviations are complex, perhaps the most important are that people are loss averse (more sensitive to losses than identical gains) and tend to use a range of heuristics – defined as simplified cognitive tools – when making demanding decisions (Morrison and Clark, 2016). As these heuristics are imperfect they lead to systematic errors and biased choices (Gibb, 2012).

Gibb (2012) notes that a reliance on heuristics and imperfect information is a particular issue for housing decisions as:

- Most people move home too rarely to become experienced with the decision-making process.
- Housing decisions involve making complex trade-offs between bundled attributes such as location, size, quality and cost.
- Residential moves are expensive and have very significant consequences, which may encourage loss aversion.
- Residential decisions may be influenced by the dynamic preferences of multiple people.

In line with the economic tradition, *geographical approaches* have concentrated on how rational households match themselves to suitable housing vacancies as their residential demands and resources change (Clark, 2021). However, these perspectives tend to focus more heavily on aggregate spatial patterns of housing behaviour and their connections to the changing social composition of places. The mechanisms producing unequal patterns of residential mobility and housing selection, as well as inequalities in housing wealth, have also been central themes in geographical scholarship.

The economic and geographical focus on quantitative modelling of housing behaviours diverges from the *sociological tradition's* broader interest in the role housing plays in the fabric of societies. Throughout the late 20th century, sociologists examined whether housing tenure divisions accentuate occupational class inequality or instead constitute a separate but related axis of social division in the sphere of consumption (Saunders, 1990). Today, these debates have been eclipsed by an explosion of work tackling a range of housing issues from multiple epistemological standpoints (Atkinson and Jacobs, 2016).

One limitation of much of the work conducted within all three traditions is that it often focuses on system dynamics or on understanding specific residential behaviours at one point in time (Clapham, 2005). While valuable, these approaches can tell us little about how decisions about housing are embedded into the longer-term dynamics of people's lives and interpersonal relationships. Tracking how people move through the housing system over time is also important for understanding how geographies of population change are, in part, the aggregate product of the residential decisions individuals make as their lives unfold in varied ways. In consequence, several interdisciplinary frameworks have been developed to try and take the more life span perspective that people tend to adopt when thinking and talking about their own residential experiences. The most influential of these perspectives – traditional models of housing careers, the housing transitions framework and ideas of housing pathways – are now reviewed in turn.[1]

Housing careers

The idea that the succession of dwellings and neighbourhoods a person passes through over time forms their housing career first emerged from Peter Rossi's (1955) *Why Families Move*. Rossi argued that people move home in order to adjust their housing consumption to meet the new residential needs that emerge as they transition between household structures. The crux of Rossi's model is that people pass through a relatively orderly family life cycle as they age. This life cycle is comprised of a fairly predictable sequence of age-graded household structures. Each of these household structures comprises a life cycle stage that is associated with a specific set of residential demands, in particular for dwelling space and local amenities. Transitions between stages in the family life cycle thus create housing disequilibrium or 'stress' (which people express as dissatisfaction with their current home) by generating new residential demands that are poorly satisfied in situ. For example, the birth of a first child to a couple living in a small inner-city flat may cause them to want more dwelling space and a garden.

To meet these new demands, households seek to adjust their housing consumption and improve their satisfaction by moving to a new dwelling which they anticipate will better satisfy their changed requirements. Over time, the succession of adjustment moves a person undertakes as they pass through the life cycle combines to create their housing career. Table 2.1 shows a stylised example of this process broadly appropriate to Rossi's 1950s world (Rossi, 1955).

Subsequent studies better integrated socio-economic disparities and cultural preferences into Rossi's model. On the one hand, scholars observed that housing career transitions are not simply a passive response to changes in family composition as an active desire to boost comfort, status and capital accumulation motivates moves to larger, higher quality, owner-occupied homes in more desirable neighbourhoods (Morris and Winter, 1975). On the other hand, housing adjustments and the general tendency for people to 'move to improve' are not inevitable but rather depend on occupational progression and income growth (Kendig, 1984). A favourable institutional

Table 2.1: A stylised traditional model of family life cycle and housing career stages

Age	Life cycle stage	Housing demands	Housing career processes
0–15	Childhood	Dependent child requiring supervision and care	Living in the parental home
16–19	Young single	Proximity to work/education; cheap flexible housing; access to urban amenities	Leave parental home to rent a small dwelling or houseshare in a city
20–24	Young married couple	Greater space and privacy; higher quality accommodation	Move into a small single-family house or flat at marriage
25–34	Family formation	Enhanced desire for space and neighbourhood safety; desire for owner-occupation	Move to a larger owned dwelling in the suburbs
35–54	Family expansion and consolidation	Increased space demands; preference to live near good schools	Trade up to a larger home
55–64	Empty nest	Reduced need for space but emotional attachment to dwelling and location	Pay off mortgage
65+	Retirement	Less need to live near work; desire to live near kin; preference for amenities	Downsize as space needs decline and in anticipation of poorer health

context and an absence of involuntary triggers (such as eviction) are also important preconditions for 'upward' housing career development.

Although the housing careers concept remains popular, it has been heavily critiqued and its detractors have assembled a long charge sheet of alleged offences. The most significant charges are that traditional models of housing careers:

1. *Are normative and unidirectional* as the word career implies an upward lifetime trajectory in housing space, dwelling quality, housing assets and so on (Forrest, 1987). This assumption of progression up the housing ladder is culturally potent in Anglophone countries but fits poorly with many people's lived experience.
2. *Are temporally and geographically specific*, especially to the post-war US where a suburban construction boom, state support for mortgage borrowing, buoyant economy and the predominance of stable nuclear families created the conditions for people to make a relatively orderly progression through the housing market as they aged. Critics argue that this linear model is now obsolete as increased family complexity and greater economic instability mean people move through the housing system in more fluid and varied ways (Beer and Faulkner, 2011). In addition, housing careers

may have always poorly described many people's experiences in countries like the UK or the Netherlands where large non-market rental sectors house many households across the life course.

3. *Focus excessively on moves and changes in objective measures of housing circumstances* such as tenure, dwelling size and so forth. This means that the concept may be less useful for understanding individuals' subjective perceptions or experiences of housing, as well as the ways these evolve during periods of residential stability (Clapham, 2005).

4. *Problematically assume people have choice* (are able to make adjustment moves) *while denying them agency* (as the model is linear and deterministic).

This charge sheet is formidable but not without weakness. To begin with, the third and fourth charges are more critiques of application than of concept. There is no *prima facie* reason why diversity, cultural prioritisation of certain types of trajectories, subjective meanings and periods of residential stability cannot be incorporated into housing career frameworks if these are detached from rigid life cycle models. Furthermore, the first, second and fourth charges are critiques of a stylised strong model of housing careers that few authors have ever endorsed. Most studies have long stressed that housing careers are not synonymous with upward progression as income, class, unpredictable life events, spatial location and social institutions all stratify moves through the housing system (Kendig, 1984; Clark et al, 2003). As we shall see, modern life course perspectives provide a useful template for reworking the core idea of a housing career to better accommodate the greater dynamism, diversity and destandardisation of 21st-century lives.

To sum up, there is insufficient evidence to convict housing careers, but some rehabilitation is required before the concept can re-enter the research community. This rehabilitation needs to involve recasting the careers concept as more akin to the way the term is used in professional sports. Here, a career is a more neutral and directionless term capable of encompassing a long-term pattern of ups and downs, successes and failures, injury and recovery as well as mobility and stability (for example between clubs). We will shortly explore how life course perspectives can be used to rework the housing careers concept in this more flexible fashion.

Housing transitions

The housing transitions framework was devised by Beer and Faulkner (2011) to address the perceived conceptual deficiencies associated with housing careers. Beer and Faulkner (2011, p 31) argue that their transitions approach:

> better reflects the complex and fluid relationship between individuals in developed economies and their housing in the 21st century. It places a

focus on ongoing change – potential or real – in housing circumstances and leaves open the possibility of identifying common housing sequences that may shift over time in response to social, economic and cultural developments ... Importantly, it leaves scope for both the subjective and objective analysis of change in housing circumstances while having scope to incorporate both structural processes and individual decision making. The term housing transitions does not imply a particular direction or set of dynamics over the life course – *a critique levelled at the concept of housing careers* [emphasis added] – but neither does it privilege the subjective dimensions of housing over quantitative assessment.

Housing decisions in this framework are shaped by five factors: stage in the life course, resources, health, tenure, and lifestyle values and aspirations (Beer and Faulkner, 2011). Social, economic and cultural changes which alter any of these five variables will thus restructure aggregate patterns of housing transition as well as how people perceive their homes and their potential housing futures. This recognition that contemporary residential behaviours are dynamic, diverse and context-dependent is a vital insight which was not adequately incorporated into traditional housing career frameworks. In addition, the transitions perspective helpfully opens up space for research conducted within a more diverse suite of epistemological traditions using both numerical and qualitative methods. This breadth makes the transitions framework very flexible and potentially applicable to a huge range of housing-related research questions (Beer and Faulkner, 2011).

However, the transitions perspective comes with its own conceptual limitations. On one level, the term transitions ironically carries similar unwanted intellectual baggage to the careers, histories and pathways concepts that Beer and Faulkner (2011) dismiss as excessively baggage laden. In sociology, transitions often refer to the passages between social roles and states which act as culturally significant life course milestones: for example the transition from school to work or the transition into marriage. In any given setting these transitions usually have a normative timing and sequencing that is culturally valued and embedded into public discourse and institutions such as the social security system (Elder et al, 2003). Such strong institutionalised scripting means that transitions which are 'ill-ordered' or which occur 'off-time' can be stigmatised, poorly supported and thus can have long-lasting adverse consequences (for example childbearing during education). By contrast, cultural and institutional scripting of other sorts of transitions (for example retirement) may be far more flexible, delinked from age-graded expectations and thus able to accommodate a much wider range of life trajectories (Grenier, 2015). This richer perspective on the cultural and institutional dimensions of transitions is largely absent from Beer and

Faulkner's (2011) framework. It is also unclear why life course factors are separated from resources and health when these are typically considered constitutive elements of the life course.

In addition, the point-in-time focus implied by the word transition is unhelpful for understanding the long-term evolution of housing experiences over the life span or the ways in which past experiences and future-oriented aspirations influence preferences, behaviours and outcomes. Beer and Faulkner (2011) are aware of this – as well as the importance of encompassing social and spatial variations – but do not provide any tools to systematically conceptualise and examine the mechanisms *producing* variation in housing transitions. This conceptual vagueness makes it rather hard to determine precisely how ideas of housing transitions should actually be used in research projects.

Housing pathways

David Clapham's (2005) housing pathways approach is perhaps the most radical attempt to reconceptualise how people interact with housing systems as they pass through life. Clapham devised the pathways framework in the early 2000s to counter the positivism he considered was dominating the housing research field. In Clapham's (2005, p 11) view, most contemporary housing analyses were positivist 'in that they assume the existence of a world of social facts to be uncovered by researchers using quantitative and empirical research methods'. He contended that too much of this literature consisted of pure empiricism (for instance policy evaluations) and research which assumed that people are rational actors with universal preferences. A further issue was that housing choices and constraints tended to be considered separately as scholars prioritised nomothetic model building over more idiographic exploration of particularity and lived experience.

Clapham (2005)'s critique of what he termed positivist scholarship has two interrelated dimensions. First, he contends that positivism simply provides an epistemologically inadequate framework for understanding the social dynamics of housing. Clapham (2005) argues that positivism's acceptance of objective social facts leads researchers to either completely ignore the subjective dimensions of housing or instead to reduce subjectivity down to crude but quantifiable constructs such as levels of dwelling satisfaction. Clapham (2005) contends that both of these approaches overlook individuals' constantly changing perceptions of and attitudes towards housing. In addition, he argues that positivist approaches pay little attention to the way that these housing-related subjectivities – as well as the actions of the individuals and institutional actors they influence – are all shaped by circulating social discourses (for example concerning what constitutes an appropriate lifestyle in young adulthood or older age).

Clapham's (2005) second argument is that these epistemological deficiencies of positivism have strengthened over recent decades as globalisation and societal individualisation erode the structure and certainty of life paths (see Chapter 1). He argues that this transition to post-modernity means that individuals now assume greater responsibility for actively constructing their own lives by making choices. Drawing on the sociology of Anthony Giddens, Clapham (2005) contends that this 'opening out' of social options means people increasingly strive to achieve personal fulfilment by making choices that will allow them build desired identities and lifestyles (sometimes this is referred to as constructing choice biographies). Housing is central to both identity and lifestyle and thus increasingly forms a means to achieve the end of personal fulfilment (Clapham, 2005). This implies that in a post-modern context, housing scholarship simply cannot afford to neglect perceptions, attitudes, values and other subjectivities.

The pathways framework was designed to address these issues by fusing elements of social constructionism with Giddens' structuration theory (Clapham, 2005). Clapham (2005, p 22) describes the pathways perspective as based on a weak version of social constructionism which 'recognises a material world outside of discourse, but argues that its nature and its impact on the social world *can be understood only through its social construction* [emphasis added]'. Integral to these processes of social construction are social practices and more specifically the interactions between the housing-related perceptions and actions of individuals and the discourses and social structures that form the settings within which they exercise agency.

Drawing together these ideas, Clapham (2005) defines housing pathways 'as patterns of interaction (practices) concerning house and home, over time and space' (Clapham, 2005, p 27). The pathway is thus a metaphorical framework that foregrounds the subjective meanings of housing and the ways people's interactions with it are embedded into the broader context of their lives, societal structures and social discourses. No assumptions are made about preferences, rationality, the direction of change or how to measure processes and outcomes. Indeed, one of the most refreshing aspects of the pathways approach is the way it prioritises in-depth qualitative analysis while encouraging generalisation 'in order to understand the relative prevalence of different pathways or their constituent meanings, or to design housing policy, or to characterise the housing system in comparison with other countries' (Clapham, 2005, p 33).

The pathways metaphor is an important innovation, yet like all frameworks it also comes with its own limitations. The most significant is that the framework's social constructionism and prioritisation of subjectivity leave it, by design, much less suited to aggregate-level analysis of the housing processes that shape material inequalities across populations. While Clapham (2005) does envisage a place for quantitative analysis, the role this plays in the pathways framework is mostly confined to generalisation – by which he means the inductive identification of pathway types and perhaps some representative survey analysis of the meanings associated with each one. A good example of such work is provided by Clapham and colleagues (2014). These authors used longitudinal data to categorise and quantify UK young adults' objective housing pathways before drawing on interviews to unpack the meanings and subjectivities associated with each route. In this work (as in much pathways scholarship), the quantification is more descriptive than explanatory and serves primarily to allow the qualitative interpretations to be scaled up.

The relatively circumscribed role that population-level analysis plays in the pathways framework means that other conceptual approaches are needed to fully understand how, on a broad level, housing matters for changing lives, places and inequalities. One valuable way to complement the pathways approach is thus to devise new frameworks which (1) focus less on subjectivity than on the *observable dimensions of housing-related processes and behaviours* and which (2) concentrate on *describing and explaining regularities and variations* across populations. This renewed focus on materiality and aggregate perspectives emphatically does not mean embracing positivism and nor does it imply the rejection of small-scale qualitative work. Today, relatively few housing scholars who work with large datasets pretend to be detached rational observers or assume that a perfectly knowable world of social facts exists completely independently from society. Scholars also seldom seek universal social laws or try to generate deterministic models based on assumptions of pure rationality. Critiques that label all quantification as positivist are outdated and care needs to be taken not to tar all aggregate analysis of residential behaviour with the stigmatised brush of post-war positivism.

As Johnston and colleagues (2014) discuss, most contemporary aggregate analyses of housing behaviours follow a more 'postpositivist' scientific approach. This means that they accept the existence of a real material world but accept that (1) it is imperfectly knowable and that (2) social constructions (for example of concepts like housing tenure) influence both how we know about it and also how people behave. Postpositivists are aware that researchers have positionality and in their work often draw on elements of critical realism (for example the idea that measurable events are produced by causal mechanisms originating within structures of relations) and structuration theory (for instance by exploring how the lives of people and changes in society constantly influence one another). Delving beneath population averages by posing research questions about difference and inequality are hallmarks of these more postpositivist approaches, which focus not on building universal models but instead on trying to understand the contingent causal relations that configure uneven patterns of behaviour and outcomes (Johnston et al, 2014). When this tradition is at its best, care is often taken to critically reflect on how categories are constructed and there are rich debates about how to define and measure housing concepts such as affordability, crowding, choice and aspiration. There is also a healthy recognition that aggregate data analyses can usually only take us so far and that qualitative work is very often essential for delivering holistic answers to housing research questions (particularly those where social construction and discourse are central considerations).

This paradigm shift means that more sensitive postpositivist analysis of large datasets can provide a rich complement to the nuanced insights gained from the more subjective, individual-level and constructionist focus of pathways scholarship. In the next section and throughout the subsequent chapters, we will explore how modern life course conceptual perspectives are being coupled with this postpositivist empirical research tradition to develop our knowledge of contemporary patterns and processes of residential behaviour.

Life course perspectives

Life course approaches coalesced within sociology during the late 20th century. Although the life course is sometimes labelled a singular theory or paradigm, these terms overstate the cohesion of life course thought, which has never coalesced around any particular topic or models (Bernardi et al, 2019). Instead, the life course is better viewed as a flexible approach, framework or perspective with some core principles that can be applied to understand how the structure of interlinked events and transitions in multiple domains of life unfold over time in relation to collective social contexts (Bailey, 2009). In this view, life course perspectives help less with formulating testable hypotheses than with the identification of research questions, study design and the interpretation of findings (Elder et al, 2003).

Life course approaches began to be applied in housing and population research from the 1980s (Feijten, 2005). Their adoption was motivated by an awareness that new residential dynamics were emerging as people's lives became longer, more fluid, increasingly diverse and more complex. The conceptual core of the life course perspective is that lives are comprised of multiple careers in separate domains which run in parallel across the life span. These careers are interrelated as events and processes in one career can affect the course of the others, for example if childbirth leads a person to move to a larger home and alter their labour force participation. Such careers are not linear or deterministic and so the life course perspective provides a powerful way to reconceptualise notions of housing careers in order to overcome the main critiques of this concept. Figure 2.1 provides a hypothetical example of a life course made up of parallel careers that sometimes interlink but at other times run largely independently of one another (see Clark and Dieleman, 1996, p 33 for an earlier representation).

Figure 2.1: A hypothetical life course

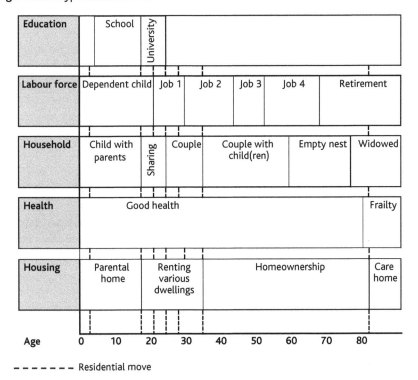

- - - - - - - Residential move

Re-thinking housing careers as one dimension of an intertwined life course is valuable because this approach:

- acknowledges that housing careers are *diverse and destandardised* as people have different preferences, resources and varied objective and subjective life experiences;
- allows for greater *non-linearity and fluidity* by de-linking housing processes from transitions between an age-graded sequence of household structures; and
- emphasises the *bidirectional connections* between housing and other life course careers.

Residential decisions

To date, most life course perspectives on housing careers have drawn on Rossi's (1955) insight that people move between residences in order to adjust their dwelling and location to meet the new needs and preferences that emerge as they pass through life. However, life course approaches recognise that these housing decisions unfold in far more varied ways than Rossi envisaged as people have agency and there is much diversity in the types and timing of the events punctuating people's lives. This means that changes in residential states are not predictable age-graded events, but rather are diverse temporal processes which can occur in varied ways across the life span. Indeed, the considerable costs and complexity of moving home means that residential adjustments often take a long time to sort out and many people thus spend long periods living in places they are thinking of leaving.

Life course approaches tend to distinguish two stylised types of residential decision-making process which combine with periods of stability to structure the housing career. On the one hand, residential dissatisfaction and desires to move can emerge relatively gradually. The underlying causes of this gradual emergence of a moving preference may be endogenous to an individual's life, for example if family growth increases dwelling space pressure or if a long commute becomes more gruelling over time. Equally, perceptions of unwelcome exogenous changes in the local area, for example neighbourhood decline or a shift in population composition, can make people feel it is a less appealing place to live (Clark and Coulter, 2015). Finally, housing dissatisfaction can be culturally induced (Morris and Winter, 1975). Examples of this include desiring to move in order to improve social status by entering homeownership or moving in order to live in a more affluent part of town. The relative importance of these different drivers is likely to vary over the life course and across social groups.

With this in mind, De Jong and Fawcett (1981) argued that residential moves are a means to obtain valued life goals including wealth, status, comfort, stimulation, autonomy, affiliation and morality. Their perspective offers a richer view of the motives for residential moves which recognises people's agency, diverse aspirations and the way that housing forms part of a broader life project (Clapham, 2005). De Jong and Fawcett's (1981) ideas – combined with the knowledge that housing is a composite good – also help us to understand how people may only be able to attain one valued residential goal by trading this off against others. For example, it may be necessary to compromise on space in order to live in an expensive city-centre location offering proximity to work and urban amenities.

A variety of stylised behavioural models comprised of different decision-making steps have been derived to describe how people respond to residential dissatisfaction. These models typically posit that people do not constantly evaluate the suitability of their current housing. Rather, rationality is bounded as a desire to move only emerges once perceived residential dissatisfaction passes a personal tolerance threshold (Mulder, 1996). After this threshold is crossed and the desire to move has emerged, people then search for a new location, plan and – if a suitable destination is available and moving is feasible – potentially go on to relocate (Coulter et al, 2011). The costs and social disruption of moving over longer distances mean that most people seeking to adjust their housing and neighbourhood consumption strive to make relatively short distance moves.

On the other hand, the need to move may emerge more quickly in order to adjust to 'trigger' events in other life course careers which suddenly generate new housing demands or which dramatically impact on resources (Feijten, 2005). If these triggers are unexpected they can disrupt pre-existing residential plans (de Groot et al, 2011). Archetypal examples of this include urgent moves driven by partnership breakdown or eviction. More positively, job changes or attending university often require relocation at a particular moment, frequently over longer distances than moves driven by housing or neighbourhood dissatisfaction. In many cases, moves triggered by these types of events may also be more spatially constrained – for example by the location of workplaces or by a lack of knowledge, time and resources to devote to housing search – than more local moves undertaken for housing reasons. This can lead people relocating in response to unexpected life events to make stopgap residential decisions that do not satisfy their long-term preferences and which thus motivate subsequent adjustments.

Contextualising housing careers

Life course frameworks recognise that diversity in housing career processes is not simply due to personal preferences or to the varied life events people experience. Instead, diversity is also produced by the ways in which social and spatial contexts shape residential behaviour over the life span. Mulder and Hooimeijer's (1999) influential model of residential preferences and behaviour outlined several ways in which contextual forces impact on point-in-time housing decisions and, by extension, the longer-term structure of housing careers. In their framework, life course careers create distinct patterns of residential needs and preferences, which, as the last section described, over time motivate people to try and make particular types of adjustment. Crucially however, Mulder and Hooimeijer's model (1999) stresses that housing decisions do not occur in a contextual vacuum as residential behaviours are directly and indirectly shaped by micro-level household factors as well as by macro-level influences.[2]

At the household level, Mulder and Hooimeijer (1999) argued that resources and restrictions generated from the life course careers of household members as well as their ties to non-resident others influence people's ability to act on their residential preferences. Resources can be defined as attributes that increase a person's ability to exercise effective residential choice (Brown and King, 2005). These resources can take many forms, including:

- economic resources such as income, savings and job security;
- social capital provided by social and kin networks able to assist with housing search and perhaps broker access; or
- cultural capital such as know-how about the housing system, for example concerning how to obtain mortgages or to access social housing.

The flip side of resources are the restrictions that to some degree limit everyone's ability to act on their residential preferences. The most obvious restriction is simply a lack of resources. However, restrictions may also relate to time budgets and the need to be able to visit particular spatial 'nodes' during daily life. Different nodes are important for different people but for many the location of workplaces, schools, religious centres and the homes of non-resident kin are especially important. According to Roseman (1971), the importance of being able to visit these nodes is such that most people generally try to avoid making long-distance moves that result in the 'total displacement' of their entire daily activity space. Instead, shorter distance 'partial displacement' moves that involve accessing the same daily nodes but from a new residential hub location are typically preferred.

Three nuances are important when thinking about resources and restrictions. First, these are not necessarily mutually exclusive labels and the same attribute can function simultaneously as both a resource and restriction. For instance, dual-career households may benefit from greater income to spend on housing than otherwise identical single-earning households. However, the spatial choice set available to a dual-career household may also be more restricted by the need to access two workplaces. Second, the same attribute can be a resource for some people at some points in the life course and a restriction in other circumstances. For example, the direction and magnitude of house price and interest rate movements influences whether mortgaged homeownership acts as an asset or a source of economic risk for recent homebuyers. Finally, Mulder and Hooimeijer's (1999) model assumes that resources and restrictions influence whether a housing preference is realised without affecting what preferences people actually express. This assumption seems problematic given that research on hedonic adaptation and adaptive preferences finds that changes in people's circumstances can generate shifts in their perceptions and preferences.

At a broader level, macro-contextual conditions create opportunities and constraints which impact on housing career processes (Mulder and Hooimeijer, 1999). The basic idea here is simple: people's ability to act on their residential preferences is structured by the characteristics of society.

These macro-level structural characteristics interact with micro-level household attributes to shape the residential choice set that is available and accessible to particular individuals. There is now a considerable literature comparing the factors that enable people to act on their housing preferences and make residential moves. In brief, this literature suggests that the balance of opportunities and constraints is configured *inter alia* by:

- turnover rates and dwelling vacancy chains, as well as the tenure composition of the existing housing stock;
- housing market and broader economic conditions including house price and rent movements, access to credit, construction levels and incomes; and
- current and historic institutional developments and policies on a range of issues including social security and planning.

Enriching the life course perspective

These applications of life course perspectives have boosted our knowledge of housing careers but left important areas of weakness. One crucial problem is that the application of life course thought still draws heavily on classic texts written a considerable time ago (Clark and Dieleman, 1996; Mulder and Hooimeijer, 1999; Feijten, 2005). This means that recent advances in life course sociology such as the importance of 'linked lives' have not fully percolated down to inform housing analysis. Furthermore, the term life course is often used fairly imprecisely in housing scholarship as a synonym for demographic events or simply as an alternative for life span. More seriously, it is still quite common to encounter studies equating life courses with the same sort of sequence of age-graded household structures as Rossi devised in the 1950s. While 'fluidity and fleetfootedness' is one of the most appealing features of the life course perspective (Bailey, 2009, p 413), it is important that this lack of agreed definitions does not lead to life course ideas being invoked in a simplistic, ill-defined or incorrect fashion.

Finally and most crucially, extant life course literature on housing lacks cohesion and is scattered across the social sciences. The preponderance of empirical articles means evidence is seldom integrated and synthesised into a broader shared framework for understanding how housing is embedded into life course dynamics in a range of interrelated ways. This lack of integration and synthesis carries two practical risks. The first is that researchers ploughing specialised furrows end up documenting the obvious, inadvertently duplicating each other's efforts or getting drawn into very specialised and often technical debates. Second, the fragmented state of life course infused housing research means the field risks being overlooked or seen as of limited relevance to policymakers and practitioners. While specialised knowledge is clearly vital for making good decisions, a broader synoptic understanding is

Table 2.2: Life course principles and conceptual tools

Principle (Elder et al, 2003)	Conceptual tools
1. Life span development	Biography
	Cumulative development
2. Timing	Ordering and sequences
	Duration
	Trajectories and turning points
	Timetables and scripts
3. Linked lives	Synchronisation and ripples
	Solidarities
	Household relations
4. Agency	Construction
5. Time and place	Cohort and period
	Changing places

just as crucial for fully appreciating the ways that interventions in one arena might have knock-on consequences elsewhere.

One solution to these issues is to refresh and hone the life course framework for 21st-century housing analysis by revisiting the fundamental elements of life course thought devised by Glen Elder. According to Elder, life course perspectives are underpinned by five principles: life span development, event timing, linked lives, agency and time and place (Elder et al, 2003). Re-examining each of Elder's five principles allows us to distil a set of twelve conceptual tools which can then be collectively applied in customisable combinations to revitalise, integrate and synthesise our understanding of housing and life course dynamics within 21st-century societies. Table 2.2 outlines these twelve conceptual tools and the underlying life course principle each one is primarily derived from.

The twelve conceptual tools shown in Table 2.2 are neither completely new nor intended to form a prescriptive list to be ticked off in every research situation. Instead, the twelve concepts are designed to provide researchers with a flexible toolbox to draw on when devising housing-related research questions, designing analyses, interpreting findings, synthesising evidence and evaluating policy and practice. Often multiple tools will need to be used together and, as Chapter 8 discusses, conducting empirical research will also normally involve supplementing the life course conceptual toolbox with insights from specific theories relevant to the topic of interest. Some of the tools also overlap with each other and fusions between two or more tools or between a tool and another life course principle (for example a study could fuse concepts to explore 'biographical timing') may prove particularly valuable for addressing some research questions.

We now turn to briefly explore each life course principle and the conceptual tools associated with it in greater depth. The rest of the book then applies these conceptual tools (sometimes singly and sometimes in combinations) to help integrate and synthesise what we know about how housing interacts with other life course dynamics.

Principle 1: Life span development

The principle of life span development stresses that lives are continuously unfolding, that important life events can occur at any age and that such events can have long-lasting consequences (Elder et al, 2003). Events are described as transitions if they involve a significant change in social roles, responsibilities, status or identities. As a result, the principle of life span development guides researchers to move away from cross-sectional analysis of particular snapshots in time in favour of longitudinal perspectives which can capture temporal interdependencies within lives and between people and their changing social contexts (Bernardi et al, 2019). The rationale for this approach is essentially that a photograph album tells us more about someone's life than a single picture of them taken at a particular moment.

Two conceptual tools are useful for taking this longer-term view of life span development: *biography* and *cumulative development*.

Biography

Viewing lives as personal biographies is a defining feature of life course scholarship (Bailey, 2009). However, the concept of biographies can be applied in many ways. Perhaps the simplest is to focus on the patterning of objective residential biographies across the population. This approach typically involves using longitudinal data to construct and analyse the sequences of residential states people pass through over time. While early studies simply described the prevalence of biographical sequence types, recent work has started to scrutinise the interrelations between housing careers and state sequences in other life domains. For instance, Spallek and colleagues (2014) document how Australian tenure biographies have become more diverse and less closely tied to marital status sequences over time. This approach has proven useful for uncovering persistent inequalities such as the association of low income with repeatedly unfulfilled moving desires (Coulter and van Ham, 2013).

A second view of biographies goes beyond description to examine biographical processes of housing career development and in particular the way agency is bounded by the 'shadows' cast by earlier decisions and experiences (Bernardi et al, 2019). A core tenet of this approach is that past experiences shape subsequent residential aspirations, preferences, resources and behaviours in many ways. These include the ways that childhood residential circumstances influence tenure preferences and whether people prefer to live in a more urban or rural setting in later life (Feijten et al, 2008; Lersch and Luijdx, 2015). Similarly, prior familiarity with migration has been posited to affect residential evaluations and make people more likely to subsequently move again (Thomas et al, 2016). The biographical timing of when an event is experienced (for example in childhood versus as an adult) may also shape its impacts and fusing notions of biographies with other conceptual tools can often help us to better understand these nuances.

Understanding biographical processes involves considering how events and transitions shape subsequent housing careers. Doing this requires distinguishing a person's factual residential biography from the almost infinite number of counterfactual or virtual biographies they could have lived (Feijten, 2005). In this view, every event or transition a person (does not) experience at a particular moment closes off some virtual biographical possibilities, opens up others, and alters the relative probabilities of taking each remaining potential path. For example, buying a house constitutes a major financial commitment that typically reduces subsequent moving propensity. Similarly, adverse events such as divorce have been shown to increase the likelihood of moving for many years afterwards (Feijten and van Ham, 2010).

A third approach focuses less on measurable housing career states and more on subjectivity and the social construction of residential biographies.[3] Here biography is both a method and a subject, with biographies defined more as 'narrations of the subjective and social meaning of events' (Bailey et al, 2021, p 3). This 'strong' biographical approach can be traced back to Halfacree and Boyle's (1993) contention that migration – and by extension any residential decision – is not simply a predictable behavioural response to external stimuli. Instead, Halfacree and Boyle (1993) argued that decisions about moving unfold over time and are bound up with people's past, projected future life course trajectory and desired cultural identities.

Halfacree and Boyle's (1993) argument implies that residential biographies are shaped by agency and personal choice as these are enacted in particular cultural contexts. However, the extent to which residential biographies are purposefully constructed identity projects varies across the population. For instance, Savage and colleagues (2010) show that older middle-class Britons frequently narrate their housing experiences as personal 'life journeys' that have culminated in them forging a deep emotional, aesthetic and often proprietary connection to a chosen dwelling and landscape. Less affluent and less mobile older Britons were, by contrast, more likely to report feeling passively 'placed' into a location which has defined the contours of their life but led them to develop a rich network of local social contacts (Savage et al, 2010). Similarly, Clark (2009) reports how residents of deprived Scottish neighbourhoods viewed these estates ambiguously as both places to exit and valued spaces.

Cumulative development

Cumulative development offers a more explanatory tool for understanding life span development. The crux of the concept is that many aspects of people's lives follow developmental trajectories (Wheaton and Gotlib, 1997). Outcomes observed at a given moment in the trajectory are thus the product of a biographical development process that is configured, in part, by unfolding patterns of past experience in both the focal career and in other interdependent domains.

For housing research, a key concern is for Matthew Effects in the cumulative development of housing careers. Matthew Effects are named after a passage in the gospels: 'For unto every one that hath shall be given, and he shall have abundance: but from him that hath not shall be taken away even that which he hath' (Matthew 25:29). In essence, a Matthew Effect indicates the divergence of fortunes over time. While advantages increasingly accrue to those who were the most advantaged to start with, the less advantaged either experience the slower accumulation of benefits or find that their disadvantages compound each other over time.

Ideas of Matthew Effects can be applied to understand how the uneven accumulation of housing assets shapes social inequality. Writing in 1990, Saunders optimistically argued that UK housing assets were being democratised as households across the social spectrum benefited from expanding access to homeownership and house price growth. More recent work contends that wealth gains are in fact much more of a Matthew process as the largest returns accrue to older and higher-income households (Arundel, 2017).

Cumulative development is also relevant for understanding locational ties. Traditional cumulative inertia models posited that people become less likely to move the longer they have lived in a place as the accumulation of local social bonds, local knowledge (for example about jobs) and subjective place attachments increases the cost of relocating. However, analysis by Thomas et al (2016) suggests this view is too simplistic as duration of stay has more non-linear and spatially varied effects on moving intentions. This could be because psychological assessments of the costs and benefits of moving vary with personal risk appetites (Clark and Lisowski, 2017). In addition, prospect theory suggests that people evaluate whether to move using dynamic personal reference points that shift in favour of staying with increased duration in a particular place as they accumulate location-specific endowments (Morrison and Clark, 2016). This approach suggests that the actual costs and the perceived risks of moving may both rise as duration of stay increases.

Principle 2: Timing

This principle states that the timing of events and transitions alters their meaning and implications (Elder et al, 2003). In this view, timing has both an absolute and a relative dimension. Absolute (or chronological) timing refers to the biological age when an event or transition occurs or does not occur. Changes in the absolute timing of residential events such as leaving the parental home, migrating or moving into assisted living are of central interest to demographers (Falkingham et al, 2016) and also underpin many policy issues, for example debates about delayed entry into owner-occupation among younger cohorts. However, these approaches often rest on an assumption that biological age has a static and homogenous meaning. This jars with scholarship emphasising the social construction of life stages and the ways that meanings, experiences and expectations of biological ageing vary over time and across populations (Mortimer and Moen, 2016).

In contrast, relative timing refers to the way the timing of a focal event relates to the timing of something else (Feijten, 2005). This could be the timing of another event (timing is relative within biographies) or the normative societal timetabling of events (timing is relative to what might be termed collective social scripts). Viewing timing as relative shifts the focus away from age-grading and opens up space for more relational understandings of housing career processes. These recognise that the meaning and effects of events are not innate but are instead produced through their temporal relations with other events as well as with social norms and institutions.

Four conceptual tools can complement notions of biography and cumulative development by helping us to better understand the timed dimensions of housing careers: *ordering and sequences, duration, trajectories and turning points* and *timetables and scripts*.

Ordering and sequences

Life courses are differentiated not only by the (non)occurrence of events and transitions but also by their biographical timing and the order in which such events occur (Feijten, 2005). The meaning and implications of a given event therefore depend on when it occurs in relation to other events. For example, consider three adverse events: (1) mental ill health, (2) losing one's job and (3) being evicted. If experienced in this sequence, the proximate cause of the eviction is being unable to work due to illness and so providing better healthcare assistance might be a good policy solution. However, the presumed causal processes look very different if the events are rearranged so that (1) being evicted is followed by (2) mental ill health and then (3) unemployment. Now eviction appears the cause of other problems and so social policy needs to improve housing security.

The elapsed time between events also matters for their sequencing. This is perhaps especially relevant for housing as the cost and complexity of residential moves means that it is often difficult to tightly synchronise relocation with other life course processes. As a result, Falkingham and colleagues (2016) note the value of analysing what occurs in the temporal 'windows' around residential events. This approach allows for analysis of anticipation and lag times (Feijten, 2005), as well as the ways in which people adapt psychologically to moving home and to periods of residential stability.

To illustrate the importance of elapsed time, the top five rows of Figure 2.2 show five examples of how two events – birth of a child and a tenure

Figure 2.2: Example sequencing of a homeownership transition with childbirth

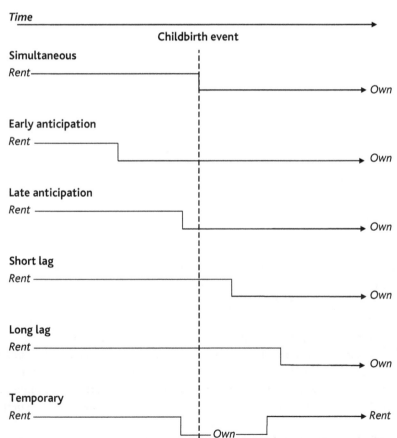

adjustment – might be temporally organised in different ways. These range from early anticipation of childbirth through to simultaneous occurrence and a long lag between fertility and tenure change. Differentiating between these different temporal orderings requires longitudinal rather than cross-sectional analysis.

Duration

Life course careers are comprised of periods in states punctuated by events or transitions marking moments of change. In addition to the ordering of these events and transitions, the duration spent in each state is important for understanding the structure of residential careers (Feijten, 2005). Indeed, some of the cumulative development models reviewed earlier can be thought of as specific forms of duration-dependent process where elapsed duration has some kind of a causal effect on the trajectory of a life career.

However, it is important to move beyond this by inverting the focus to consider duration as an outcome rather than a cause of other processes. This can help us to understand what leads people to spend more or less time in particular types of dwelling and residential location, as well as what these states mean to the individuals concerned (Clapham, 2005). The bottom row of Figure 2.2 illustrates why this is important by showing that some transitions into homeownership may be temporary rather than lasting. As was the case with temporal ordering, distinguishing states that are short-term and temporary from those that last longer requires longitudinal data.

Trajectories and turning points

Adopting this type of longer-term lens allows us to assess whether segments of the life course form a trajectory. Life course careers are on a trajectory if they show a continuing direction towards a particular outcome (Wheaton and Gotlib, 1997). This does not mean that trajectories are periods of stability: a trajectory can encompass events and transitions so long as these do not dramatically change the probability of a destination outcome. For example, a housing career comprising leaving home and a period renting could be considered a trajectory towards homeownership if the probability of buying a home is progressively increasing as a person saves.

Life events leading to a significant change in the trajectory of life course careers are known as turning points (Stone et al, 2014). These come in many forms, ranging from anticipated and advantageous turning points (for example leaving the parental home to go to university) through to negative turning points induced by external shocks (such as recession-induced job loss). For an event to be considered a turning point it must:

1. create a significant, long-lasting change in the trajectory of one or more life careers; and
2. form a transition by leading the person to assume new roles, responsibilities and potentially identities (Wheaton and Gotlib, 1997).

These criteria mean that whether an event forms a turning point usually depends on its biographical timing, personal attributes (for example gender, class or ethnicity) and its occurrence in calendar time and geographical space (Stone et al, 2014). These factors also shape the type of turning point a given event constitutes. For instance, having a child while a lone teenager living in the parental home is a qualitatively different turning point to childbearing when aged 35, employed and living independently with a spouse. This example points to the interdependence between turning point events and trajectories, as well as the way neither can be understood in isolation.

Trajectories and turning points have advantages over the other conceptual tools discussed thus far. Both turning points and trajectories better highlight the directionality of lives than the related but more descriptive concepts of biography, ordering and duration. In addition, both better accommodate non-linearity and shocks than the idea of cumulative development, while the notion of turning points provides an effective tool for identifying causal processes. However, making use of the turning point and trajectories concepts is challenging because both are inherently retrospective. It is not possible to tell if an event is a turning point or whether someone is on a trajectory without knowing about their subsequent experiences (Wheaton and Gotlib, 1997).

Timetables and scripts

The meaning and implications of life events depends partly on how closely their timing aligns with shared cultural scripts (Elder et al, 2003). These timetabled scripts circulate as social discourses and they set out the normative timing and sequencing of life events and transitions, as well as the 'correct' turning points to experience during particular life phases. Whether an event occurs on- or off-time can thus have a major impact both on how it is experienced and on its subsequent effects. An internalised desire to follow a prevailing cultural script – especially if encouraged to do so by significant others – can also strongly affect residential preferences and behaviours.

Grasping how timed cultural scripts shape housing careers requires appreciating that these scripts vary geographically and across social groups (Grenier, 2015). These variations can have major consequences for residential preferences and behaviours (for example by creating differing patterns of household structure across ethnic groups), as well as for subjective experiences of housing. The pace at which socially accepted housing scripts change over time is also relevant for understanding housing careers. For example,

Crawford and McKee (2018) argue that an 'aspirational gap' is opening up in younger cohorts' housing careers as they find it increasingly difficult to follow the script of early homeownership they grew up expecting and which their parents wish to see them attain.

Some of the most powerful effects of cultural scripts come from the way these are embedded into social institutions. This is a fundamentally political process that the most powerful groups' normative scripts and timetables usually dominate. For instance, in Britain eligibility for various housing-related benefits is dependent on age and thus entitlements rest on a particular social script about what constitutes appropriate housing needs over an age-graded life course. For example, the restriction of housing benefit support for single under-35s to the cost of renting a room in a shared dwelling draws on and reproduces an assumption that sharing with unrelated people is a normal part of young adulthood (Wilkinson and Ortega-Alcázar, 2017). This assumption fits poorly with the residential needs of less well-off young separated parents who are not following the prevailing cultural script and thus can expect limited state support (Berrington and Stone, 2014).

Principle 3: Linked lives

This principle asserts that individuals are not atomised actors as the course of people's lives is profoundly influenced by the life course dynamics of others they are 'linked' to in ways that range from kinship bonds through to friendship ties (Elder et al, 2003). Such interconnections influence everyday experiences of housing and decisions about where to live through a huge variety of mechanisms that stretch far beyond resources and restrictions. In addition, the role linked lives play in housing careers varies greatly over space, time and across axes of social differentiation such as gender, class, ethnicity and health status. The links between lives are also not static but are themselves transformed over time by the housing behaviours of those who are tied together (Holdsworth, 2013). This means that residential behaviours are relational processes that help to drive change within families and other social groupings.

Three sets of conceptual tools can help us better integrate linked lives into work on housing careers: *synchronisation and ripples*, *solidarities* and *household relations*.

Synchronisation and ripples

Synchronisation and ripples are two related ways to understand how housing processes bind together multiple life courses. Synchronisation has many meanings in life course scholarship but is defined here as the ways in which events or behaviours in one person's life are timed to intersect or coincide with those in the life of someone else (Bailey, 2009). This synchronisation can occur within everyday life, for example when working partners coordinate daily routines to juggle childcare and workplace demands. However, synchronisation can also take place over broader scales, for example through family reunification migration or internal migrations to provide physical support to non-resident kin. In both cases, the way that housing structures daily activity space makes it an integral aspect in the synchronising of careers.

Ripple effects meanwhile refer to the ways in which events and processes in one person's life have consequences that ripple out to affect the lives of others. While many ripple events are likely to involve life course synchronisation, some may take longer to emerge or to attain significance. For example, parental divorce during childhood could alter the resources available to subsequently help children to enter the housing system (Hubers et al, 2018). Crucially, the significance of synchronisation and ripple effects are likely to vary across social groups and across country contexts.

Solidarities

Synchronisation and ripples are valuable for understanding how linked lives shape residential decisions and housing careers. However, neither concept effectively grasps why people synchronise their life courses, the extent to which the effects of linked lives vary, or the way linked life connections are simultaneously transformed by housing behaviours. To understand these issues we can draw on the rather complex concept of solidarities.

The basic idea of solidarity is that people typically want to work together to promote the well-being of others they are linked to by virtue of their joint membership of a group with a collective identity and shared norms of mutual support. For many people, the most significant collective group in their life will be their family, although groups of friends, neighbours, religious believers or migrants from a particular origin may also exercise solidarity by helping each other out with housing-related matters. Such solidarity practices can take many forms, including:

- bodily support such as childcare or caring for the frail or sick;
- financial support ranging from transfer payments and loans through to providing guarantees or security to smooth access to credit;
- knowledge or informational support;
- direct housing support in forms ranging from co-residence, cheap accommodation and transfers of property through to DIY help or the provision of hand-me-down items.

Three issues are important for understanding the role solidarities play in housing careers. First, solidarity demands as well as people's ability to support others are likely to vary across the population and across countries with different cultural norms and systems of public welfare provision. Second, the provision and acceptance of housing-related support does not just passively flow along linked life connections but instead actively transforms the lives of those involved. For example, becoming a part-time childminder for grandchildren reshapes intergenerational relations and so changes in the housing domain that necessitate new forms of solidarity help to drive broader changes in family and community relations. Third, solidarities can have a dark side and veer towards control and coercion if housing-related support is conditional ('I'll help you buy a house but you must take me in when I'm old') or motivated less by altruism and more by a desire to maintain group cohesion by enforcing a particular way of living ('no, you cannot move away to go to university as girls should stay home until they get married'). It is therefore always important to consider uneven power relations when thinking about housing-related solidarities.

Household relations

Understanding how linked lives matter for housing careers requires rethinking how we conceptualise households. Traditionally, much housing scholarship assumed that households are unified actors with distinct sets of preferences and goals. This tendency to treat multi-person households as cohesive units is most evident in planning but it also surfaces more incongruously in Clapham's (2005) housing pathways approach. Here, Clapham (2005, p 26) reasons that as households consume housing 'there is no practicable alternative but to use the concept of household [sic] as the basic unit of analysis in housing *while accepting that there are substantial difficulties in its use* [emphasis added]'.

These difficulties are certainly substantial! On the one hand, people can and do change their domestic living arrangements and so it makes little sense to think of households as having a longitudinal housing pathway or career. Careers and pathways are more appropriately conceptualised as individual-level attributes that may involve crossed paths and interwoven development. Meanwhile, on the other hand, there is no logical reason why the joint consumption of housing means that each household member must perceive their residential situation in the same way or have the same preferences or aspirations. As Clapham (2005) rightly goes on to acknowledge, these difficulties mean that we need to open up households and view them as dynamic units of housing consumption that are produced by the changing relations between their constituent members.

These household-scale relations can have major implications for housing careers and life course development. Differences in preferences and residential needs among household members who wish to continue living together may only be soluble through negotiation and compromise. Bargaining power models indicate that the outcome of these interactions depends on personal attributes like the relative ages, genders and economic positions of the parties involved (Abraham et al, 2010; Mulder and Wagner, 2010), as well as how these interact with broader cultural norms about whose needs and views should be prioritised. The linking of lives within households may thus act as unequal ties that bind some people to residential situations they personally consider suboptimal. At present, relatively little is known about these processes outside of a literature on the gendering of long-distance family migration (see Chapter 5).

Principle 4: Agency

This principle stresses that people actively make choices which affect how their lives unfold (Elder et al, 2003). In the housing domain, agency is often exercised in a purposeful fashion, for example as people move and select dwellings in order to satisfy particular goals. However, exercising agency in other life domains and much earlier in life can also shape housing careers in less deliberate or even in inadvertent and unwanted ways (Feijten, 2005). This highlights how agency is bounded by personal biographies and access to resources, as well as by people's linked lives and the broader times and places they have lived in.

The concept of *construction* can help us better understand how bounded agency influences housing careers.

Construction

Construction refers to the ways that people actively make choices, which, over time, configure their residential careers (Clapham, 2005). In part, these choices are informed by idiosyncratic personal tastes and preferences although people with a particular attribute (for instance class or ethnicity) also often exhibit shared patterns of housing experience due to the ways their agency is bounded by similar constellations of opportunities and constraints. For example, Preece (2018) documents how working-class residents of northern English cities rely on local knowledge and informal help from local family and friends to navigate precarious labour markets. This reduces their propensity to migrate relative to more advantaged middle-class workers whose occupational careers may bound their agency by requiring long-distance moves. Similarly, minority groups' preferences for residential clustering are likely to occur partly because the agency of group members is bounded in common ways by resource access, perceived threats and demands for particular amenities or services (Peach, 1996).

Although there has been much qualitative analysis of agency in housing careers, the social constructionism of much of this work means it tends not to engage with more quantitative life course scholarship. This is problematic as setting agency in the context of the other life course principles can help us understand the mechanisms through which choices are systematically bounded in ways that help to produce aggregate inequalities. For example, the principle of linked lives helps us grasp how the geography of kin networks may more strongly bound the residential options of less advantaged groups who rely more heavily on face-to-face family support than those with greater economic resources (Mulder, 2018).

Principle 5: Time and place

The principle of time and place emphasises that lives do not unfold in a contextual vacuum. Instead, the events, transitions and development processes which collectively create life course biographies are shaped by the temporal context and places people pass through as they age (Elder et al, 2003). This is not a one-way causal process as changes within people's lives combine over time to restructure places and societies.

Two conceptual tools are valuable for understanding these issues: *cohort and period* and the broad notion of *changing places* (see Chapter 7).

Cohort and period

Cohort and period effects allow us to move beyond timeless models of residential decision-making and behaviour. Instead, these concepts guide us to scrutinise how the age-graded timing of events, transitions and processes are given structure and meaning by their location in particular collective social and historical times (Elder and George, 2016). A cohort can be defined as 'a group of individuals who experienced an event of interest at the same time' (Elder and George, 2016, p 60). Most often this event is birth, although analysing birth cohorts does make it almost impossible to disentangle the effects of ageing processes and measurement time from the effect of cohort differences: the so-called Age–Period–Cohort problem (Elder and George, 2016).

The concept of cohorts has two uses in housing research. First, birth cohort comparison helps assess how the age-graded patterning of residential careers have changed over historical time (Myers, 1999). The basic idea here is that the times in which cohorts enter the housing system have consequences for their housing demands and expectations, resources and the housing opportunities and constraints they encounter as they age. This interplay between age and cohort development is integral for understanding how and why contemporary younger adults are in many countries entering owner-occupation more slowly than their predecessors. Similarly, Falkingham and colleagues (2016) show that the late 20th-century increase in divorce rates and female higher educational enrolment have altered the residential mobility biographies of successive cohorts of British women to a greater extent than men. Cohort effects may thus be felt selectively by people with certain attributes.

Second, the impact of cohort attributes on housing systems is vital for understanding how changes in people's lives reshape contextual conditions. In a basic sense, the raw size of birth cohorts influences housing demand over historical time and thus alters housing system dynamics. Myers and Ryu (2008) argue that the sheer size of the US baby boom cohort has impacted housing market dynamics by driving a competitive housing boom during their peak years of market entry in the 1970–80s followed by a projected bust when this cohort starts to sell up or die in the 2020s. In Britain, the unprecedented affluence of the baby boom cohort has further impacted the housing market through their ability to invest in second homes and buy-to-let dwellings (Ronald and Kadi, 2018). In addition, Mannheim's idea of social generations suggests that cohorts' collective childhood experiences could influence their residential demands, potentially leading housing aspirations and preferences to change over time as cohorts with different values and attitudes replace one another (Preece et al, 2020).

In contrast, period effects refer to contextual shocks that impact on everyone exposed to them. These shocks can range from events in the business cycle or dramatic policy changes through to natural disasters, wars or, more recently, the COVID-19 pandemic. Although period effects impact everyone exposed to the event, their effects are not necessarily uniform and identifying the severity, selectivity and duration of effects is vital for understanding housing inequality. For example, Clark (2013a) documents how the 2008 US housing crash had a more damaging impact on marginal homeowners and recent buyers than on those more established and affluent owners who were less exposed to the downturn. Hamnett (1999) meanwhile likened the volatile UK housing market to a casino where the time and place of purchase load the roulette wheel of capital gain in ways that are unknowable to the buyer.

Understanding the impact of period effects and the ways these vary requires tracking those affected for long periods of time. Exploiting natural experiments – for example geographically specific events or policy changes – to compare the experiences of those 'treated' to the experiences of a control group is also a valuable research strategy.

Changing places

There are deep connections between housing career processes and the social dynamics of places. These connections can be approached from two angles. On the one hand, much scholarship seeks to describe and explain spatial variation in housing careers. This approach draws on the idea that places have contingent causal impacts on life courses (Johnston et al, 2014). However, several difficulties make it hard to convincingly unpack how places influence housing careers:

- *Scale*: Although most studies focus primarily on one spatial scale (for example cross-national patterns or localised neighbourhood effects), contextual influences on residential careers are likely to operate at multiple scales and interactions between processes spanning different levels may be important (Piekut, 2021). In addition, the level of aggregation used in any study and how the boundaries of geographical units are drawn can greatly affect the results from statistical analyses.
- *Timing*: The biographical timing of exposure to particular contexts may matter, for example if deprivation has more damaging impacts on child than adult health (Chapter 6).
- *Dimensions*: Spatial effects are likely to occur through multiple mechanisms ranging from material opportunities and constraints on housing behaviour through to the less visible and more indirect ways in which the characteristics of neighbours or the institutional and cultural setting shape preferences, resources and events in other life course careers.
- *Social selectivity*: The role spatial processes play in structuring housing careers is likely to vary across people with different attributes, for example if only less affluent households are priced out of owner-occupation in costly markets.

Work on the spatiality of housing careers tends not to consider how aggregate patterns of residential behaviour also drive changes in places. This has been the subject of a largely separate set of often discrete literatures examining different neighbourhood dynamics. These include work exploring socio-economic sorting, ethnic or racial 'segregation', gentrification and studentification.

  More closely integrating work on the geography of housing careers with these geographical studies of population dynamics can provide a richer framework for understanding how changes in residential behaviours connect broad-scale changes in economies and societies to changing lives and local population dynamics. In this view, trends such as the gentrification of city neighbourhoods are not the inevitable consequences of abstract structural forces. Rather, these are embodied processes produced by the residential decisions people make by exercising bounded agency within the context of their own lives and particular constellations of contextual circumstances. Understanding the ways in which social trends shape life courses and residential decisions is thus vitally important for grasping why places change in particular ways. Crucially, this is not a one-way process as changing places can, in turn, affect residential decisions and through this alter the structure of society. A good example of this is the way in which social inequality deepens when working-class residents displaced from gentrifying neighbourhoods cannot profit from the financial gains associated with subsequent house price uplift. We return to these issues of changing places throughout subsequent chapters and especially in Chapter 7.

Summary

This chapter has argued that existing frameworks provide only a partial lens for understanding 21st-century housing behaviours. To overcome these issues, the chapter presented a modern life course perspective on housing career dynamics which can form the conceptual framework for a more nuanced understanding of residential behaviours. This approach was sketched by revisiting Elder et al's (2003) five principles of life course approaches and using these to derive twelve conceptual tools that can be applied in research projects and when synthesising evidence. These tools are intended to be used flexibly in ways tailored to the needs of a particular research application. The twelve conceptual tools outlined in this chapter can also be operationalised using multiple methods, including both quantitative and qualitative techniques. Regardless of the approach taken, the chapter has consistently emphasised the value of viewing life course processes through a longitudinal lens. The rest of the book now takes the framework developed in this chapter and applies it to integrate and synthesise the disparate literature on 21st-century housing and life course dynamics.

3

Households and families

This chapter examines the connections between housing careers and the dynamics of households and families. As Chapter 2 explained, Rossi (1955) was the first to recognise that family dynamics play a pivotal role in structuring housing careers. Decades of subsequent research have supported Rossi's thesis that events in the family life course frequently generate new residential demands which then prompt housing adjustments (Clark, 2021).

However, this prevailing focus on how family processes drive housing careers provides only a partial view of how these two life course domains interact. For a start, causality can flow in the other direction as housing opportunities and constraints impinge on family dynamics, for example the choice to have children (Mulder, 2006). More fundamentally, housing moves and housing-related support practices also actively reshape kin relations (Holdsworth, 2013). Housing and family therefore constitute such deeply intertwined careers that neither can be fully understood in isolation.

Changing families

Changes in housing behaviour are deeply bound up with the ongoing transformation of households and families that has occurred with the post-war demographic restructuring of Global North societies. Broadly speaking, population change since the Second World War has influenced family dynamics in two ways. First, *new family behaviours and patterns of domestic living arrangement* have emerged as countries have moved through the Second Demographic Transition (Lesthaeghe, 2010). To illustrate this process, Table 3.1 compares data on family-related behaviours and household structures in England and Wales from two census years: 1951 and 2011. The table highlights several trends, including:

- delayed marriage and the emergence of unmarried cohabitation, most notably among younger couples for whom cohabitation is now both an alternative to marriage as well as the normal precursor to it;
- increased partnership instability since the 1960s driven partly by higher divorce rates and partly by the replacement of marriages with less stable cohabitations;
- declining fertility due to postponed childbearing and lower levels of completed fertility;

- the decoupling of childbearing from marriage;
- reductions in average household size associated with ageing, lower fertility and increased solo living (ONS, 2014).

These trends have been accompanied by the growth of reconstituted or 'blended' families and an increase in the proportion of children dividing their time between the households of separated parents. Greater acceptance of same-sex partnerships and their legal recognition from 2005 have injected further variety into family structures. As we shall see throughout this chapter, these changing family behaviours are a crucial force which is helping to drive the increased dynamism, diversity and destandardisation of 21st-century residential careers.

Second, *changes in population composition* driven by ageing and immigration have profoundly altered family dynamics. In 1951, male and female life expectancies at birth were 66 and 72 respectively but by 2011 had risen to 79 for men (+13 years) and 83 (+11) for women (ONS, 2015b). This elongation of the life course has opened up space for new family behaviours (such as remarriages and divorce in later life), has transformed intergenerational relationships and also reshaped household structures (for example declining sex differentials in life expectancy mean older adults are now spending longer living as couples).

In addition, post-war immigration streams have significantly altered the composition of the British population. Between 1951 and 2011, the share of overseas-born residents of England and Wales swelled from 4.3 to 13.4

Table 3.1: Changing family behaviours and household structures in England and Wales

Indicator	1951	2011	Source[c]
Marriage rate/1,000 unmarried (M)	69	23	ONS (2020a)
Marriage rate/1,000 unmarried (F)	52	21	ONS (2020a)
Mean age at marriage (M marrying F)	29	36[a]	ONS (2020a)
Mean age at marriage (F marrying M)	26	34[a]	ONS (2020a)
Divorce rate/1,000 married	3	10	ONS (2020b)
Percentage of adults cohabiting	–	12	ONS (2015a)
Total Fertility Rate (TFR)	2.1	1.9[b]	ONS (2021a)
Percentage of births outside marriage	5	47	ONS (2021a)
Average maternal age at birth	28	30	ONS (2017)
Average household size	3.2	2.4	ONS (2014)

[a] Both averages had increased by a further two years in 2017.

[b] Down to under 1.7 by 2019.

[c] Contains public sector information licensed under the Open Government Licence v3.0.

per cent (ONS, 2013a), while the share of births to foreign-born mothers doubled to 26 per cent in the three decades to 2011 (ONS, 2021a). The composition of migrants has also diversified over time – the top ten origin countries supplied 60 per cent of the overseas-born population in 1951 but only 45 per cent in 2011 – and helped drive the growth of ethnic minority populations to around 13 per cent of the 2011 UK population (ONS, 2013b).

The rest of this chapter uses the life course framework and the conceptual tools outlined in Chapter 2 to examine how these changes in households and families intersect with housing career dynamics. The chapter focuses primarily on four family-related dynamics which, taken together, strongly drive aggregate patterns of household formation, dissolution and housing demand (Mulder, 2013): (1) leaving the parental home and entering the housing system, (2) partnership formation, (3) fertility and (4) relationship dissolution.[1]

Entering the housing system

Youth research has long viewed leaving the parental home as an important milestone in the transition to adulthood (Berngruber, 2016). The basic idea is that leaving home is often a life course turning point which enables young adults to attain greater autonomy and take on new roles, for example concerning household management. In Britain, this turning point model probably adequately described the way that children born immediately after the Second World War entered the housing system. Their early lives were marked by rising affluence, plentiful jobs, a supportive welfare state, early marriage norms and good access to owner-occupation and a secure public rental sector. This context provided young people with the incentives, resources and opportunities to leave home early and fairly quickly enter the 'lifetime' tenures of either homeownership or council housing (Ford et al, 2002). Berrington and Murphy (1994) show how initial exits from the parental home in the post-war decades often coincided with higher education or marriage. However, the timing and destination of home-leaving varied considerably by gender (with earlier home-leaving among women), across time (with falling direct exits to partnership from the 1970s) and by socio-economic status (with university attendance accelerating middle-class departures).

Berrington and Murphy (1994) demonstrated that young adults' household formation patterns were already becoming more complex by the 1980s. These trends have continued as leaving home has become a more protracted, precarious, reversible and destandardised process across the Global North (Berngruber, 2016). Several macro-structural shifts explain these trends, including:

- enhanced job instability, lower incomes for young workers, curtailed benefit support, and the expansion of debt-funded higher education reducing locational stability and young people's resources and economic security (Berrington et al, 2017);
- delayed partnership and family formation together with prolonged educational enrolment dampening preferences to quickly enter the long-term tenures of homeownership or social housing;
- strengthening housing constraints induced by a shortage of social housing, increased income and deposit barriers to home purchase, and, in Britain, post-2010 austerity cuts to young people's benefit entitlements.

Taken together, these trends have altered the *ordering, sequencing and durations* of young adults' initial routes into the housing system while also heightening the importance of *intergenerational solidarities* and *place* in shaping early housing careers.

Ordering, sequencing and durations

Writing in 2002, Ford and colleagues divided young people's pathways out of the parental home into five types. Yet just over a decade later, Clapham and colleagues (2014) found that young people were now following nine types of residential pathway. In addition to this greater diversity, Clapham et al (2014) noted that private renting and the parental home were assuming greater prominence in early housing careers as young adults' access to owner-occupation declined, in particular in the years after the 2008 crisis.

Clapham and colleagues' (2014) analysis is borne out by official statistics. Between 2003–4 and 2013–14, the owner-occupation rate of 25–34-year-old householders in England fell from 59 to 36 per cent, while the proportion renting privately climbed 27 percentage points from 21 to 48 per cent (MHCLG, 2020a). Although by 2019–20 both rates had converged to around 41 per cent as mortgage borrowing became easier, it is clear that since 2000 private renting has become a far more common aspect of young Britons' housing careers. Crucially, this transition in age-graded tenure experiences – encapsulated by the popular term Generation Rent – has happened extremely quickly and seems evident across the entire country (Corlett and Judge, 2017).

One problem with focusing purely on the tenure circumstances of young households is that this assumes stable rates of household formation. However, household formation among the under-35s is being postponed across the Global North as home-leaving becomes a more protracted and reversible process. In Britain, the ONS (2018a) estimate that the proportion of 20–34-year-olds living in the parental home rose from 21 to 26 per cent between 1996 and 2017. This growth in parental co-residence has had a clear regional geography with more pronounced increases in London and the South East (7.9 and 9.1 percentage point rises respectively) than in northern England (with 3 and 3.3 percentage point rises in the North East and North West). Wales and Northern Ireland, meanwhile, posted reduced co-residence figures between 1996 and 2017 (down 0.7 and 0.1 percentage points respectively). Patterns of parental co-residence are also gendered with a higher proportion of young men than women living in the parental home, especially between the ages of 24 and 32 (ONS, 2021b).

No single factor can explain these trends and surprisingly little is known about the extent to which delayed exits versus higher rates of return are responsible for increasing parental co-residence among the under-35s. On one hand, living at home is a coping mechanism for the growing numbers of young people who lack the resources and job security to enter a less affordable and less accessible housing system. This interpretation is bolstered by evidence that co-residence in Britain – especially past the age of 30 when living at home tends to become less socially acceptable – is more common among the less economically advantaged (Berrington et al, 2017). For these groups, co-residence is an intergenerational support practice that allows lower-income young adults to boost their standard of living. It is therefore perhaps unsurprising that, across Europe, the probability of exiting the parental home is greater when young people have a job and higher income (Iacovou, 2010). From a parental perspective, the economies of scale and opportunities for income pooling produced by intergenerational co-residence make living together a more efficient housing support mechanism than financial transfers to pay children's rent.

Research into boomerang moves shows that parental housing also provides an important safety-net for young adults navigating precarious labour and housing markets. Stone and colleagues (2014) show that moving back in with parents is a way for young people to adapt to life course shocks such as unemployment. However, the likelihood of returning home following these events is mediated by other factors as higher ages, incomes and parental affluence all buffer against boomerang moves (Arundel and Lennartz, 2017). Gender and family status are also relevant in Britain as the welfare system directs housing support towards custodial parents. This means that those without children, as well as non-resident parents (usually fathers), are particularly vulnerable to shocks and are more reliant on either shared accommodation, cramped bedsits or the parental safety-net (Berrington and Stone, 2014).

Crucially, living in or returning to the parental home is not simply a passive response to housing constraints and economic risk. For a start, differences in family formation behaviour across ethnic groups (such as later home-leaving among South Asians) signal that culturally differentiated norms shape co-residence patterns (Stone et al, 2011). Furthermore, more advantaged young adults often use the parental home more strategically as a springboard into the labour and housing markets. For example, delayed home-leaving can allow young people to save up and amass the larger mortgage deposits required to enter owner-occupation (Clapham et al, 2014; Suh, 2020). The expansion of higher education since the 1990s (both in numerical terms and to non-traditional social groups) has also increased levels of parental co-residence. In part, this is because a greater proportion of first-generation and lower-income students live at home while studying locally (see Chapter 4). Moreover, many students who do move away subsequently return home after course completion before oscillating between the parental home and private renting as they remain spatially flexible while trying to enter competitive graduate labour markets (Sage et al, 2013).

The increased prominence of the parental home in early housing careers has a number of implications. Lewis et al (2016) document the ambiguous consequences of extended parental co-residence which can bring families together but also generate intergenerational friction. This ambiguity came to the fore during the COVID-19 pandemic when young adults' lockdown returns generated significant family stress and strife (Evandrou et al, 2020). Nevertheless, spending longer at home and returning during one's twenties are increasingly viewed as a normal aspect of early 21st-century life courses (Lewis et al, 2016). This suggests that age-graded housing norms are changing as people from all cohorts recognise that the transition to adulthood has become a more difficult, fuzzy, reversible and drawn-out phase marked by prolonged semi-independence (Arundel and Ronald, 2016). This may be partly due to increased precarity and housing uncertainty, but it also seems that the late teens and early twenties are often viewed – at least by the middle-classes – as a phase of 'emerging adulthood' where young people should be free to experiment with jobs, relationships, identities and residential arrangements (Arnett, 2000). Changing residential behaviours may therefore be bound up with broader shifts in the normative cultural scripting of transitions to adulthood.

Panel data tracking young people through time provides an ideal way to robustly explore how early housing careers have changed in the 2000s as new birth cohorts have entered the housing system. Britain is fortunate here in having long-running nationally representative panel survey data collected by the BHPS (1991–2008) and its successor, Understanding Society (UKHLS, from 2009/10 onwards). For this analysis, two birth cohorts were selected from these datasets. Members of the first cohort were born from the mid-1970s to 1981 and were aged 18–24 in 1999 (the year of the ninth wave of BHPS), while members of the second cohort were born from the mid-1980s to 1992 and were aged 18–24 in 2009/10 (the years of the first wave of UKHLS). Each cohort's housing experiences were then tracked as its members aged from 18–24 (at the baseline wave in either 1999 or 2009/10) for nine waves through to around ages 27–33 (at the final wave of each survey's follow-up period in either 2008 or 2018/19). Figure 3.1 visualises the housing states of each birth cohort over their nine-year follow-up period while Table 3.2 provides key statistics summarising their housing careers.

Figure 3.1 and Table 3.2 confirm that recent cohorts of young adults have come to rely much more heavily on the parental home. In particular, Table 3.2 shows that the percentage of young adults who spend an extended period of time living with their parents has increased sharply through the first decades of this century. Both Figure 3.1 and Table 3.2 also show significant tenure restructuring over this period as entry into homeownership has been much slower for the latter cohort. While 69 per cent of young adults aged 18–24 in 1999 had some experience of owner-occupation during their nine-year follow-up period, this fell to just 48 per cent among those aged 18–24 in 2009/10. Decreasing rates of long-term owner-occupancy indicate that delayed purchases lie behind this trend. This pattern has to a large degree been counterbalanced by increased private renting and especially longer spells of renting privately. Table 3.2 shows that the proportion of young adults experiencing a long spell of private renting approximately doubled across these two cohorts, while the proportion who ever rented rose far more modestly. Overall, Figure 3.1 and Table 3.2 reiterate that young adults' early housing careers have changed dramatically over the past twenty years as more recent cohorts rely much more heavily on private renting and the parental home while making slower transitions into owner-occupation.

Intergenerational solidarities

The growth of parental co-residence in young adulthood is one dimension of the broader 'familialisation' of early housing careers (Forrest and Hirayama, 2018). This rather ungainly term captures how young adults' routes into the housing system are now strongly shaped by family support. In essence, intergenerationally linked lives powerfully structure early housing events and transitions, which, in turn, have consequences for lifetime housing trajectories. In one sense this is neither a new nor a particularly surprising observation. Exchanging support has always been at the heart of the intergenerational contract and housing (along with land and property more generally) has always been a key site for these exchanges.

The problem confronting policymakers is that family support has become an increasingly important force in young adults' housing careers as the early lives of recent birth cohorts have become more fluid, marked by economic risk, the state has retreated from welfare provision and the housing system has become less accessible. This growing importance of family assistance conflicts with governments' espoused commitments to social mobility as differential access to family housing support transmits inequality down the generations

Figure 3.1: Housing states of two cohorts of young Britons tracked for nine years

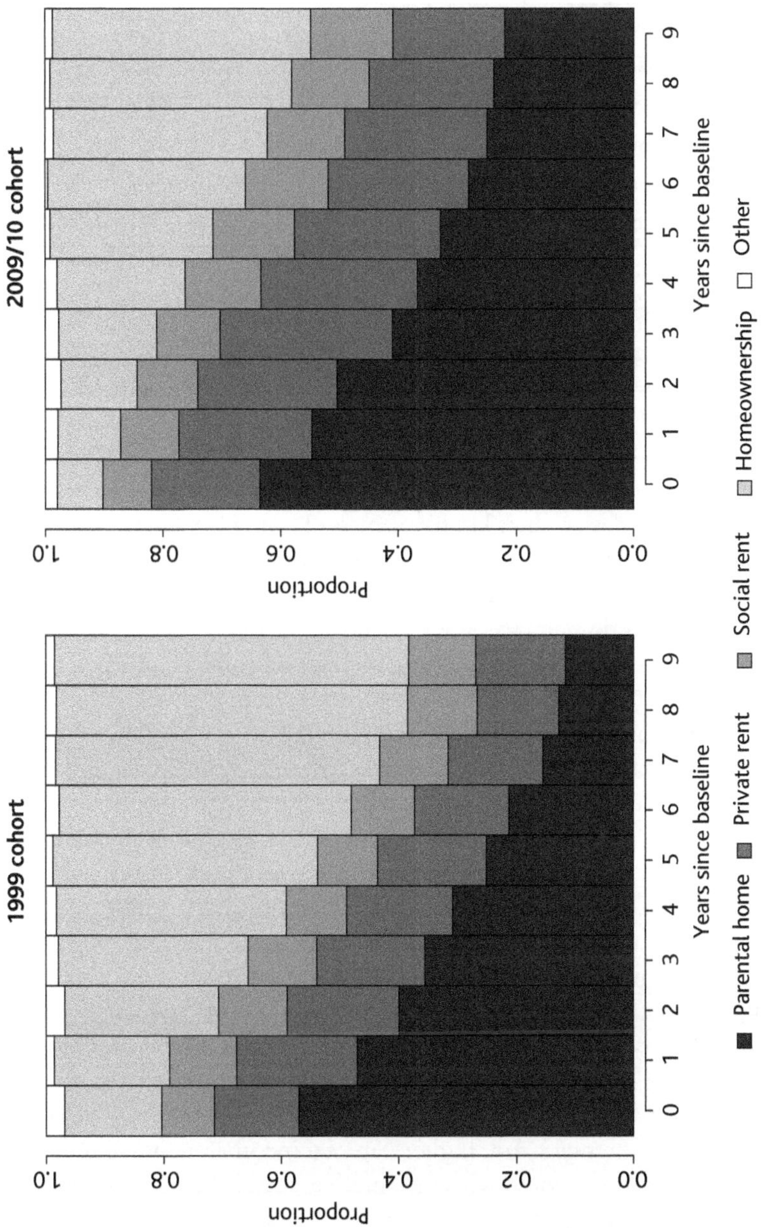
1999 cohort
2009/10 cohort
Proportion
0.0
0.2
0.4
0.6
0.8
1.0
Years since baseline
0
1
2
3
4
5
6
7
8
9
Parental home
Private rent
Social rent
Homeownership
Other

Source: Own analysis of weighted BHPS/UKHLS data.

Table 3.2: Housing career attributes of two cohorts of young Britons tracked for nine years

Characteristic (% of individuals)	1999 cohort	2009/10 cohort
Ever a private renter	45.5	48.3
Ever a homeowner	69.4	48.1
With long spell[a] in parental home	22.8	35.2
With long spell[a] of private renting	10.3	22.3
With long spell[a] of homeownership	41.8	25.7
Unweighted n individuals	563	491

[a]Defined as lasting more than five consecutive waves.

Source: Own analysis of weighted BHPS/UKHLS data.

(Christophers, 2018). In consequence, Forrest and Hirayama (2018) argue that housing dynasties are now emerging to re-stratify 21st-century societies. While the children of renters and owner-occupiers in low-value areas can expect little housing support, those from real-estate accumulator dynasties benefit from the assets their kin have amassed from homeownership in prime locations, perhaps supplemented by additional buy-to-let and property investments. In essence, early housing careers are now structured not just by what work you do but also by what land and property your family owns.

These types of intensifying intergenerational solidarities operate in two ways. First, family relationships affect home-leaving and household formation as research shows that the probability of leaving home to different household destinations varies with the structure of parental households and with the quality of intergenerational relationships (Bayrakdar and Coulter, 2018). This literature indicates that while troubled relationships accelerate departure to destinations other than higher education, the odds of returning home are higher for children with good intergenerational relationships and lower for those from blended families (South and Lei, 2015). New social scripts created by ethno-religious diversity may also be relevant here. For example, compared with White Britons, young Pakistani and Bangladeshi migrants are more likely to live with parents in their twenties but by age 30 are more likely to have formed their own families (Stone et al, 2011).

The influence of parental socio-economic status on home-leaving is more complex. On the one hand, higher parental income encourages departures to coincide more tightly with age-graded social scripts. Iacovou (2010) documents how higher parental income discourages early exits to partnership while accelerating departure at older ages when living at home usually becomes more stigmatised. These findings chime with qualitative evidence that middle-class British parents support their children to leave home and live independently 'on time' in ways ranging from buying property and big-ticket items through to defraying household expenses (Heath and Calvert, 2013). Crucially, these intergenerational support practices change family relationships in ambiguous ways as accepting parental assistance ironically highlights young adults' continued dependence (Druta and Ronald, 2017).

On the other hand, higher socio-economic status can deter exits if affluence enables parents to provide a more spacious and comfortable family home (the 'feathered nest' hypothesis). In essence, the incentive to leave the family home to attain independence may be reduced if living at home is cheap, comfortable and provides enough privacy to still live an autonomous life (Mulder, 2013). Middle-class parents may further encourage children to live at home in their twenties in order to launch them into the housing and labour markets by supporting them to 'reach' for homeownership and a career job instead of 'settling' for renting and less rewarding work in order to leave home (Lewis et al, 2016; Suh, 2020).

Second, intergenerationally linked lives influence the residential destinations and early housing careers of home-leavers. Indeed, it is difficult to understand leaving home without considering housing and household destinations as these decisions are usually made jointly (Mulder, 2013). One issue of particular importance is the way in which family support – often colloquially termed the 'bank of mum and dad' – propels young adults into homeownership, thereby laying the foundations for wealth accumulation as well as enhanced housing control and security over the life span.

There is now convincing evidence that Global North children are *ceteris paribus* more likely to become owner-occupiers if their parents are homeowners. A number of mechanisms could explain this correlation, including:

- homeowning parents having greater ability to provide financial support for mortgage deposits through *inter vivos* gifts, loans, as well as leapfrog inheritances from grandparents;
- direct gifts of property – sometimes from repurposed buy-to-let investments or with the intention of subsequently letting the dwelling (for example when parents buy housing in university towns for their children before renting it out after they graduate);
- specialist financial products allowing children to use parental savings in mortgage applications;
- parental role model and childhood socialisation effects on tenure preferences (Lersch and Luijkx, 2015);
- a desire to live close to parents in the same housing market, potentially generating intergenerational correlations in tenure (Mulder et al, 2015). This explanation seems less convincing as it assumes children have the resources to enter homeownership and that location determines tenure rather than vice versa.

Strengthening intergenerational correlations in owner-occupation have been documented in Britain since the 1990s as the financial barriers to house purchase have increased and as lending became more constrained after the GFC (Coulter, 2018). Greater reliance on familial financial support partly explains this pattern as Suh (2020) estimates that receiving a monetary gift significantly increased the probability that younger adults entered homeownership between 2008–10 and 2014–16. Of course, many parents do not have the luxury of providing large sums of money to help their children buy housing. A 2014 British survey estimated that 49 per cent of parents supporting child housing purchases came from the most advantaged AB social grades while parents from less advantaged CDE grades dominated the group of parents not providing assistance (Jessop and Humphrey, 2014). Those parents providing support also had an average of £36,000 in savings compared to around £20,000 for those who did not. These data not only signal that inequality between parents is being transmitted to their children through the housing system, but also that the moral economy underpinning the intergenerational contract is being restructured by restricted housing affordability. Indeed, Druta and Ronald (2017) show that giving and receiving gifts towards home purchase creates new forms of intergenerational interdependence as childrens' continued financial reliance on parents is paradoxically rationalised as a way to promote their independence and keep wealth in the family.

Intergenerationally linked lives affect homeownership trajectories in other ways. As research suggests that parental background has the strongest effect on the homeownership outcomes of higher socio-economic status children (Coulter, 2017), it follows that family assistance might primarily influence the timing rather than the occurrence of home purchase.[2] Receiving family support also seems to structure the type and location of housing purchases by enabling young borrowers to afford larger dwellings in more desirable neighbourhoods, potentially as part of a broader intergenerationally negotiated strategy of dynastic wealth-building (Galster and Wessel, 2019). This points to the way place stratifies intergenerational support as access to homeownership in prime locations becomes limited to affluent children from families owning property in the same type of areas (Galster and Wessel, 2019). This evidence fits with the quip that carefully picking your parents is probably the fastest route to homeownership in 21st-century London.

Place

As previously mentioned, geography plays an important role in the structure of young people's housing careers. Within countries, the location of the parental home influences home-leaving preferences, as well as the extent to which household formation is necessary for other transitions such as attending university or finding a career job (see Chapter 4). For example, rural Britain is ageing partly because large numbers of young people in their late teens and early twenties leave home and move to cities in order to study and find a job (Stockdale and Catney, 2014). More limited economic opportunities at home may then dissuade immediate returns.

This tight temporal coordination of home-leaving with education and employment transitions is less evident among urban youth. Those growing up in or near to major cities are more likely to be able to access education and job opportunities while living in the parental home, decoupling their household formation decisions from events in the employment and educational careers. This is probably especially true for those from less advantaged backgrounds who lack the resources to sustain independent living. One consequence of this is that the parental home probably forms a more advantageous social mobility springboard if it is located in or close to a major city. By contrast, children from more peripheral areas have to migrate and rent in order to access the same educational and job opportunities. High costs of living in some cities make this impossible for children from less affluent outsider families, thereby exacerbating social and spatial inequalities. As former Prime Minister Theresa May put it in 2018: 'It's not so hard to accept that door-opening internship in London if your parents own a large house in Central London. It's a much greater challenge if you share a room with your siblings in a North Wales terrace' (May, 2018).

Local geographies of dwelling stock and housing costs further shape the housing opportunities and constraints young people encounter. This is likely to be especially true for working-class youth who are more likely to lack the economic incentives and family mobility traditions that boost long-distance migration among middle-class children. In rural areas, working-class youth will often find that limited private rental housing (coupled with high housing prices in amenity-rich regions) make it difficult to leave home to attain independence or form families. By contrast, opportunities for home-leaving are likely to be better in urban areas with large private rented sectors and lower housing prices (Bayrakdar and Coulter, 2018). Housing prices also shape locational choices through young adulthood as those motivated to enter homeownership flow out of expensive cities in order to buy and access larger dwellings. This dynamic partly explains why London exports adults in the family formation life stages, many of whom flow to surrounding districts and commute back into the capital (Lomax and Stillwell, 2018).

On a broader spatial scale, a large literature demonstrates how national contexts shape young adults' home-leaving. Across Europe there are clear differences in home-leaving behaviour with countries in Northern Europe characterised by earlier initial departures to more varied household destinations. In contrast, exits in Southern Europe typically occur later and are more often synchronised with marriage and entering owner-occupation (Mandic, 2008). There are many reasons for these patterns but a lack of rental housing, less developed mortgage markets, stronger family norms, weak systems of public welfare and the difficulty of entering the labour market in Mediterranean countries are typically seen as key determinants (Mandic, 2008). Cross-national diversity in young adults' housing seems to have been accentuated by the GFC which triggered falling homeownership across Europe but with a switch to private renting in some countries and increased parental co-residence or sharing in others (Lennartz et al, 2016). These housing trends could have major knock-on implications for partnerships and fertility and it is to these processes we now turn.

Partnership formation

Until the 1980s, most research linking partnerships with housing focused on how housing attributes and the propensity to move varied with household structure. For example, studies documented higher rates of mobility and renting among single person households than among families with children (Clark and Dieleman, 1996). Underpinning this literature was Rossi's (1955) idea that life cycle transitions in household structure motivate residential adjustments. However, without representative longitudinal data it was difficult to examine the actual processes of residential adjustment or the ways these vary with age, cohort, place and resources (Kendig, 1984).

The maturation of panel studies has since enabled a more dynamic life course perspective on partnership to emerge. Central to this is the idea that forming a co-residential partnership is a significant transition or turning point across both the family and housing careers. At least one person must relocate when co-residential partnerships form and new relationships are known to trigger a substantial proportion of all residential moves and household formations (Clark, 2021). As a result, the fact that people now transition in less predictable ways between a greater variety of partnerships over a wider range of ages than ever before has profound implications for housing dynamics. SDT trends of delayed partnership formation and destandardised relationship careers are thus a crucial force driving both the *diversification* of housing careers and the *postponement* of significant residential transitions such as leaving home and entering homeownership. However, understanding precisely how partnership trends are bound up with this restructuring of housing careers requires careful consideration of three issues: (1) the changing timing and sequencing of events in the two domains, (2) the importance of 'living apart together' relationships, and (3) how partnership configures residential preferences and resources.

Event timing and sequencing

SDT trends of delayed marriage, increased unmarried cohabitation and greater partnership instability have several implications for housing behaviour. First, the growth of pre-marital cohabitation has severed the traditional connection between getting married and forming a new household (Flowerdew and Al-Hamad, 2004). Yet although 90 per cent of British couples cohabit before getting married (ONS, 2020a), marriage remains associated with residential mobility and household formation for at least two reasons:

1. Rates of pre-marital cohabitation vary significantly across the population and living together before marriage is still uncommon among some groups.
2. Getting married is a symbolic commitment to a relationship that is likely to be coordinated with new residential commitments (in particular entering homeownership) as well as anticipative moves to dwellings suitable for childrearing (Michielin and Mulder, 2008).

Second, the greater prevalence of serial monogamy combined with increased longevity is affecting mobility tempo and the demographic structure of places. Delays in forming stable relationships are thought to be deterring young adults from counter-urbanising out of cities in search of homeownership and larger dwellings (Moos, 2016). Later partnership formation means that social amenities and more advantageous partner markets may also 'pull' young singles to remain longer in urban areas. Meanwhile, increased partnership formations later in life – often after separating from previous relationships – means that new partnerships are now a potent trigger of residential mobility across the entire life span rather than being something mostly associated with younger adulthood (Evandrou et al, 2010). However, the association of moving with partnership formation is usually more complex for older than younger adults. This is because older adults forming a new relationship will usually both already have households and so the question becomes who moves and the way this decision is influenced by factors including gender, resources and children from past relationships.

Living apart together

Thus far this chapter has followed the common practice of equating partnership with co-residence. In this perspective, partnership formations are viewed as triggers of residential events as family processes cause housing adjustments. Yet it is becoming increasingly clear that the connections between these two careers are in fact much more complex. Jamieson and Simpson (2013) argue that data on de jure marital status and de facto living arrangements are not sufficient for capturing contemporary partnerships as not all of those who are unmarried and without a live-in partner are actually single. In Britain, around 10 per cent of adults report that they have a stable partner who lives outside their household and these types of living apart together (LAT) relationship help explain why the increased prevalence of living alone over the late 20th century is not indicative of social isolation or a retreat from intimacy. Research shows that LAT relationships vary considerably in form and function over the life span from typically being a short-term stage in early adulthood through to being a longer-term state in later life or when a separated parent (Coulter and Hu, 2017).

Recognising the existence of LAT relationships provides a richer view of how housing resources, opportunities and constraints influence partnership careers. Early in the life course, LAT tends to occur while at least one partner is living in the parental home, with 70 per cent of these couples intending to cohabit (Coulter and Hu, 2017). Qualitative evidence suggests that residential constraints – for example workplace locations or limited income – as well as feeling unready help to explain why many such couples are living apart (Duncan et al, 2013). Further evidence that housing factors into these decisions is provided by German analysis showing that gendered resource access and the costs of moving influence the probability of converting LAT relationships into cohabitation (Wagner et al, 2019). As most LAT couples live near to each other (Coulter and Hu, 2017), this implies that local geographies of housing access and affordability shape partnership careers by influencing the ease with which couples can form a joint household. This could have major implications for fertility, well-being and relationship stability as institutionalising a partnership by progressing to co-residence helps to create and signal greater commitment (Wagner et al, 2019).

Housing is relevant in different ways to later-life LAT relationships. Coulter and Hu (2017) estimate that older groups of single parents and seniors comprise around a quarter of all Britons in LAT relationships. Unlike young adults, these groups are much more likely to view LAT as a choice, many have been in a co-residential relationship before and few seniors have any intention to cohabit. Qualitative evidence indicates that housing considerations are a key reason why these couples live apart. For example, keeping separate spaces for children from past relationships as well as preserving autonomy and assets (including housing wealth) were cited by one study's interviewees as reasons why they chose to live apart from their partner (Duncan et al, 2013).

Preferences and resources

This discussion indicates that the relevance of partnership dynamics to housing behaviour extends far beyond residential mobility. Indeed, a large literature has shown that dwelling and neighbourhood selection decisions are strongly configured by partnership careers. On the one hand, co-residential partnerships clearly influence residential preferences for dwelling attributes including housing type, space, location and tenure. In countries with homeownership norms, buying a house is a particularly important way for couples to signal and strengthen their joint commitment (Mulder,

2013). Research shows that forming a co-residential partnership is closely associated with entering owner-occupation in Britain but to a lesser extent in Germany where renting is a less stigmatised and a more attractive long-term option (Bayrakdar et al, 2019).

On the other hand, the growth of dual-earner and dual-career partnerships means that couples also generally have more resources to devote to housing than singles. This helps explain why couples have higher rates of homeownership than singles across Europe (Thomas and Mulder, 2016). The importance of partnership for homeownership does, however, vary across time and space. At the country level, Thomas and Mulder (2016) show that owner-occupation is more tightly associated with marriage in Germany than in Britain or the Netherlands where cohabiting and married couples have more similar homeownership rates. The authors attribute these patterns to the countries' differing welfare regimes, tenure structures and Germany's more traditional demographic context.

In Britain, the data strongly suggest that trends in partnership are closely bound up with tenure restructuring. The left bars in the left panel of Figure 3.2 show that the homeownership rate among 25–44-year-olds – traditionally the principal years for entering owner-occupation – fell from 63 per cent in 1999 to around 51 per cent by 2019. The right-hand panel indicates that this trend may partly be driven by compositional changes in partnership status as the proportion of married adults (the group most likely to be homeowners) declined from 1999 to 2019, while the proportion cohabiting and of never married singles (groups less likely to own) rose considerably. In addition, the left-hand panel of Figure 3.2 shows that while ownership rates fell among people in all partnership statuses, the drop was much more pronounced among the expanding pool of singles (down 11.5 percentage points from a lower base) than among cohabiting adults or among the dwindling proportion of married individuals (down 6.7 and 6.2 percentage points respectively). While we cannot draw firm causal conclusions from this cross-sectional analysis, overall these trends suggest that homeownership has become more closely tied to partnership over time and that postponed partnership formation and delayed marriage are two demographic shifts that are tightly bound up with changes in housing careers.

Family formation

For most people, having a child – and especially becoming a parent for the first time – is a life course turning point. Fertility is not just a family-related event as employment and housing careers often impinge on childbearing decisions. Although demographers traditionally devoted little attention to the housing–fertility nexus, this has now changed and there is growing interest in analysing how childbirth is synchronised with residential moves and housing

Figure 3.2: Trends in the partnership status and owner-occupation rates of 25–44-year-old Britons

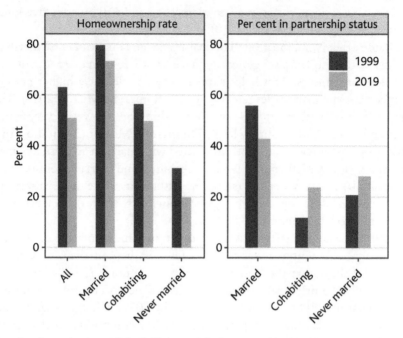

Note: Bars for previously married cohabitants and singles are not shown as these groups made up a small and declining share of the 25–44-year-old population over this period.

Source: Own analysis of weighted LFS data.

transitions (Mikolai et al, 2020). Much of this work follows Rossi (1955) by conceptualising fertility as a trigger of housing events. The basic idea is that couples' residential needs and preferences change when they plan to start a family or actually have a child. Often this involves looking for:

- greater space within dwellings and externally through access to a garden or yard;
- higher quality housing located in a safer, quieter and more environmentally desirable neighbourhood;
- access to family-friendly amenities and in particular to good schools; and
- residential security and stability so that children can stay in the same school.

Satisfying these new demands means couples often relocate in the temporal window around childbirth. Studies conducted across Europe show that, in the main, couples tend to anticipate fertility by moving to larger, single-family and often owner-occupied housing in more suburban or rural areas in the period immediately before children are born (Feijten and Mulder, 2002; Kulu and Steele, 2013). Further cultural impetus for anticipative moves probably comes from traditional social scripts emphasising (at least in Anglophone societies) that homeownership is the best tenure for childrearing as it offers security, control and an inheritable accumulating asset (Lauster, 2010).

Ordering and sequences over time and space

It is tempting to stop here and conclude that childbirth and housing events are purposively sequenced as people adjust their housing consumption to match their fertility preferences. However, analysis of Finnish data by Kulu and Steele (2013) suggests this provides only a partial view of the connections between fertility and residential behaviour. These authors demonstrate that housing and fertility are co-determined processes which are both influenced by unobserved individual-specific factors, which they speculate may include personal values such as whether women are more family- or career-oriented.

More importantly, Kulu and Steele (2013) also show that the way couples adjust their housing circumstances around childbirth varies geographically. In rural Finland, couples tend to move to single-family dwellings before women fall pregnant. By contrast, in large cities with tighter housing markets, moves are more often to flats or terraced houses and are more likely to occur in pregnancy or soon after childbirth. This evidence suggests that the way housing and fertility events are sequenced depends on local patterns of housing access and affordability. Where family-friendly housing is less attainable, couples may be less likely to make moves ahead of childbearing and may be more likely to instead move just before or soon after a child arrives (Kulu and Steele, 2013).

Kulu and Steele's (2013) work suggests that causality may also flow from housing to fertility as housing opportunities and constraints impinge on family formation decisions. This could occur in indirect as well as direct ways (Mulder, 2013). Housing opportunities could indirectly affect the timing and level of childbearing if, as discussed earlier, the ease with which young adults can leave home, form partnerships and ultimately start families depends on their access to housing. More directly, couples might delay or reduce their fertility if they either cannot find suitable accommodation or if moving into this type of dwelling would be prohibitively expensive.

A growing body of work documents how fertility varies with housing opportunities and constraints. At the micro-level, Tocchioni and colleagues (2021) show that the fertility of British homeowners has declined since the 1990s – especially at younger ages – at the same time as accessing the tenure has become more difficult. This means that owner-occupiers' fertility has converged with the lower levels of fertility among the expanding pool of private tenants. The authors speculate that reduced fertility among owner-occupiers may be because the increased costs and uncertainty of homeownership are 'crowding out' younger cohorts' ability to enter the tenure before starting a family. This delinking of fertility from homeownership is most pronounced in medium-cost districts where buying a house is neither affordable nor so difficult as to be attainable only to an elite few with abundant resources (Tocchioni et al, 2021). These trends are problematic for younger families as high rents, short contracts and limited rights regarding the control and use of privately rented housing (particularly in England) makes it hard for tenants to settle down and create a family-friendly home (Hoolachan et al, 2017).

Housing opportunities and constraints also correlate with fertility at broader scales. Clark (2012) shows that US fertility rates are lower in metropolitan areas with high housing costs, although this pattern seems mainly attributable to the higher education levels of the women who live in these places. Meanwhile at the national scale, Mulder and Billari (2010) posit that homeownership rates and access to mortgage finance are correlated with fertility rates. Very low fertility is especially evident in those countries with a 'difficult' homeownership regime (such as Greece and Italy) where scarce rental housing coupled with limited access to mortgages impede home-leaving and family formation (Mulder and Billari, 2010). Although these results are interesting, as yet few studies linking housing system characteristics to fertility patterns have gone beyond correlation to convincingly present evidence of causal relationships.

Ripples and solidarities

An additional issue with much of the literature on housing and fertility dynamics is that most studies focus purely on individual or household behaviour without considering the way lives are linked together into family networks. This is problematic as fertility is a quintessential example of an event whose effects ripple out across the family in ways that reshape kin relationships. For example, becoming a grandparent is often a life course turning point, but this is not a transition one can control.

The ripple effects of childbearing decisions are likely to be relatively strong in Britain where many women work, public childcare provision is scarce and private childcare is extremely expensive. This context means that intergenerational family relationships often change after children are born as older generations step in to provide unpaid childcare. Official figures indicate that around a third of British pre-schoolers are cared for at least partly by extended family members (usually grandparents) and that use of formal childcare is lower among poorer households and in more deprived areas (DfE, 2019a). A desire to receive or provide informal childcare probably thus factors into the residential decision-making of many (potential) parents and grandparents.

Consistent with this view, Thomas (2019) reports that around 20 per cent of UK internal migrants cite family reasons for moving. This figure varies little with the distance moved but migrants with fewer resources and those with children – precisely the groups most likely to rely on informal support and unpaid family childcare – are *ceteris paribus* more likely to report moving to live closer to family. These conclusions chime with Swedish evidence that the location of family members is a particularly important factor in the residential moves of people from ethnic minorities and lower-income brackets (Hedman, 2013). Moving forward, the challenge for research is to disentangle whose moving behaviour is most strongly affected by childcare needs, and whether childcare assistance actually triggers moves or just affects the destination choices of people relocating for other reasons (Mulder, 2018).

Partnership dissolution

Elevated levels of partnership instability are a hallmark of the SDT. In England and Wales, divorce rates and the number of divorces both rose sharply through the late 1960s and then more gradually through the 1970–80s before plateauing off at the unprecedented annual level of around 13–14 divorces per 1,000 married adults until the mid-2000s (ONS, 2020b). The last fifteen years have witnessed a gradual decline in divorce rates attributable at least partly to marriage becoming a more selective state as a greater proportion of younger and less committed couples opt to cohabit (ONS, 2020b). Although cohabitations are known to generally be shorter and less stable than marriages, their informality means that official statistics do not chart trends in the dissolution of cohabiting relationships.

The growth of separation and divorce through the late 20th century sparked public concern about the extent to which dissolutions harmed society by propelling families into poverty. Exploiting newly available longitudinal datasets, US studies demonstrated that separation triggered a larger fall in disposable income for women than men due to women having lower human capital, a weaker labour market position and also typically taking custody of any joint children (Smock, 1993). UK data from the 1990s to 2000s broadly support this view with Brewer and Nandi (2014) showing that British women – especially those with children and those from higher-income couples – experienced a larger decline in their living standards after separation than men.

Building on these analyses, a growing literature has examined the impact of partnership splits on the housing careers of men and women. These studies typically conceptualise separation as a turning point that has major impacts not only on dwelling type and residential location but also on people's emotional connections to housing (Gram-Hanssen and Bech-Danielsen, 2008). Much of this work focuses on housing dynamics around the time of separation. One consistent finding is that partnership dissolution is a potent trigger of residential mobility as at least one partner must quickly leave the family home. Studies by Mulder and Wagner (2010) and Gram-Hanssen and Bech-Danielsen (2008) indicate that which partner leaves (or whether both do) is determined by a complex cocktail of factors, including:

- the partners' relative resources and the expected costs each faces in either moving out or staying in the family home;
- whether the couple has children, their ages, and their future custodial arrangements; and
- which partner initiated the split.

Regardless of who leaves, exit moves are typically unusually constrained as those splitting up often have reduced resources and lack the time to conduct an effective housing search (Cooke et al, 2016). This means that separation often triggers 'downward' housing career moves involving exits from owner-occupation, reduced housing size and quality, moves to less desirable neighbourhoods and possibly a loss of independence if people move into shared housing or back to the parental home (Feijten and van Ham, 2010; Mikolai and Kulu, 2018).

Most existing work on housing and separation concentrates on the individual-level residential adjustments taking place around the time of the dissolution. However, this approach provides only a partial view as four additional issues also need consideration.

Duration and turning points

There is growing evidence that separation is a housing turning point with long-lasting as well as immediate impacts. Longitudinal analyses show that mobility rates remain high for several years after separation as people often struggle financially, adjust to changes in their housing needs and try to find somewhere better to live than the stopgap accommodation they settled for after abruptly leaving the former family home (Mikolai and Kulu, 2018). As moving is typically a costly process, this extended period of residential instability has long-term implications for the finances of separated individuals.

Separation also has long-term impacts on housing quality and tenure circumstances. Research shows that both separation and widowhood reduce the probability of homeownership in later life across Denmark, the Netherlands and Sweden (Herbers et al, 2014). While a developed mortgage market and large homeownership sector enables many UK separators to remain in owner-occupation or to quickly re-enter the tenure, those with fewer qualifications and lower incomes are much less likely to regain homeownership than their better-off peers (Mikolai and Kulu, 2019). These socially selective patterns of housing recovery help exacerbate inequalities in wealth and quality of life through mid- and later life.

Synchronisation and solidarities

The role linked lives play in the housing career often changes drastically after separation. On the one hand, the geography of the natal family network often assumes a new importance in determining where a person lives. In part, this is because the risk of returning to the parental home is high after partnership dissolution, especially for younger adults, men and those without children (Stone et al, 2014). Furthermore, Dutch analysis indicates that many of those ex-partners who manage to stay living in their own household still move closer to their parents when they relocate (Michielin et al, 2008). The authors interpret this as evidence that the enhanced need for support from family members after separation is a potent driver of ex-partners' destination selection. Over time, this support provision is likely to change family relationships.

On the other hand, the end of a co-residential relationship does not always sever the linked lives of former partners. British and US research demonstrates that ex-partners with joint children tend to stay living in close proximity, particularly if they have shared responsibility for childrearing (Cooke et al, 2016; Thomas et al, 2017). This indicates that ex-partners with shared custody strive to live near each other in order to synchronise their daily lives to support co-parenting. Forming new relationships does, however, seem to break these connections and especially when the father is the one forming a new partnership (Thomas et al, 2017). In general, residential moves after separation are typically relatively short distance as these adjustments are spatially constrained by a combination of continuing workplace ties and co-parental responsibilities (Mulder and Malmberg, 2011).

Place

The relationship between separation and housing career dynamics varies with contextual housing opportunities and constraints. For example, Lersch and Vidal (2014) show that those exiting owner-occupation at separation are more likely to quickly re-enter homeownership in Britain than Germany. The authors attribute this to the high rate of owner-occupancy and greater availability of mortgages in the UK. A stronger gendering of Germans' labour market participation may also inhibit women from recovering their housing position after separation.

However, Mikolai et al (2020, p 46) caution against over-emphasising cross-national variation in the residential aftermath of separations. They report 'striking similarities in post-separation residential moves and housing outcomes across the study countries [Australia, Britain, Germany and the Netherlands] despite differences in their housing markets and welfare systems'. One tantalising conclusion that could be drawn from this is that it might be more valuable to focus research effort on the way local housing provision influences the residential outcomes of separation. This topic has not yet received much attention.

Reverse causalities

Separation does not just trigger housing adjustments as residential circumstances and the characteristics of the wider housing system both seem to affect partnership stability. Coulter and Thomas (2019) suggest three micro-level mechanisms through which housing conditions could affect the risk that a co-residential relationship ends:

1. The legal conditions of housing contracts can create commitments binding partners together, for example through joint dwelling ownership. On the flip side, the costs of separation may be lower if only one partner is the legal owner or tenant of the dwelling. Unpacking these hypotheses is tricky given that more committed and stable couples selectively take on commitments such as joint ownership (Lersch and Vidal, 2014).
2. Space pressure or physical problems with the dwelling could damage relationships by reducing privacy and creating friction between partners.
3. Housing affordability problems and in particular payment arrears are likely to reduce psychological well-being and cause strife between partners. This may persist even after controlling for general economic hardship as housing is so integral to personal identity and one's sense of security.

Using British data, Coulter and Thomas (2019) find support for the first and third hypotheses, while Krapf and Wagner (2020) report that unaffordable housing undermines German partnerships. UK analysis also suggests that house price shocks destabilise partnerships (Rainer and Smith, 2010). Taken together, these studies indicate that housing policy actions to support vulnerable households through hard times are likely to have knock-on benefits for family stability and ultimately for household and societal prosperity.

Summary

This chapter has shown how housing and family behaviours are interconnected in ways that go far beyond those originally posited by Rossi (1955). While family changes clearly trigger residential adjustments and shape the structure of housing careers, residential experiences and the broader housing context also have implications for demographic processes such as the timing of home-leaving, partnership formation decisions, fertility and possibly even whether co-residential relationships last into later life. Crucially, grasping the connections between family and housing dynamics requires that we look beyond individual behaviours to explore how these are embedded into geographically distributed kinship networks as well as uneven flows of intra-family care and support. This approach reminds us that all housing dynamics are, to some degree, also family dynamics. It is thus impossible to understand either the SDT or ongoing processes of housing restructuring without appreciating the way these proceed in tandem. Adopting the modern life course perspective developed in Chapter 2 provides a useful way to do this.

As this chapter focused only on four family processes, it is inevitable that not all the demographic dimensions of contemporary residential behaviour have been covered. Space precluded a detailed review of, for example, the housing dimensions of widowhood or the dynamics of specific household structures such as single persons. However, by concentrating on four sets of process the chapter has demonstrated how the twelve life course conceptual tools set out in Chapter 2 can help us to better grasp the contemporary connections between housing and family dynamics. Chapter 4 now moves on to apply the life course perspective to understand the interconnections between housing and educational careers.

4

Learning and training

Learning and training are central topics in life course research as variations in educational participation, pathways and attainments form an important axis of social inequality. In contrast, housing scholarship often considers education to only be crucial to a specific set of residential processes, such as long-distance migration or neighbourhood dynamics around university campuses. While qualification variables are almost always used when modelling residential behaviour, these are typically treated as controls or are instead interpreted as proxy measures of resources or lifestyle preferences. Surprisingly little attention has thus been devoted to understanding how changes in education and housing systems interact to alter lives, places and patterns of inequality.

The post-war transformation of education is one arena where public policy has had particularly potent impacts on the structure of life courses. Since the Second World War, Global North education systems have expanded as compulsory schooling has been prolonged and become less selective, vocational training pathways have been formalised and participation in higher education (HE) has grown and widened to formerly excluded populations (for instance women, the less affluent and ethnic minorities). This transformation of extended education into a mass activity has altered residential careers by changing the type and timing of life events while also altering aggregate patterns of housing preference, resources and restrictions. Crucially housing has, in turn, become an influential determinant of educational success as where families live often has an impact on the quality of the schooling their children receive (Piekut, 2021).

This chapter uses life course perspectives to examine these two-way connections between education and housing dynamics. It argues that understanding how education interacts with housing processes requires recognising that:

- Education is not just relevant to housing in early adulthood but rather matters over the entire life span.
- Education is not just about measurable qualifications but is also a biographical process of gaining competencies, skills and knowledge about subjects, activities and places while developing new perspectives, worldviews, peer groups and tastes.

- Educational qualifications are, to an extent, positional goods as their economic value is inversely related to their prevalence, while the disadvantages of not possessing a given qualification increase the more ubiquitous it becomes (Green, 2017).

Adopting this richer life course perspective allows us to grasp how processes of learning and training interact with two aspects of residential behaviour: (1) patterns of longer-distance migration and decisions about where to live, on the one hand, and (2) domestic living arrangements, housing tenure and neighbourhood selection on the other. Many of the connections linking education and housing run at least partly through labour market processes and so this chapter segues into Chapter 5's discussion of housing, work and money.

Educational inequalities

British children complete compulsory schooling around age 16, but restrictions on their next steps vary across the home nations. In Scotland, Wales and Northern Ireland there are no further constraints but in England 16–18-year-olds must either stay in full-time education, start an apprenticeship/training programme or combine part-time study/training with work/volunteering. These extra requirements were introduced to address concerns that pupils leaving school at 16 lack the advanced skills needed for 21st-century workplaces. Indeed, successive British governments have long viewed raising educational attainments and skills as the best way to improve job prospects and thus reduce poverty, boost social mobility and tackle the UK's low productivity problem (Hoare and Corver, 2010).

According to Green (2017), the fragmented and confusing British education system with its diversity of providers, varied and shifting pathways, large number of qualifications and weak provision of both adult learning and higher vocational training (all of which vary across the devolved regions) creates ideal conditions for social stratification. This sets in early, with pathway choices and attainments during compulsory schooling varying significantly by gender (with girls on average outperforming boys), ethnicity (with Chinese and Indian children doing better on average than White children and with lower attainment among Black boys), social class (with children from poorer families doing less well than their affluent counterparts) and with the social composition of school catchment areas (Manley and Johnston, 2014). Table 4.1 shows that pathways out of compulsory education also vary systematically along these axes. The first column shows that boys, pupils from disadvantaged families and those from White ethnic backgrounds are less likely to progress to

Table 4.1: Percentage of state school pupils in England progressing to a sustained higher education or training destination, 2018–19

Characteristic	Progressing (%)	To HE (%)	To top third HEI (%)
Not disadvantaged	65	61	18
Disadvantaged	59	55	9
Chinese	87	84	41
Asian or Asian British	82	79	20
Other ethnic group	80	78	21
Black or Black British	79	76	14
Mixed	69	66	20
White	60	55	16
Female	66	63	17
Male	61	56	16
Total	64	59	17

Source: Based on data from DfE (2020). Contains public sector information licensed under the Open Government Licence v3.0.

HE or advanced training than their peers. Progression to HE is also less likely for pupils attending schools with a working-class intake (Manley and Johnston, 2014).

However, the latter column of Table 4.1 shows that these headline progression rates mask variation in the types of higher education institution (HEI) pupils go on to. While rates of progression to HE or advanced training are only slightly lower for disadvantaged children than for their non-disadvantaged counterparts, disadvantaged children are much less likely to progress to the most prestigious HEIs. Moreover, the general HE progression advantage all ethnic minorities enjoy over White pupils is greatly reduced – or even reversed for Black children – when looking at entry to prestigious top third institutions (with the notable exception of Chinese pupils). Entry to elite universities thus remains particularly stratified by class, ethnicity and school composition.

Figure 4.1 shows that there are also clear geographies in the share of school leavers staying in education or embarking on an apprenticeship. Progressing into post-compulsory learning and training is most common in and around London, in the Midlands and across northern England, with lower progression rates in rural areas across southern and western England where more young adults go straight into work. Figure 4.2 meanwhile indicates that the highest rates of leaving school to no stable destination are found in disadvantaged ex-industrial areas (for instance the North East

Figure 4.1: Percentage of state school pupils progressing to higher education or training, 2018–19

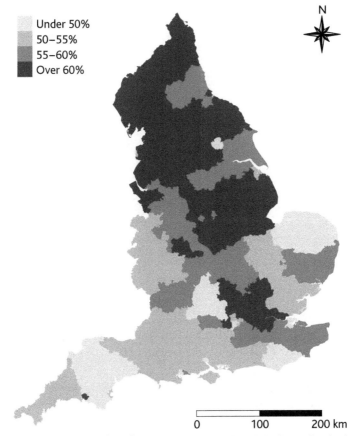

Source: Based on data from DfE (2020) and Office for National Statistics licensed under the Open Government Licence v3.0. Contains OS data © Crown copyright and database right [2022].

and parts of Yorkshire and Humberside), more peripheral rural areas (for example Cornwall and Norfolk) and relatively deprived coastal areas.

At first glance, these socially and spatially uneven patterns of educational success and progression seem of little relevance to housing careers. However, education and housing dynamics are in fact tightly intertwined over the life span through (1) migration and locational decision-making as well as through (2) living arrangement decisions, tenure selection and neighbourhood attainments. These tight interlinkages means that educational inequalities laid down early in life often have long-term cumulative implications for residential behaviour and housing outcomes. The rest of this chapter integrates and synthesises what is known about these processes using Chapter 2's toolbox of life course concepts.

Figure 4.2: Percentage of state school pupils with no sustained education, training or employment destination, 2018–19

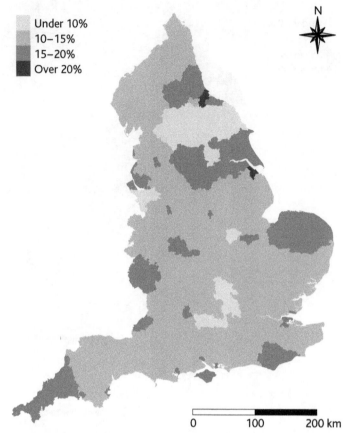

Source: Based on data from DfE (2020) and Office for National Statistics licensed under the Open Government Licence v3.0. Contains OS data © Crown copyright and database right [2022].

Education and residential location

Migration dynamics

Population geographers have long recognised that HE systems profoundly influence internal migration patterns (Green, 2018). This is because entering HE is an educational transition that often triggers at least one residential adjustment. However, moves related to HE differ from other relocations in several ways:

- *Destination location:* This is largely fixed in advance and cannot easily be adjusted during a course of study.
- *Resources:* Waged income is often not the sole way students cover their living costs as grants, loans and family transfers are often more relevant resources.

- *Timing*: The seasonal timing of residential moves is strongly timetabled by institutional term dates, while the biographical timing of HE-related migration is largely determined by the age-grading of the educational system.

Institutional timetabling is particularly important in Britain where over 80 per cent of full-time students live away from home and migrating to attend university is a culturally engrained milestone in middle-class transitions to adulthood (DfE, 2019b). Although a large share of these student migrations take place over long distances, Faggian and McCann (2009) show that students attending HEIs created after 1992 (former polytechnics which tend to be less research-focused) typically move shorter distances than their peers going to older research-intensive institutions. Students are also more likely to live at home if they attend a post-1992 institution or if they live in London (Faggian and McCann, 2009). This is probably because post-1992 institutions tend to recruit less students from more localised catchment areas while the density of HEIs in London – together with high living costs and excellent public transport – dissuades young Londoners from leaving home to go to university. However, overall, the general picture is that UK students are predominantly young, migratory and are drawn to a specific set of towns and cities with HEIs. Anyone who has lived in one of these will be familiar with how the ebb and flow of students over the year gives particular spaces (or even the entire place in the case of smaller university towns) a distinct seasonal rhythm.

This culture of educational mobility in young adulthood has major impacts on UK patterns of internal migration. Globally, the probability of migrating peaks during the late teens to mid-twenties when many of the educational, family and employment transitions that trigger geographic mobility typically occur (Bernard et al, 2016).[1] National age-graded migration rates constructed by Clark (2021) show that UK migration rates peak sharply around ages 20–24 when young adults typically attend university and move into work. However, Clark's analysis shows that this UK peak occurs earlier and is more pronounced than in the US or Australia. In the case of Australia, lower rates of long-distance migration among 20–24-year-olds may occur because HE enrolments are more local and there is a weaker cultural impetus to go straight from school to university (Bernard et al, 2016). It therefore appears that the UK's educational tradition and system script long-distance migration to frequently occur early in the adult life course.

It is not just the migration of new students that drives high levels of HE-related mobility through young adulthood. In Britain, the provision of student housing – together with cultural norms of student life as a transient phase of experimentation – generates much residential mobility among student populations. Although many students spend their first year

Figure 4.3: Neighbourhood-level rates of private renting and population mobility increase with the concentration of student households

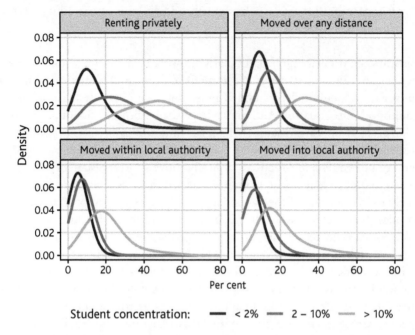

Student concentration: ▬ < 2%   ▬ 2 – 10%   ▬ > 10%

Note: Roughly 80 per cent of England and Wales's 34,753 LSOAs have under 2 per cent student-headed households, 18 per cent have 2–10 per cent students and just over 2 per cent of neighbourhoods have over 10 per cent of their households headed by a student.

Source: Based on 2011 census tables and migration flow data for LSOAs in England and Wales. Census output is Crown copyright and is reproduced with the permission of the Controller of HMSO and the Queen's Printer for Scotland.

living in purpose-built accommodation, students often move out to spend their subsequent terms in privately rented housing that is often shared with other students and/or recent graduates. Leases are frequently offered only for (part of) one year and moving to come and go from the parental home, to change flatmates, and to find better or cheaper accommodation is very common and seen as part-and-parcel of student life. This means that attending HE is typically a biographical spell characterised by repeated moves (sometimes termed residential itinerancy) accompanied by frequent changes of household composition.

These biographical patterns of student mobility have spatial consequences for university towns and cities. Neighbourhoods with high concentrations of students typically have lots of privately rented stock and high rates of population turnover. Figure 4.3 shows how the distribution of four tenure composition and mobility rate variables (the panels) differs across English and Welsh neighbourhoods with different shares of student-headed households (the lines). The top-left panel shows that neighbourhoods with larger student populations (the lighter coloured lines) tend to have a larger share of privately rented dwellings. Of course, we cannot tell from this whether an expanding private rented sector attracts students or whether a growing student population encourages landlord investment. The balance probably varies depending on the local context.

The rest of the panels show that neighbourhoods with high concentrations of student-headed households also tend to have higher rates of both long-distance in-migration and shorter-distance residential mobility, while neighbourhoods with few students typically have much lower turnover rates. The flatter distribution of all variables for neighbourhoods with over 10 per cent student households reflects the diverse profile of these areas. These range from mixed neighbourhoods containing sizeable pockets of student housing intermingled with other stock through to neighbourhoods dominated by student halls.

High levels of mobility among students mean that policy-induced shifts in the timing of HE entry, in the number of people going to university and in student finance can dramatically change the migration patterns of new cohorts as they enter the housing system. At the biographical level, Falkingham et al (2016) document how migration in early adulthood has become more common among more recent birth cohorts of women, in part because of increased female participation in HE. Meanwhile, at the aggregate level, Champion and Shuttleworth (2017) argue that a sharp increase in migration intensity among those aged 16–24 during the 1990s was due to the rapid expansion of HE at this time.

Although the UK's student population has continued to climb from 1.9 million in 2000/01 to 2.5 million in 2019/20 (HESA, 2022), two trends have helped depress student mobilities among cohorts of young adults entering HE in the new millennium. These trends have both weakened the trigger effect that entering HE has on migration and thus may go some way towards explaining why migration intensities for 16–24-year-olds fell back from their 1990s peak during the 2000s (Champion and Shuttleworth, 2017). First, student maintenance support has shifted from a grants-based system into one dominated by repayable loans while tuition fees have risen since they were first introduced in 1998. In England, top-up fees were introduced in 2006 and then trebled in 2012 so that home-domiciled students now pay upwards of £9,000 per year for tuition (upfront HE costs are generally lower in the devolved regions whose governments provide more financial support). Overall, this means the burden of paying for HE has been transferred from the exchequer onto students (who are eligible for student loans repaid from graduate earnings) and their parents (as loan entitlements are means-tested and higher-income parents are supposed to cover more of their offspring's living costs). In this context, it is probable that less affluent students are increasingly choosing to live at home and commute to a local university in order to save money. Second, both HEIs and government policy have driven the expansion of HE to non-traditional populations who are in general less likely to migrate to university. We now turn to explore how housing-related factors play a role in creating these social disparities in HE-related mobilities.

Housing and university choice

Thus far this chapter has examined how educational careers drive events and transitions in the residential career. This is the direction of causality that has most preoccupied population and housing researchers. However, to fully grasp how education and housing careers intertwine, it is vital to recognise that housing-related factors may also influence educational trajectories in ways that can help to perpetuate inequalities.

To grasp how housing matters for post-compulsory education we first need to understand two things about educational decisions. First, these decisions – for instance the decision about whether to apply to university or college and if so which ones – are not made by individuals operating in a contextual vacuum. Instead, multiple family members usually have some input into educational decisions which are also influenced by how each person perceives the likely costs and benefits of particular pathways. Second, residential costs and perceptions are likely to be a significant contextual factor that people integrate into their educational deliberations. As a result, the role housing-related processes play in creating educational inequalities needs careful examination. While housing may contribute to uneven school results (for example due to a lack of space to study at home) and thus to unequal progression rates, a potentially more insidious form of inequality may result if housing factors help bound or restrict decisions about which HEI to attend. These decisions are important as the economic value of university degrees is produced by institutional reputation as well as by subject and grade attainments.

There is ample evidence that residential issues contribute to UK HE disparities as differences in housing-related resources, restrictions, opportunities and constraints help explain why patterns of university choices vary with ethnicity, gender and class. Looking first at ethnicity, objective and perceptual barriers related to the residential environment are thought to help to create the ethnic inequalities in enrolment to prestigious HEIs shown in Table 4.1. Finney's (2011) analysis of 2001 census data showed that the conventional assumption that students are highly migratory was only true for young people from certain ethnic groups (most notably White British, White Irish and Chinese). By contrast, she found that young Black African and Pakistani adults were actually less migratory if studying for a degree than if they were not studying. Finney (2011) argued that this is because Black

African and Pakistani youth often live at home while studying. Differences in the proportion of younger group members moving away to university probably also partly explains why Chinese, White Irish and White British 16-to-24-year-olds were considerably more migratory than their South Asian and Black Caribbean peers (Finney, 2011). Although 2001 census data are now rather old, updated analysis by Darlington-Pollock's team (2019) confirmed similar patterns of ethnic disparity in long-distance migration propensities among UK-born young adults in 2010–11.

Both objective and perceptual housing-related factors probably help explain why young adults from some minority groups are less likely to migrate to university than their White British peers. On the objective side, lower migration rates among Black, Pakistani and Bangladeshi youth could be attributed to the fact that these groups are among the most economically disadvantaged in Britain. In 2019, the unemployment rate among Black, Pakistani and Bangladeshi individuals (8 per cent apiece) was double the rate among White Britons, while average rates of pay for these groups were well below the national average (Race Disparity Unit, 2021). Perceived or actual resource constraints as well as tighter local support networks may well deter young people from these groups from moving to study an expensive course in a far-off city. In addition, the fact that many young people from ethnic minority backgrounds grow up in large cities means they often have better access to multiple local HEIs than their White British peers and so they may have less need to move away to study (Gamsu et al, 2019).

However, both quantitative and qualitative evidence indicates that the university choices of ethnic minorities are bounded by how potential applicants perceive the diversity of the population they will be mixing with on campus and in the local area. Modelling of 2014–15 entry data by Gamsu and colleagues (2019) demonstrates that more ethnically diverse HEIs tend to be less prestigious and that some minority students – in particular Black Caribbean and Bangladeshi, but not Indian or Chinese students – are disproportionately likely to 'stay local' and look for an ethnically diverse institution. The authors argue that these findings are in line with qualitative evidence that working-class minorities avoid applying to prestigious far-off universities as these are seen as privileged White spaces unwelcoming to those from other backgrounds (Gamsu et al, 2019). These types of perception are particularly likely to deter minorities from applying to universities in smaller peripheral towns and cities where the local population is, on average, likely to be much less ethnically diverse than they are used to at home (Gamsu et al, 2019). While there is, of course, nothing wrong with wanting to attend a diverse local institution, the fact that these tend to be less prestigious and that the value of a degree depends so much on institutional reputation means that the lower educational mobility of some minorities may help perpetuate their economic disadvantages.

These ethnic inequalities in HEI choice are hard to comprehend without considering intersections with gender, religion and intergenerationally linked lives. Research by Khambhaita and Bhopal (2015) shows that South Asian young women are more likely to live in the parental home or locally while at university than their White British counterparts, even after adjusting for class, regional origin and school attainments. Moreover, their work reveals that getting better grades at school boosts the HE mobility of South Asian women to a lesser extent than for their White British peers. When combined with qualitative evidence on students' destination choice processes, Khambhaita and Bhopal (2015) argue that South Asian young women's university selection is constrained first by wanting to attend a diverse HEI and second by more specific cultural views and expectations concerning appropriate female behaviours. British Pakistanis and Bangladeshis are predominantly Muslim and fears about socialising with men, encountering alcohol, and worries about discrimination based on clothing practices may encourage young women from these groups to opt for the safety of living at home while studying (Khambhaita and Bhopal, 2015). Home-leaving decisions for young Pakistani and Bangladeshi women may also be bounded by family members' cultural views on appropriate living arrangements in early adulthood. These can bound girls' residential options (and through this their educational choices) for those whose parents subscribe to more traditional gender norms emphasising that girls should only leave home at marriage.

Finally, and as alluded to previously, differences in residential behaviour across social classes crosscut and contribute to the ethnic educational disparities discussed previously. Both Gamsu et al (2019) and Khambhaita and Bhopal (2015) show that young adults are less likely to move away to university if they come from a working-class family or have grown up in a deprived neighbourhood. Pupils from schools in working-class areas are also less likely to go on to elite institutions and are more likely to attend less prestigious universities or colleges in their local area than those educated in middle-class schools (Manley and Johnston, 2014).

While these patterns are partly due to resource disparities, class-based educational cultures within families, neighbourhoods and schools play a role in explaining the more local orientation of working-class students. Across the Global North, the middle-classes define themselves in part through their mobilities for education, work and leisure. Many children in middle-class families have two university-educated parents who both have experience of long-distance migration. In these families, moving away to university is a well-trodden normative path in the transition to adulthood, even if returning home after graduation is now more acceptable than it used to be (Chapter 3). Schools with middle-class catchments thus tend to be better practised and better resourced (in terms of both financial and social capital) at supporting their pupils into prestigious far-off universities. Pupils going to these schools are also likely to mix with peer groups where applying to elite universities is the norm and there are plenty of successful role models (Manley and Johnston, 2014).

By contrast, working-class students from families where no one has previously gone to university are not following this cultural script and may well find it so alienating they wish to attend a local university with a less socially exclusive student body. Furthermore, schools with working-class catchments are less likely to have the resources to devote to encouraging and supporting talented students to apply to elite universities, while peer groups are less likely to socialise this trajectory (Manley and Johnston, 2014). These explanations fit with Holdsworth's (2009) argument that UK discourses of 'going away to uni' culturally privilege middle-class educational mobilities while overlooking the very different residential experiences of less advantaged students who tend to live at or close to home while studying.

Residential biographies

Thus far this chapter has concentrated on the rather narrow phase of early adulthood when people typically enter HE. However, adopting a longer-term biographical perspective helps us appreciate how educational processes shape residential behaviour over the entire life span. To develop this perspective, it is necessary to conceptualise attending HE as a life course transition or turning point that can have lasting implications for locational preferences. Indeed, on a basic level the familiarity with migration many students acquire may predispose the degree-educated to make further moves later in life (Faggian and McCann, 2009).

Many studies dealing with the long-run residential effects of education focus on graduate migration and settlement patterns. Underpinning this literature is the notion that education, skills and training form embodied human capital resources (Faggian and McCann, 2009). The basic idea here is that people invest in their human capital via education and training in order to gain competencies to improve their future productivity and job prospects. In this literature, HEIs and graduate migration flows are viewed as working together to drive the production and distribution of human capital across the economy. In a well-functioning system, talented but untrained adults flow to HEIs where they are equipped with new skills (evidenced through credentials) before going on to 'match' these to suitable job and further training vacancies. Often this matching process will require migration to take up the new opportunity and high mobility after graduation is a defining feature of the biographies of highly educated adults. These patterns are, however, contingent on graduating into a buoyant economy as busts like the post-GFC recession often reduce graduate vacancies and so dampen graduates' job-related mobility while encouraging returns to the parental home (Sage et al, 2013).

Analyses of longitudinal data tracking students' origins, HEI choices and residential locations after graduation demonstrate that these pathways are geographically patterned. First, and most obviously, graduate residential decisions are influenced by the spatial distribution of skilled jobs which act as potent locational pull factors. London provides a classic example of this as the capital not only attracts large numbers of students (especially from London but also from elsewhere) but also pulls in very large numbers of the highest achieving graduates from other regions (Hoare and Corver, 2010). This importance of London (and to a lesser extent other large cities) within graduate residential biographies is largely because the city's highly skilled jobs market functions as an 'escalator region' which offers unique opportunities for career progression (Fielding, 1992). Escalating processes will be examined in greater depth in Chapter 5, but for now it is sufficient to say that moving to London after graduation is particularly crucial for those entering sectors concentrated in the capital such as financial services, central government, some professional services and the arts, media and creative industries.

Overlaying this effect of economic geography is the way the location of the home residence and the HEI both help to structure graduates' residential pathways. Many students stay in their home regions to go to university and in more peripheral regions like the North East, Scotland, Wales and Northern Ireland the graduate labour force contains a large share of people who grew up in the region, were educated there and stayed on to work (Hoare and Corver, 2010). Many graduates also return to find work in their home region and nowadays this frequently involves spells in the parental home. Nonetheless, Faggian and McCann's (2009) data demonstrate that in 2000 around a quarter of students stayed on in their university town or city after graduation to enter the local labour market. This indicates that, for some, the choice of which university to attend has long-lasting housing consequences as the HEI forms a new gravitational centre to the residential biography. The extent to which this occurs will vary across HEIs depending on the size and buoyancy of their local graduate labour markets.

Imeraj and colleagues (2018) suggest that location-specific capital helps explain why graduates often return to their home region or stay on to work in the area around their alma mater. They suggest that non-transferable forms of location-specific capital are amassed with duration spent in a place and encompass things that make subsequently living there more attractive. These forms of location-specific capital include:

• knowledge about the local jobs market and housing opportunities;
• workplace contacts gained through family or social networks, job experiences, placements and so on;

- local friendships or romantic partnerships; and
- emotional place attachments.

Imeraj et al (2018) argue that it is not just the local labour market or personal stocks of location-specific capital that determine the probability of staying in or leaving the vicinity of universities. Rather, they contend that liveability also factors strongly into 21st-century graduate mobility decisions. Access to suitable and affordable housing are key aspects of liveability that, in general, becomes a higher priority with age as many people move into the family formation life phase. This probably explains why large cities with HEIs often attract young people in their late teens and export adults in their thirties and forties.

One final trend that has transformed how education intersects with housing biographies is the globalisation of HE. One indicator of this globalisation is the growth in international student enrolments shown in Figure 4.4. In the space of 14 academic years since 2006–07, the number of overseas domiciled first-year students attending British HEIs rose by 81 per cent to 320,000, with much of this growth driven by a fourfold increase in Chinese enrolments (Figure 4.4). These overseas arrivals are not randomly distributed, as some HEIs – typically prestigious large urban institutions – attract particularly large

Figure 4.4: Trends in overseas domiciled first-year students at UK HEIs

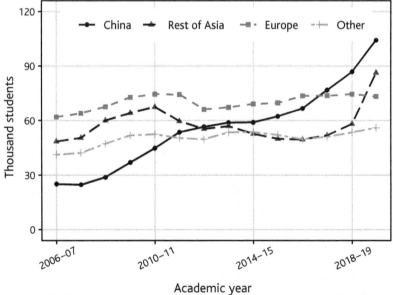

Academic year

Source: Based on data from HESA (2022) published under the Creative Commons Attribution 4.0 International (CC BY 4.0) licence.

volumes of overseas students. Specific patterns of recruitment and institutional tradition explain some of the more eye-catching departures from this general trend, for instance the fact that more US students studied at the University of St Andrews in 2019–20 than at many much larger universities (HESA, 2022).

On one level, this growth in international students adds extra pressure to housing markets near institutions with expanding overseas enrolments. Meanwhile, on a biographical level, the globalisation of HE means that the residential biographies of contemporary young adults increasingly involve international migration and periods of transnational living. While many international students return home after completing their course, some stay on to work, and indeed many countries' immigration policies aim to retain the most talented foreign-domiciled graduates. For these students, HE marks a significant turning point in the residential career by acting as a conduit for settlement in a new country. This may not be simply an individual-level process, as Samuel (2012) suggests that affluent families in some parts of the Global South (in his case Bangladesh) purposefully send their offspring to UK HEIs in order to smooth their path to British citizenship. Such moves are part of a long-term residential strategy on the part of the extended family as the naturalised graduate is then expected to help other family members immigrate to Britain (Samuel, 2012).

Education and housing arrangements

Thus far this chapter has explored how decisions about education and residential location (at the broad scale of the city, region and country) interlink over the life course. Much of the focus has been on HE as this aspect of education has potent impacts on locational decision-making. Yet if we think more broadly about education, it becomes obvious that location is not the only dimension of the housing career that intersects with learning and training as decisions related to household structures, tenure and neighbourhoods are all influenced by educational experiences and attainments. Education matters for these aspects of the housing career in two ways: (1) by influencing residential preferences, and (2) by shaping the resources and restrictions which bound housing career decisions. These two issues are now examined using the life course conceptual tools of biographies, intergenerational solidarities and cohort processes.

Housing biographies

Life course notions of biographical development are useful for understanding how student housing experiences can influence the subsequent household structures and formation decisions of highly educated adults. In Britain, the long 20th-century decline of the private rented sector (PRS) from its peak around the First World War had, by the time of the 1991 census, left only a rump sector housing under 10 per cent of households. What remained of the PRS catered in part to the demands of university students who needed cheap flexible housing in cities that offered amenities as well as access to jobs and educational institutions (Kemp, 2015). Restricted resources together with the UK's culture of migrating to HE meant that it was common for students to rent in houseshares with unrelated adults.

This tradition means that the expansion of HE over recent decades has fuelled demand for shared privately rented accommodation (Kemp, 2015). Large student rental submarkets now exist in all university towns and students' specific demands mean that these submarkets are normally quite separate from the mainstream PRS.[2] While the typical image of a student house remains a group of twenty-somethings sharing a dilapidated flat or terraced house, the economic and cultural diversification of student populations means that student housing markets are now far more variegated. An influx of investment has flowed into purpose-built student accommodation in recent years and in some places there has been an increase in upmarket city-centre apartment blocks and all-inclusive developments catering to affluent students looking for an exclusive lifestyle (Core Cities, 2019).

Most studies of student housing focus on either individual experiences or on local impacts at a particular moment in time. This cross-sectional focus reflects a tacit assumption that students are a distinct population group whose housing experiences are time limited. This approach fits poorly with the life course notion that housing careers are continuously unfolding biographies where past experiences can shape future decisions. To fully grasp how HE sculpts residential careers, it is therefore important to focus on individual life courses and explore how student housing experiences might have longer-term biographical implications for housing preferences. These processes may be becoming increasingly crucial determinants of housing behaviour as more adults have been to university and have experienced student housing.

Shared housing

Pioneering qualitative work published twenty years ago showed that shared housing is attractive to English graduates (Kenyon and Heath, 2001). Sharing a rented house makes it easy to move for career development, while income pooling allows sharers to obtain better housing conditions and live in a more desirable location than they could afford alone. However, Kenyon and Heath's interviews with young professionals revealed that social and lifestyle benefits were also a powerful motivation for sharing and that many sharers did so repeatedly and after having lived with others at university. Their data indicate that student houseshares may create a familiarity with sharing's benefits, as well as experience in minimising problems with flatmates, which taken together increase the appeal of sharing after graduation (Kenyon and Heath, 2001). Student housing experiences thus need to be set in the context of the longer-term biographical development of housing careers as residential experiences at university may have long-lasting impacts on preferences regarding domestic living arrangements.

This view that sharing with unrelated others has become a normal part of early housing careers was repurposed by the 2010–15 coalition government to reduce the housing benefit bill. This had nearly doubled from £11.6 billion in 2001–02 to £22.8 billion in 2011–12 as the number of private tenants rose, rents inflated and economic insecurity increased after the GFC (DWP, 2019). One of the austerity cuts the Cameron–Clegg coalition government implemented in response was raising the age threshold for the Shared Accommodation Rate (SAR) of housing benefit from 25 to 35. SAR restricts private tenants' housing support to the local cost of renting a room in a shared dwelling and so raising the upper age threshold amounted to a major cut to the entitlements of single 25–34-year-olds. The stated justification for extending the SAR was that this created fairness by preventing young benefit claimants from being able to afford better housing conditions than their working peers. Ministers' thinking went something like this: as sharing is a normal part of young adulthood and many young graduates and workers can only afford to share, then why should the state support benefit claimants to live alone? Why not adjust the housing benefit system so everyone follows the same age-graded housing script?

Restructuring the housing benefit system so that young singles are forced to share was a deeply regressive move for two reasons. First, young benefit claimants are a much more vulnerable population than students or graduates as many are grappling with health problems, difficult housing histories, family trouble and economic insecurity. Second, *choosing* to share with friends is very different from *having no choice* but to share with strangers – indeed, the benefits of sharing largely depend on having choice over who to live with. Qualitative work on SAR's impacts has shown that pushing vulnerable people into sharing with strangers (who often come and go frequently and have their own problems) in often poor-quality housing has damaged young adults' health and well-being, parenting and personal relationships (Wilkinson and Ortega-Alcazar, 2019). Such problems also spill over into communities, and all major UK cities now have areas where concentrations of cheap, high-turnover shared housing generate localised problems with social cohesion, crime, dwelling upkeep and neighbourhood management (Core Cities, 2019).

Locational tastes

Educational experiences influence subsequent residential preferences in ways that go beyond graduates potentially developing a taste for shared housing.

Writing in 2007, Smith and Holt argued that HE students should be seen as 'apprentice gentrifiers' whose university experiences prime them to subsequently take part in state- or capital-led gentrification. They contend that as HE students tend to live and socialise in tight-knit urban communities, this means they often develop particular shared cultural tastes – for example for communal living and for urban amenities such as cafes, bars, nightlife, lively music and arts scenes and so forth. Smith and Holt (2007) propose that graduates subsequently disproportionately opt to stay in or move to major cities not simply to find work but also to satisfy these amenity preferences.

Smith and Holt's (2007) contention that lifestyle preferences inculcated while at university subsequently pull educated youth to vibrant inner cities chimes with North American evidence that higher education predicts high-density urban living (Moos et al, 2019). It also fits with evidence from various countries that processes of middle-class suburbanisation and counter-urbanisation slowed during the early part of the new millennium as those with economic and cultural capital increasingly opted to remain in cities for longer periods of the life course (Damhuis et al, 2019). Cities across the Global North have subscribed to these ideas and have integrated creativity and cultural development into their urban plans in a competitive bid to provide the lifestyle-related amenities that are thought to attract skilled workers.

Intergenerational solidarities

The life course principle of linked lives is very important for grasping how housing matters for educational careers. Within middle-class families, choosing a residential location which enhances the educational success of one's children by enabling them to go to a good school is a powerful (and normative) expression of intergenerational solidarity. The relevance of school quality to family residential decisions is a situation generated partly by education policy. The fact that places in oversubscribed state schools are often allocated in part using residential criteria (which usually prioritise those living locally) inevitably means education factors into families' housing decisions. However, the importance of schools to locational decisions is heightened by two additional factors: significant variations in UK school quality (as gauged from assessment results) and crucially the way these variations are publicised through school league tables designed to promote competition and parent choice. Taken together, these factors mean that the housing decisions of (would-be) parents are also decisions that have a bearing on their children's educational futures and through this their life course attainments.

As a result, it is perhaps unsurprising that local school quality is a major factor in middle-class families' locational decisions. Schooling is particularly important to middle-class residential decisions because:

- The middle-classes are most likely to be able to afford to pay a premium to live near a good school as prized schools can add many thousands of pounds to local house prices.
- Prioritising educational success is a key plank of middle-class identities.
- Gaining good grades is more likely to be seen as the passport to a successful career by parents who are themselves highly educated.
- Middle-class parents are more likely to have the nous, social contacts, resources, skills and time to understand and exploit bureaucratic systems like those governing the allocation of school places.

Smith and Higley (2012) describe how for middle-class couples, decisions about where to live before children are born or while they are young are made strategically to buy into good school catchments or to locate in places where children can be driven outside the neighbourhood to a particularly successful local school.[3] Crucially, this strategising is not just an intra-urban phenomenon as longer distance moves out of major cities during the family formation phase are also motivated by a blend of lifestyle factors and a desire for one's children to gain a good education in a cleaner, safer and more wholesome environment (Smith and Higley, 2012). Overall, it is safe to say that middle-class housing career adjustments are partially a means for purposefully *constructing* children's educational careers. For the middle-classes, residential decisions are thus an expression of intergenerational solidarity and a vehicle for ensuring class reproduction through the education system.

Life course resources

The final way educational careers interact with residential careers comes through the effect education has on monetary resources over the life course. On average, higher levels of education translate into higher employment rates and better lifetime incomes, with the median UK graduate earning 80 per cent more than the median non-graduate by age 40 (IFS, 2021). However, these averages mask considerable variation in resources over the life course and between cohorts. Both of these dimensions matter for housing and each is now briefly examined in turn.

Biographical timing

Education does not have a constant effect on the resources people can devote to housing. Rather, the impact of education on housing-related resources varies over the life span as people move from investing in their human capital to – on average at least– reaping the returns of this investment as they grow older and experience accelerated occupational advancement. Investing in post-secondary education usually happens at younger ages and is costly because of upfront fees and foregone earnings while studying. These educational costs mean that students and recent graduates typically have relatively few resources to devote to housing and so are likely to live in the parental home, share or rent low-quality dwellings in cheaper neighbourhoods. However, over time the higher salaries and better career prospects of highly educated workers allow those with degrees to more easily move into homeownership and more desirable neighbourhoods than their less qualified peers. The overall picture therefore is of higher education reducing housing resources at younger ages but boosting them as the life course progresses.

The impact this has on the biographical timing of housing events is neatly illuminated by Shiffer-Sebba and Park (2021). They show that homeownership rates among White US baby boomers were relatively low among the college-educated through their twenties. However, once the cohort moved into their thirties the homeownership rate of the college-educated caught up with and then surpassed the rate among boomers who had not attended college. While these findings are undoubtedly specific to a particular cohort and place, the general pattern fits with tenure choice models' consistent finding that being in education depresses entry into ownership while higher educational qualifications have the opposite effect.

Cohort patterning

Finally, the resource implications of educational attainments vary across birth cohorts. This is partly because educational qualifications are, to a degree, positional goods whose economic value depends on how prevalent they are. For example, while the UK government's drive to boost participation in HE has largely been successful, the expanding number of degree-educated adults means that the meaning and value of a degree has changed. Over time, the economic premium attached to degrees has become lower and more varied, under-employment among graduates has increased, and having no degree has become a greater penalty in the labour market (Green, 2017). In addition, the shift in HE funding from a grants-based system to one based around repayable student loans has hit graduates' disposable incomes and helped delay their homeownership transitions (Andrew, 2012).

Summary

Housing scholarship has devoted surprisingly little attention to understanding how educational careers and housing behaviour are interconnected. In much of the literature, education is usually reduced to being either a trigger of residential moves or qualifications are instead treated as proxies for resource access and particular sorts of residential preference. There is also a widespread assumption that education only matters significantly for residential behaviour during the early phase of the life course.

This chapter sought to address these issues by showing how the contemporary links between education and housing careers are deep, varied and integral to the reproduction of social and spatial inequalities within both the housing and education systems. Crucially, the chapter has demonstrated that the connections between education and housing are not confined to young people but rather span the entirety of adulthood. Throughout the chapter, the life course concepts of biographies, timed events, cohorts, intergenerational solidarity and changing places have proven particularly useful for illuminating the complex interactions between education and residential careers. These interactions have a considerable bearing on the world of housing, work and wealth examined in Chapter 5.

5

Employment and money

As the GFC illustrated, it is difficult to overstate just how integral housing is to 21st-century economies and to the global financial system. Yet to fully understand how housing matters for economic prosperity and inequalities, we must look behind the national statistics at the ways in which housing careers are bound up with the labour market position and financial well-being of individuals and families over the life span.

This chapter uses the life course perspective to take a fresh look at how the deep interactions between housing and labour market careers influence economic outcomes at both the micro- and macro-levels. It shows how the ways people engage with both the labour market and the housing system over the course of their lives play a crucial role in determining the social distribution of resources. The chapter begins by using Chapter 2's life course conceptual toolbox to review how employment influences housing behaviour and housing system dynamics. It then inverts the focus to consider the role housing resources, opportunities and constraints play in shaping employment careers and the broader operation of labour markets. Finally, the chapter examines how differential accumulation and use of housing wealth influences contemporary patterns of social and spatial inequality.

Labour markets and residential behaviour

In *Why Families Move,* Rossi (1955) argued that housing transitions are adjustments undertaken to satisfy the new residential demands which emerge as people pass through the family life cycle. However, scholars quickly recognised that Rossi's demographically driven model said too little about labour force participation and in particular how a desire to improve one's economic position or social status can be a powerful motive for residential adjustments (De Jong and Fawcett, 1981). Moreover, the housing choice set available to people and thus their ability to act on their residential preferences is stratified by employment status, class and income (Kendig, 1984).[1] Early housing career models often downplayed these factors by simplistically assuming that occupational careers generally progress upwards over the life span as age brings promotions, higher wages and accumulated savings.

Since the 1970s, economic restructuring across the Global North under what has been variously termed the transition to post-Fordism, advanced capitalism or post-industrialism have shattered this optimistic assumption of occupational progression over the life span. Although economic restructuring processes have been mediated by governments and regional economic histories, common bundles of changes are also evident across most advanced economies (Clapham, 2005). Some of the most significant of these shared trends include:

- globalisation of production and goods flows, as well as of finance and labour markets;
- automation of routine manufacturing work (and increasingly service-sector jobs), offshoring to reduce labour costs and more flexible production and distribution enabled by information and communication technologies (ICTs);
- growth in knowledge-intensive work involving the use of ICTs, not only in production but also in an expanded and digitalising service sector;
- deregulation and reduced state intervention in economic affairs along with reduced labour bargaining power;
- the financialisation of economies through the greater penetration of financial instruments and institutions into everyday life.

These structural processes have had deep impacts on labour markets and some of the most important are shown in Table 5.1. The table summarises overarching UK trends but these have played out quite differently across regions with varying economic histories and occupational structures. Broadly speaking, the trends set out in Table 5.1 have created greater complexity, fluidity and inequality in the ways people engage with labour markets. This has had implications for housing as employment influences residential behaviour by (1) shaping locational preferences, life events and housing transitions, (2) configuring residential opportunities and constraints, and (3) altering housing resources and restrictions. These three pathways through which labour markets influence contemporary housing careers are now examined in turn.

Locational preferences, events and housing transitions

Neoclassical models posit that people evaluate where to live by comparing the expected wages and employment prospects available in different regions less the costs of moving (with more advanced formulations also factoring in living costs, non-economic utility, knowledge imperfections and other complexities). Such models predict that people will typically migrate from areas of lower wages and higher unemployment to places offering better pay, lower employment risk and greater opportunity for occupational advancement (Green, 2018). In this view, migration plays an important macro-economic function by enabling social mobility, equilibrating regional economies and matching workers to jobs. However, theories of labour

Table 5.1: UK labour market trends affecting housing careers

Trend	Description
1. Sectoral change	• Decline of resource extraction and manufacturing alongside the growth of service-sector employment • Reduced regional occupational specialisation (for example in mining or textile manufacture)
2. Skills	• Increased demand for skilled workers in knowledge-intensive sectors, often agglomerated within or around major cities • Decline of intermediate forms of employment such as skilled manual jobs and clerical work • Strong demand for low-skilled and casual workers
3. Economic security	• Decline of the job-for-life and structured occupational career paths within a single firm or sector • Growth of casualised gig employment, fixed-term employment and zero-hours contracts • Relatively low unemployment since the mid-1990s (although with a spike after the GFC)
4. Incomes	• Sluggish productivity growth and a declining share of economic growth accruing to labour leads to anaemic income growth • Socially polarised income growth • Increased in-work poverty despite minimum wage legislation
5. Working practices	• Greater autonomy and flexibility over hours and work locations for highly skilled workers, accelerated by COVID-19 • Increased part-time work, self-employment, multiple job holding and complex working patterns
6. Household divisions of labour	• Decline of single-earner couples and increases in dual-earner households driven by rising female labour force participation • Increased no-earner households as the population ages

Source: Compiled partly from Arundel and Doling (2017) and Green (2018).

market segmentation contest this perspective by arguing that labour markets are actually divided into separate non-competing segments which are each accessible only to workers with specific attributes (for example certain skills). Segmentation theories are important as they remind us that the geography of labour market opportunities and constraints varies across population groups.

In these economic frameworks, three considerations factor heavily into the cost-benefit calculations people make when deciding precisely where to live: (1) workplace locations, (2) the geography and affordability of accessible housing, and (3) the time and expense of commuting between home and work (Clark et al, 2003). Each of these variables can be adjusted but this always involves making trade-offs along the other dimensions. For example, those wanting to live near a city-centre workplace will often need to devote a larger share of their income to housing or reduce their housing consumption as compared with those commuting longer distances from cheaper residential locations. Moreover, if housing search spaces are centred on a fixed workplace and are bounded by an acceptable commute time (a common assumption of 20th-century urban models), then residential choices are effectively limited to the dwelling types, tenures, cost profile and so on that are available within the commute tolerance zone. For example, the fact that poverty was historically centralised in inner-cities while the middle-classes made longer commutes from suburban homes was attributed to land prices falling with distance from city-centre workplaces while demand for housing space rose with income at an accelerating rate (Zhang and Pryce, 2020).

In contrast, other people adapt their workplace to minimise commuting in order to achieve family or housing goals. This may involve taking a suboptimal but more local job, working fewer hours, working from home or entering self-employment. Meanwhile, countless TV property programmes attest to the way that some people accept very long commutes in order to be able to maximise their housing consumption or satisfy particular lifestyle preferences (for instance to live in a bucolic village). Overall, the exact strategy a person adopts to geographically juggle their housing and employment careers varies idiosyncratically as well as more systematically with life course position (for example with age or with factors affecting time constraints such as children) and with personal attributes such as gender or qualifications.

In Britain, there is good evidence that people are, on average, stretching their commutes to access urban workplaces from areas of cheaper housing located further away from city centres. Judge (2019) shows that commute zones have expanded in recent decades as trips to work have got longer, particularly for younger more resource-constrained workers. Indicative of this trend is the way the number of statistical travel to work areas (TTWA) – functional labour market zones defined so that few commuters cross zonal boundaries – has fallen with each decennial census from 308 in 1991 to 228 in 2011 (ONS, 2016). Multiple factors are thought to have driven this growth in longer commutes. On the positive side, these include employment-related changes such as:

- growth in managerial and professional occupations offering higher pay rates and more autonomy;
- ICTs that enable working on the go and working from home; and
- decentralisation of workplaces and more flexibility over where to work, especially in the wake of COVID-19.

More ambiguous or less favourable drivers of longer commutes include:

- increased numbers of spatially constrained dual-earner households;
- heightening problems of housing affordability in jobs-rich cities forcing people to move out and commute further in order to satisfy their residential preferences; and

- reduced real costs of car ownership, which have contributed to increased use with damaging consequences for congestion, air quality and greenhouse gas emissions.

Despite these trends and the fact that many job changes take place within local labour markets, employment transitions such as entering the workforce and changing job are still potent triggers of moving home, particularly over longer distances and for those with higher skills. As Böheim and Taylor (2002, p 369) put it, 'job and employer changes often require house moves, and housing demand will reflect patterns in employment turnover and labour market trends'. Their UK analysis demonstrated that changing labour force status or jobs correlates with residential moves. This result has been corroborated for the US by Clark and Davies Withers (1999) – who found a particularly strong job-trigger effect for spatially flexible single renters – and for the Netherlands by De Groot and colleagues (2011). These findings have prompted some to hypothesise that slower rates of job changing might explain the otherwise somewhat mysterious fall in US internal migration rates over recent decades (Molloy et al, 2017). In addition, as people know that job changes or finding work may require moving, anticipating future job shifts (as is particularly common for younger workers) deters home purchases and leads people to opt for more flexible private rental housing where transaction costs are lower. While retirement can theoretically trigger housing adjustments by freeing people from the need to access workplaces, there is relatively little evidence this happens on a significant scale in Britain (Ermisch and Jenkins, 1999).

Not all labour market events are, of course, beneficial or planned. Employment shocks may force residential adjustments, either by motivating in situ shifts in household composition (for example increased household size to offset cost pressures) or by triggering moves to cheaper housing. For example, Clark (2013b) shows that lay-offs trigger relocation in Australia while Rabe and Taylor (2010) demonstrate that opposite-sex UK couples are more likely to move to more deprived neighbourhoods when the man loses his job. The probability of experiencing these types of forced adjustments varies across the business cycle as illustrated by the post-GFC spike in US foreclosures or by the large number of repossessions during the early 1990s UK downturn (Hamnett, 1999).

Another strategy to cope with reduced resources following job loss is exiting homeownership. In Britain, shifting from owning to renting is uncommon but particularly attractive for those who will receive high priority in social housing allocations (for example people with health problems) and those with few assets eligible for benefit support to cover their rent. In their analysis of homeownership exits, Wood and colleagues (2017, p 212) found that those in full-time employment in both Britain and Australia were far less likely to leave the tenure than those who were unemployed or not in the labour force. Becoming unemployed also appears to motivate returns to the parental home among younger Britons (Stone et al, 2014). For some, unemployment may thus form a turning point in the housing career with long-lasting adverse effects akin to those of partnership dissolution. Biographical timing matters here as unemployment spells in early adulthood scar future employment prospects, which then has detrimental long-term housing career consequences.

Opportunities and constraints

The effects job-related events have on housing behaviour and the likelihood of experiencing such events both depend on the broader economic context. In temporal terms, migration propensities generally track the business cycle as falls in job vacancies, uncertainty, pay restraint and greater risk aversion during recessions mean people have less reason and are more reluctant to relocate (Green, 2018). Cyclical period effects on mobility are especially relevant for owner-occupiers as low or negative equity caused by (fears of) slumping house prices – plus psychological aversion to incurring losses from house sales – causes owners to wait out the bust in their current home (Ferreira et al, 2010). Figure 5.1 shows this in Britain where annual rates of address changing among mortgaged owners have, broadly speaking, moved with GDP growth rates since the mid-2000s.

The impact labour market conditions have on housing careers varies for workers with different skills profiles who operate in segmented labour markets (Böheim and Taylor, 2002). When the economy is doing well, long-distance migration for jobs is much more common for highly skilled managerial and professional workers as these groups:

• conduct wider job searches as suitable vacancies are less spatially ubiquitous and so progression in highly skilled occupations is more dependent on moving long distances;
• possess greater resources to overcome the transaction costs of moving;
• gain more in wage terms from migration than lower-skilled workers as the latter's pay levels are less spatially variable (Rodríguez-Pose and Storper, 2020); and
• are more likely to work in sectors where internships, placements, transfers, secondments and home move support packages are common.

Fielding's (1992) 'escalator region' (ER) hypothesis integrates notions of biographical development with economic geography to explain the connections between employment and housing career progression over the life span. The ER model divides the life course into three broad stages. First,

Figure 5.1: Annual mobility rates of owner-occupiers follow the business cycle

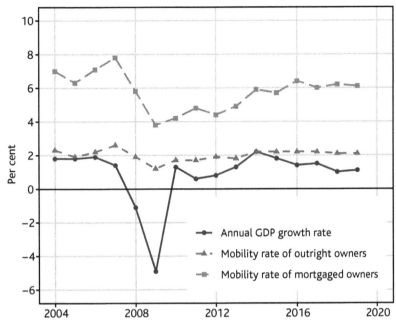

Source: Own analysis of weighted APS data supplemented with ONS GDP figures licensed under the Open Government Licence v3.0.

talented young adults *step on* the escalator by migrating to city-regions with dynamic labour markets which offer plentiful opportunities for education and professional development through job-hopping and firm switching. Chapter 4 described how this stepping-on process occurs in London as the city attracts large flows of students and high-achieving graduates from across Britain and overseas.

Second, the ER's thick labour market provides excellent opportunities for accelerated social mobility by enabling those living in the region to *ride up* the occupational advancement escalator (Gordon et al, 2015). In Fielding's (1992) original formulation, riding up also involved the accumulation of housing wealth as ER residents benefit from the way that local house prices usually rise much faster in areas with buoyant labour markets than in places where housing demand is weak due to a depressed jobs market. Third, successful workers cash in the assets they have amassed by *stepping off* the escalator around retirement when workplace ties are severed. This involves moving out of the ER to an amenity-rich location where housing costs are lower.

The ER hypothesis is elegant and many of its core predictions have largely been confirmed in subsequent work. For example, Gordon and colleagues (2015) show that smaller city-regions function as mini-ERs and that escalating effects are particularly pronounced in knowledge-intensive sectors and in labour markets with a dense agglomeration of knowledge-intensive jobs. Yet enhanced housing affordability problems in precisely these places calls into question the way Fielding (1992) imagined employment and housing career escalators to operate in a lock-step manner. Housing asset escalator effects within ERs are conditional on owner-occupation and yet the increased financial difficulty of buying a home in recent years has depressed young adults' owner-occupation rates across Britain's metropolitan areas as entering ownership here becomes more contingent on family support (Corlett and Judge, 2017). This suggests that Fielding's dual job–housing escalator may have been a cohort-specific process which depended on the more accessible housing market conditions he was analysing.

Moreover, evidence that people often leave ERs more quickly than Fielding predicted hints that the tricky job–housing career trade-offs discussed previously are required in these areas (Champion, 2012). Greater problems of housing affordability in today's ERs are likely to have placed job and housing career progression in direct conflict with one another as living in an ER facilitates occupational advancement but restricts the housing career. Resolving this conflict without compromising on either occupational or housing priorities can best be achieved by moving out or to the periphery of the ER and accepting a longer commute, perhaps coupled with working from home some of the time. This elongation of commutes is precisely what Judge's (2019) analysis suggests is occurring and there is growing evidence that COVID-19 lockdowns have embedded working from home into the lives of skilled British professionals (Felstead and Reuschke, 2021).

Labour market structures have very different implications for the housing careers of less skilled workers. Workers with fewer qualifications typically have a lower commute tolerance, are more prone to only search for nearby jobs and so are more likely to find their employment opportunities constrained by what the local labour market supplies. Judge (2019) argues that spatial convergence in wage rates (caused in part by minimum wage legislation), unemployment and disposable incomes (caused partly by housing cost inflation eroding disposable incomes in buoyant areas) has, over time, further dampened the economic incentives to low-skilled and younger workers moving between labour markets. She contends this reduces job changing and can explain Figure 5.2's pattern of falling rates of address changing in the UK private rented sector (PRS). Similar arguments have been advanced for the US where productive cities now fill their low-skilled jobs using immigrant labour rather than with internal migrants (Rodríguez-Pose and Storper, 2020).

Qualitative work has supported these arguments by examining the housing implications of low rates of pay growth and a rise in insecure and casual gig work. Research by Preece (2018) shows that remaining rooted in a local area (even one with a depressed economy) allows those on low incomes to

Figure 5.2: Annual mobility rates of private renters have fallen over time

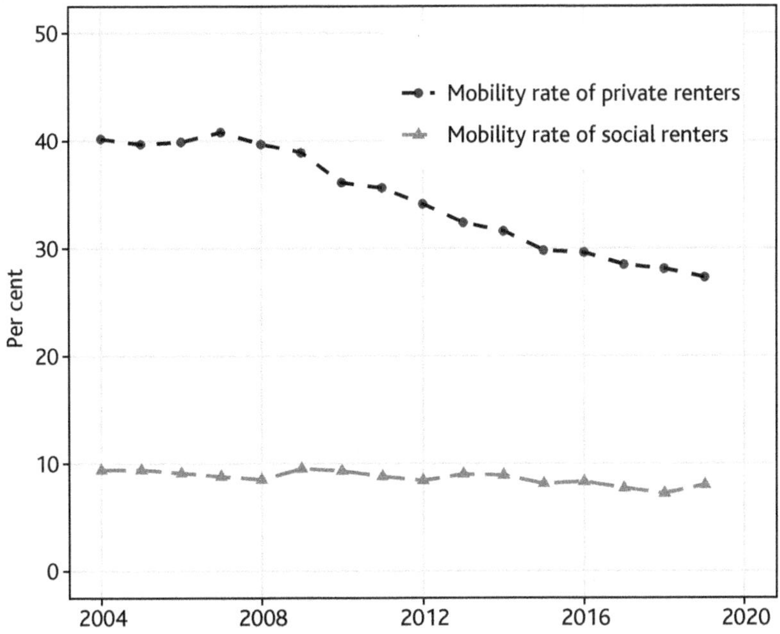

Source: Own analysis of weighted APS data.

navigate a precarious labour market by harnessing their local knowledge and social networks to find work and get by. For these groups, migration to a more prosperous area is not viable as moving would not significantly boost their wages or job prospects but would sever the local exchanges of support and job information they rely on (Preece, 2018). Linked life connections and local solidarities are thus a powerful resource tying those exposed to a precarious low-waged labour market to particular localities.

Labour market resources

For most people, paid work is their principal way of obtaining income to pay for housing. This is especially true early in life when few people have significant assets and it is rare to be an outright homeowner. Overall, greater earned income is usually associated with housing advantage along one or more of the following axes:

- owning rather than renting;
- having more residential space and better dwelling facilities;
- living in a better-quality dwelling; or
- living in a more desirable neighbourhood offering better access to opportunities.

There are numerous reasons for these patterns. The most obvious is that higher incomes allow people to pay the higher prices commanded by larger, better-quality dwellings located in more desirable areas. Higher incomes and job security are also prerequisites for mortgage borrowing, especially in contexts like Germany where lending has traditionally been more cautious (Bayrakdar et al, 2019). More informally, higher incomes may smooth housing access by signalling to lenders and landlords that a person is a more reliable borrower or tenant. In addition, the income elasticity of housing is generally quite high as 'households are willing to devote a relatively large proportion of extra income to buy more housing, and/or more quality of housing' (Clark and Dieleman, 1996, p 80). This willingness to devote extra income to housing is a further reason for pro-cyclical residential mobility, as people often opt to spend their wage gains on housing (Cho and Whitehead, 2013).

International evidence supports these ideas, as study after study shows that being employed, having a working partner, having a higher income and working in a more secure and skilled role predicts owner-occupation or homeownership entry as well as neighbourhood quality. British evidence corroborating these findings is given in Table 5.2 and Figure 5.3. The top four rows of Table 5.2 show that midlife adults (aged 35–54) are much more likely to own their home or live in an advantaged neighbourhood if they have higher incomes. The bottom rows of Table 5.2 meanwhile show that where owner-occupied housing is located and the self-reported value of owned dwellings also varies significantly with income as affluent owners possess more valuable dwellings and are far more likely to own homes in advantaged neighbourhoods than their lower-income peers. Meanwhile, the cohort trajectories in Figure 5.3 show that higher incomes predict entry

Table 5.2: The residential characteristics of midlife adults by income, 2018–19

Residential characteristic	Low	Middle	High
Per cent owner-occupied	27.5	63.6	91.9
Per cent social rent	40.7	18.3	<1
Per cent private rent	19.1	15.2	7.3
Per cent living in advantaged neighbourhood	10.3	16.0	38.5
Per cent homeowner in advantaged neighbourhood	4.7	12.5	36.3
Median value of owner-occupied homes	£150,000	£215,000	£350,000

Note: Incomes are measured at the family level with low indicating the bottom and high the top quarters respectively. Advantaged neighbourhoods are defined as the least deprived quintile of LSOAs/Scottish datazones.

Source: Own analysis of weighted UKHLS data enriched with Indices of Multiple Deprivation.

Figure 5.3: Residential trajectories of a cohort of 25–44-year-olds tracked for nine years

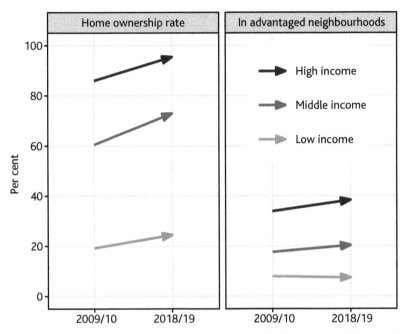

Note: Incomes are measured as median real family income over the observation period, categorised as in Table 5.2.

Source: Own analysis of weighted UKHLS data enriched with Indices of Multiple Deprivation.

into homeownership and more advantaged neighbourhoods as adults move into and through midlife.

The significant role that resources play in motivating and enabling housing transitions means that any trends in job types, vacancies, wage rates, economic security and so forth will profoundly alter aggregate patterns of housing careers. Deterioration in incomes and job security – trends pre-dating the GFC but also exacerbated by it – have helped delay entry into owner-occupation and depressed space consumption among younger Britons through recent decades (Andrew, 2012; Corlett and Judge, 2017). While a recessionary shock may trigger adverse housing events (for example evictions) across society, the housing impacts of labour market restructuring often emerge as spatially and cohort-graded processes that begin by most strongly affecting younger adults in the most exposed regions. There are two reasons for this. On the jobs side, older labour market insiders are often protected from restructuring by their employment contracts, wealth and accumulated entitlements (Arundel and Doling, 2017).[2] In contrast, younger outsiders do not have these protections and so are vulnerable to being hired on less favourable terms or not being hired at all. This age-graded process of labour market change means that resource accumulation trajectories vary across cohorts to create differences in their housing careers. Meanwhile, on the housing side, most residential events and transitions occur in early adulthood and so it is during this life stage that housing careers are particularly exposed to shifts in resource access. This became evident after the GFC when economic uncertainty and constrained lending delayed first-time home purchases but had much less impact on the housing careers of older, more established owner-occupiers.

The housing effects of labour market processes are moderated by context. At the regional level, variations in the type and severity of economic change as well as in pre-existing occupational and housing structures act as important moderators. At the macro-level, how societies provide housing, support people to obtain and sustain it as well as broader housing market conditions (sometimes collectively termed the housing regime) all configure how labour market processes influence housing careers. These moderation effects can be thought to range on a spectrum from housing contexts which *buffer* people against labour market difficulties (such as low wages or job insecurity) through to those that *amplify* these problems.

Since the 1980s, economic restructuring combined with two sets of housing changes have made life more economically precarious for low-income UK households. First, house prices and rents have inflated faster than wages and this has eroded disposable incomes while limiting housing choices. Between 2000 and 2015 mean UK nominal house prices rose 173 per cent (roughly 135 per cent in real terms) and this has helped push owner-occupation out of reach of those without high salaries and job security (Hamnett and Reades, 2019). This is particularly problematic in parts of southern England where average price-to-income ratios are now extremely high. Cross-national analysis by Lersch and Dewilde (2015) shows that job security is an especially important prerequisite for entering homeownership in Britain because most people strive to own and buyers rely heavily on commercial mortgages. Prior to the GFC, the affordability gap generated by wage growth lagging house price inflation was masked by two household strategies: greater borrowing and drawing on family transfers. Although these are neither equitable nor sustainable strategies, further house price inflation in a low interest rate environment since the mid-2010s (and especially through the pandemic) has driven their resurgence.

Shifts in tenure structure and social security have exacerbated these housing resource problems. Between 1919 and 1979, council housing became more common across Britain as governments of all stripes viewed building affordable, decent and secure public housing as a way for the state to improve public welfare. This consensus ended with the 1979 election of a Conservative government led by Margaret Thatcher who believed that free markets and individual self-reliance yielded better social and economic outcomes than state provision. One of the earliest of her government's expressions of these convictions was the Housing Act 1980. This started the

Right to Buy programme of mass council house sales which went unmatched by new construction (Murie, 2016).[3] Private renting and housing finance were also later deregulated in a broader bid to liberalise housing and these policies were continued by the subsequent New Labour government, which also presided over a boom in buy-to-let PRS investment (Kemp, 2015).

The net effect of these interventions has been contraction of the social housing sector and an expansion of private renting. Lower-income households who might a few decades ago have been allocated a council house are now dependent on the private rental market where rents are higher, tenancies are less secure and contracts often restrict usage rights (Hoolachan et al, 2017). This situation is especially acute in areas of high demand and the pressure has been exacerbated by the 2010–15 coalition government's package of cuts to housing benefits and other social security entitlements (policies which have been continued by subsequent Conservative administrations). Taken together, the overall effect of these trends has been to layer housing insecurity onto the growing problems of low incomes and precarity experienced by less advantaged groups. Housing today thus amplifies the hardship caused by low pay and job insecurity instead of providing a buffer against these problems. This is especially true in England as the Scottish and Welsh governments are taking a more interventionist stance by protecting social housing and more strongly regulating the PRS (McKee et al, 2017b).

Employment career restrictions

Labour market restrictions on housing careers are also generated through a person's ties and relationships with others. These types of linked life restrictions have traditionally been neglected by housing scholarship, which often either looks purely at individual behaviour or instead conceptualises households as unified social actors. One problem with these approaches is that neither can handle the complex spatial restrictions encountered by people in dual-earner or dual-career partnerships. Such couples have become more numerous since the 1960s as women have entered the workforce and increasingly sought to pursue their own careers.

Dual-career couples – defined as those where both partners (usually highly educated) are not just in work but are striving to develop their occupational careers – face particularly strong linked life restrictions in what has been termed the co-location problem (Chen and Rosenthal, 2008). This problem is quite straightforward to grasp: how can a couple find a single residential location that will allow both partners to develop their occupational careers? For highly skilled dual-career couples confronted by a low spatial density of jobs, finding somewhere to live does not simply involve trading off workplace location, housing costs and commutes – it also involves coordination and synchronisation of these across two intertwined life courses, as well as consideration of each person's future needs. This complexity and the associated costs of coordination explains why dual-career couples rarely move home (Green, 2018).

Dual-career couples can circumvent the difficulties of coordinating home and work in multiple ways. These are not necessarily mutually exclusive and they include:

- one or both partners accepting a long commute;
- making strategic choices about where to live in order to maximise access to workplaces, usually by living in or near to at least one major city;
- splitting the household across two residences during the working week (commuter partnerships);
- adapting working practices, for example by working from home; or
- one or both partners accepting an economically suboptimal location for the sake of their partner's career and/or for net family gain.

Particular research attention has been devoted to the latter strategy and especially to the gendered nature of opposite-sex couples' residential decisions. The basic idea is that the difficulty of optimising both partners' occupational needs from a single residential hub means that one or both are often restricted to being 'tied' movers or stayers. Partners are understood to be tied if they have sacrificed their own occupational career interests by moving to (tied movers) or staying in (tied stayers) a location that is personally suboptimal (Cooke, 2008).

Throughout the late 20th century, research showed that women were disproportionately the tied partner as couples predominantly moved or stayed for male occupational gain. In contrast, female partners – especially mothers with young children – typically adjusted their labour force engagements to fit around male needs (Cooke, 2008). Debate has centred primarily on two issues: how these outcomes emerge through bargaining and whether female losses are due to purely rational calculations about what will be best for the couple or are instead caused by gender norms devaluing women's contributions (Abraham et al, 2010). Cooke's (2008) evidence that egalitarian couples make more de-gendered decisions points towards the latter, although this area has been less well-researched in recent years and far less is known about how ties to non-resident others (for example ageing parents or adult children) shape decisions about work, home and commuting (Mulder, 2018).

Housing and employment careers

The connections between labour markets and housing flow both ways and there is growing concern that unaffordable urban housing is preventing people from moving to growth centres to improve their skills, job prospects and incomes. Such housing barriers to mobility are thought to cause a host of social ills ranging from poor productivity through to income inequality, social stratification and class-based residential segregation. Thus 'housing, in this view, is no longer a local issue: it is central to debates about national growth and the effects of globalisation on communities' (Rodríguez-Pose and Storper, 2020, p 224). This idea that housing affordability problems are damaging job prospects comes through strongly in the prime ministerial forewords to two recent UK government housing policy documents:

> Our broken housing market is one of the greatest barriers to progress in Britain today. (Theresa May, in DCLG, 2017, p 5)

> Thanks to our planning system, we have nowhere near enough homes in the right places. People cannot afford to move to where their talents can be matched with opportunity. Businesses cannot afford to grow and create jobs. (Boris Johnson, in MHCLG, 2020b, p 6)

However, there are several limitations to this prevailing view of how housing affects employment careers. First, the evidence that urban housing affordability problems reduce growth by preventing cityward migration is at the very least contested and may not be as clear-cut as politicians often assume. Second, focusing solely on housing affordability overlooks how other attributes of the housing system – namely the tenure structure and the way housing is regulated and taxed – also have impacts both on population dynamics and employment. Third, empirical work shows that housing is not just a workforce restriction as homes can, for some people, act as a resource which enables entrepreneurship. We now explore these three issues in turn to try and create a more nuanced appreciation of how housing matters for employment careers and labour market dynamics.

Housing as a restriction and constraint

Current policy thinking about housing and employment is dominated by what Rodríguez-Pose and Storper (2020) term the 'housing as opportunity' (HOP) school. A core HOP argument is that enhanced problems of housing affordability in economically buoyant cities (blamed largely on inadequate dwelling supply) prevent people from moving there to improve their incomes and career prospects. This inability to move towards job opportunities not only damages individual prosperity but also harms the local and national economy by reducing productivity and stopping the benefits of growth trickling down to depressed regions (Rodríguez-Pose and Storper, 2020). To deal with these problems, HOP advocates propose deregulating planning to unleash house-building around economic hubs which they argue will reduce urban housing prices and thus enable greater in-migration.

Affordability, migration and growth

It is difficult to dispute the HOP school's point that urban housing affordability problems have grown over time and are damaging many people's lives. Likewise, high housing costs in opportunity-rich locales may plausibly dissuade in-migration by eroding the gross income gains of living in these places (Judge, 2019). Yet this does not mean that deregulation of planning to boost housing supply will automatically boost the number of affordable homes – Rodríguez-Pose and Storper (2020) contend it will not – or that improving affordability is sufficient to unleash a wave of economically beneficial migrations. Indeed, there are several reasons why HOP models may overstate how significantly an urban housing affordability crisis is preventing economically beneficial migrations from happening. These are all surprisingly poorly understood and they include:

- *Labour market trends*: As discussed earlier, there is good evidence that labour market processes rather than housing are key drivers of migration as greater spatial evenness in wages and unemployment rates along with the growth of precarious work is reducing migration incentives (Judge, 2019).
- *Better transport and communications*: Highly skilled workers have traditionally been among the most migratory populations. However, such workers are the best placed to exploit faster transport links and ICT-facilitated remote working – now normalised by COVID-19 lockdowns – to avoid the costs of migrating for work. If these trends mean occupational progression for the highly skilled is no longer so contingent on moving home, then declining migration to growth centres need not signify damaged careers or lower productivity.
- *Better job matching*: The ease of accessing online information should improve job matching and reduce the chance of making 'failed' migrations (Molloy et al, 2017). Again, this implies that lower migration rates may not be an economic problem.
- *Satisficing*: There is evidence that a large share of migrations are enabled rather than motivated by jobs, as continuity of income allows people to move for other reasons such as family or quality-of-life (Morrison and Clark, 2011). If this is the case, then easing housing affordability might increase migration, but this may not have much of an economic payoff.

Tenure structures

Whatever its merits, the HOP perspective undoubtedly misses other ways in which housing systems can shape employment outcomes. This is particularly problematic in Britain where poor labour market outcomes have often been blamed on the structure of both the traditional lifetime tenures of social housing and homeownership. Social housing has attracted most of the attention with numerous studies arguing that the structure and governance of the sector produces unemployment by preventing work-related migration. Cho and Whitehead (2013) list several mechanisms through which the structure of the social housing sector might dampen work-related mobility and thus damage employment careers:

- Tenure security and low rents supported by complex means-tested benefits reduce the incentive to move for what are often relatively small income gains.
- Bureaucratic and locally administered allocations systems inhibit long-distance moves.
- Long waiting lists in high demand areas make it difficult to move there to fill job vacancies.

Longitudinal analysis demonstrates that social tenants do have a lower tendency to move long distances than those living in other tenures and that they are also more likely to experience prolonged unemployment (Battu et al, 2008). However, two cautionary notes are important. First, the disadvantaged profile of many social tenants means that they would be very unlikely to migrate for work even in the absence of tenure barriers (Cho and Whitehead, 2013). Most tenants simply do not have the resources or skills to make migrating for work either feasible or beneficial and so most would probably search only for local jobs even if there were abundant housing opportunities elsewhere. Second, residential security and local ties are valuable resources for those facing precarious labour market conditions (Preece, 2018). Instead of fracturing these by forcing tenants to move around in search of low-wage work, bringing better employment opportunities to their locales is likely to have more beneficial overall impacts across the entire gamut of life course careers.

Given that boosting owner-occupation has long been a central UK policy objective, it is curious that policymakers seem to have paid scant attention to economists' arguments that high rates of homeownership may undermine growth. The possibility that widespread homeownership damages economies by increasing unemployment was first raised in the 1990s by Andrew Oswald who argued that 'by making it expensive to change location, high levels of homeownership foster spatial mismatch between workers' skills and the available jobs' (Oswald, 2009, p 44). Oswald advanced five mechanisms through which high homeownership levels could boost unemployment:

1. High housing transaction costs make it more costly for owners to move to avoid unemployment.
2. High homeownership prevents capital-poor unemployed workers (especially the young) from entering housing markets to take up jobs.

3. The spatial fixity of owner-occupiers leads to poor matching between skills and vacancies as homeowners take suboptimal local jobs.
4. Homeowners inhibit entrepreneurship by lobbying against local development.
5. Owner-occupiers' spatial fixity leads to inefficient long commutes.

Van Ewijk and van Leuvensteijn (2009) have suggested two additional mechanisms:

6. Owner-occupation ties up money which could be used for more productive investments.
7. State support for homeownership (through policies such as capital gains tax exemptions, mortgage interest tax deductions, one-off payments to home purchasers and zero taxation of owner-occupiers' imputed rents) require compensatory government revenue-raising elsewhere. This usually takes the form of economically harmful but more easily levied taxes on labour or firms.

The validity of Oswald's hypothesis seems to depend on whether homeownership is viewed as an individual-level restriction on employment careers or an aggregate-level constraint (or externality) which impacts on the entire labour market. At the individual level, the evidence indicates that owner-occupiers are not more likely to experience unemployment than those living in other tenures (Battu et al, 2008; Blanchflower and Oswald, 2013). A desire to safeguard homeownership seems, in fact, to boost owner-occupiers' workforce attachment and lead unemployed homeowners to search especially widely and intensely for work (van Ewijk and van Leuvensteijn, 2009). In contrast, high rates of homeownership are associated with higher unemployment both across countries and within them over time (Blanchflower and Oswald, 2013). This finding indicates that homeownership could act as a constraint on labour market outcomes regardless of individual tenure. Although the precise mechanisms producing this effect remain somewhat unclear, Borg and Branden (2018)'s analysis of Swedish data hints that high levels of homeownership in smaller labour markets may lead to worse job matching in these locales.

Taken together, tests of the Oswald hypothesis have two policy implications. First, dampening residential mobility by taxing dwelling transactions is economically harmful (Blanchflower and Oswald, 2013; van Ewijk and van Leuvensteijn, 2009). In Britain, Stamp Duty housing transaction tax regularly tops a crowded field jostling for the dubious accolade of the country's worst designed tax and replacing this with some form of progressive general property taxation would have immense benefits for both residential mobility and social equality (Murphy, 2018). Second, policies to boost homeownership need at the very least to consider that this might have adverse side-effects on labour markets.

Spatial mismatch

A separate literature indicates that housing restrictions and constraints on employment are especially pronounced for more disadvantaged groups. The spatial mismatch hypothesis was proposed in the 1960s in the US to explain the poor labour market position of African Americans and their concentration in declining inner-cities (Kain, 2004). Kain's thesis was that the decentralisation of blue-collar work together with poverty and housing discrimination meant that African Americans experienced a mismatch between the location of potential workplaces (increasingly located towards the outskirts of cities) and accessible housing (restricted to poor inner-city neighbourhoods). Essentially, African Americans' residential locations were relatively fixed and so work had to be found from the dwindling number of workplaces accessible from the inner-city (Kain, 2004). At the time, Kain estimated that 'restrictions on residential choice cost Afro American workers as many as 9,000 jobs in Detroit and as many as 24,600 jobs in Chicago, and that, in the absence of the elimination of housing market discrimination, continued employment dispersal would lead to even greater job losses' (Kain, 2004, p 10).

Kain's insights were developed in a context where the causes, severity and geography of labour market disadvantage were very different from those of 21st-century Britain. However, the spatial mismatch hypothesis has been repurposed to understand how job access varies with income and class across UK cities. In recent years, housing affordability pressures in inner cities together with poor households' increased reliance on private renting have displaced poverty out of city centres to the suburbs and urban fringe (Zhang and Pryce, 2020). Zhang and Pryce (2020) show that this de-concentration has reduced poorer households' access to jobs, especially in larger labour markets. More analysis of the impacts this has on employment careers is needed but it does appear that housing constraints may be limiting the economic opportunities of poor Britons.

Housing as an employment resource

While research and policy tend to concentrate on the ways housing restricts and constrains employment careers, for some people housing can be a resource which supports their workforce participation in two ways. First, housing careers can widen the choice of employment type by shaping the decision to become self-employed and especially to run a business from home (Reuschke, 2016). The proportion of self-employed workers in

Britain has risen over time from around 12 per cent of the 2001 workforce (3.3 million people) to 15.1 per cent in 2016 (4.8 million), with particularly strong growth among women, older workers and the highly qualified (ONS, 2018b).

While self-employment is a very varied state, Reuschke (2016) proposes that three attributes of housing careers affect decisions to become self-employed and especially to set up a home-based business:

1. *Housing assets*: these can be released or harnessed for borrowing to fund business start-ups. While 28.3 per cent of self-employed workers aged over 55 have over £500,000 of net property wealth, this drops to just 12.7 per cent among their employed peers (ONS, 2018b).[4]
2. *Tenure*: rental contracts often prohibit running a home-based business while owner-occupation provides the security and control to support start-ups.
3. *Type and space*: greater dwelling space and access to a garden or garage where workspace can be created could boost the probability of starting a home-based venture.

Reuschke's analysis supports these hypotheses as owner-occupiers, those with more space and those in detached homes are more likely to set up home-based businesses. Interestingly, renting privately predicts starting up a business based outside the home and Reuschke (2016) speculates that this may be because owner-occupation consumes savings that could be devoted to entrepreneurship. While more work to confirm these findings is needed, they do hint that housing careers may directly influence self-employment behaviour.

Second, the COVID-19 shock has highlighted how housing affects working practices and in particular people's ability to use their homes as a working location. Estimates suggest that around 43 per cent of jobs can theoretically be done remotely (most commonly highly skilled managerial and professional work) and the sudden pivot to homeworking during COVID-19 lockdowns was surprisingly productive (Felstead and Reuschke, 2021). However, even if a job is amenable to working from home, pandemic experiences indicate that smaller dwellings and role conflicts (with parenting demands in particular) dampen how effectively this can be done. This indicates that the feasibility of effective homeworking depends on the intersection of one's family and housing career circumstances (Felstead and Reuschke, 2021). Nonetheless, survey data suggest that pandemic experiences of homeworking have generated enthusiasm for this among firms and workers, with 88 per cent of those working at home in June 2020 reporting they want to continue after lockdowns eased (Felstead and Reuschke, 2021). This raises the prospect that the pandemic shock may have long-term implications for commuting behaviour, locational choice and the connections between housing, family and employment careers.

Housing wealth and welfare

Prosperity over the life course is determined not simply by employment and income, but also by wealth and thus by the trajectory of the housing career. Housing is crucially important for wealth in the 21st century as most households' principal debt and main store of wealth lies in their home(s) in the respective forms of residential mortgages and housing equity. The sums involved here are enormous: in 2018–20 British households held around £5.5 trillion of property wealth – mostly in owner-occupied housing (ONS, 2022a) – while in 2021 outstanding UK mortgage debts totalled roughly £1.6 trillion (FCA, 2021).

Three trends help explain the growing importance of housing for the distribution of wealth:

1. higher rates of owner-occupation and especially increased rates of outright homeownership as the large and relatively affluent baby boom cohorts pay off their mortgages;
2. long-run inflation of real house prices; and
3. increased private landlordism and second homeownership which have generated a secondary circuit of property wealth accumulation.

Debates about the social significance of these trends have concentrated on two questions: how evenly distributed is housing wealth and how is it used? While Saunders (1990) asserted that the expansion of owner-occupation had democratised wealth, more critical views are now more dominant with Arundel and Ronald (2021) arguing that homeownership can never be a widespread, equalising or secure asset. These critical perspectives are underpinned by concern that access to housing wealth is becoming an increasingly important welfare resource as states shift from providing collective support towards systems where individuals are responsible for investing to secure their own future well-being (Lowe, 2011).

These are broad debates and much of our knowledge about housing wealth comes from time-series analysis of aggregate data about entire populations. While valuable, this approach tells us little about the life course processes which configure the uneven accumulation and use of housing wealth across space and social groups. Wealth is never static and it is only through longitudinal analysis that we gain a rich picture of how assets are unevenly accumulated as people move through life. The rest of this chapter therefore draws on Chapter 2's conceptual toolbox to review the somewhat scanty evidence on the distribution and use of housing wealth.

Housing asset accumulation

Housing wealth is not evenly distributed in any society. Differences in owner-occupation rates, mortgage debts, levels of multiple property holding and in property values are usually stark and combine to produce disparities in housing assets. Three sets of life course concepts provide useful tools for understanding how these disparities are created and maintained: (1) timing and cohort effects, (2) changing places and (3) cumulative disadvantage.

Timing and cohort

Conceptual models of housing wealth accumulation often assume that lives follow a predictable cycle. For example, models of tenure selection frequently assert that people enter homeownership in early adulthood to frontload their lifetime housing costs, gain a mortgage-free retirement, and accumulate a bequeathable stock of equity. While these models are useful heuristics, their focus on shared biographical processes provides only a rather simplistic view of how time structures housing wealth trajectories. Time also has more collective impacts as long-run house price trends, short-run market cycles and fluctuations in interest rates all shape the money people gain and lose from housing purchases. This implies that when people enter homeownership and move between owner-occupied dwellings must be considered as crucial determinants of their equity trajectories (Hamnett, 1999). Time thus needs to be seen as having two dimensions, biographical time (how old people are when they buy and how do home purchases relate to other life events?) and historical time (at what historical moment do people buy?), with the interaction between the two conditioning equity accumulation over the life course. Timing of purchases is particularly important in countries like Britain that have very volatile housing markets.

The impact of housing market and borrowing conditions on access to homeownership and on equity gains can be thought of as a cohort effect. In many countries, the conventional wisdom is that the baby boom cohort (born 1945–64) have done particularly well out of the housing market as easy access to homeownership and subsequent house price inflation have allowed them to accumulate large equity stocks (Meen, 2013). This argument has prompted a popular narrative of generational housing conflict and the emergence of various pressure groups that have an explicitly generational agenda (for example Generation Rent in Britain). While understandable, the danger here is that focusing on cohort averages masks the very significant wealth inequalities that exist between people born at the same time but who have little else in common.

Spatial disparities

Housing is mostly geographically fixed and location strongly determines house values. In Britain, the geography of land values underpins the housing market as the proportion of house prices attributable to land costs has risen over time to around 70 per cent in 2016 (Murphy, 2018). This importance of land helps to explain the long-term persistence of stark national and local geographical patterns in housing prices per areal unit.

Spatial patterning of both housing prices and rates of house price inflation have two implications for life course inequalities. The first is that the equity gains that flow from dwelling purchase depend heavily on where homes are located. Two identical purchasers buying identical homes at the same time but in different parts of the country or city can easily end up accumulating very different volumes of equity depending on differences in local house price movements. These disparities do not reflect differences in either investment or effort and yet they go largely uncorrected by the tax system as owner-occupied homes are usually exempt from capital gains tax. A second problem is that differences in housing prices could restrict north-to-south migration as homeowners in cheaper northern areas lack the equity to maintain their housing standards if they move to southern areas where housing prices are much higher.

Cumulative (dis)advantage

Another key question is whether social and spatial differences in housing wealth trajectories exacerbate or counterbalance labour market inequalities. Unfortunately, the evidence suggests that those with the most advantaged labour market positions tend also to profit the most from the housing market. For instance, Arundel (2017) shows how British housing equity stocks are heavily concentrated among households in the top income deciles. Lower-income households are, by contrast, far more likely to rent and have no property wealth.

Cumulative disadvantage across the housing and labour market careers does not just arise within owner-occupation. Today, housing careers themselves increasingly encompass owning multiple dwellings, as better-off households expand their portfolios by investing in property. Since the 1990s, this has primarily involved becoming a private landlord and estimates suggest that around 2 million British adults now receive some rental income with average gross rental streams ranging from around £9,000 per year in the North East to £20,000 in London (Bangham, 2019; MHCLG, 2019b). Landlords benefiting from rental income and potential capital gains are not a random slice of the population, as older adults, those with higher incomes, those with more housing equity and those living in southern England are more likely to be landlords than their younger and less advantaged peers (Arundel, 2017; Bangham, 2019). A similar pattern is evident among Britain's estimated 1.4 million second homeowners who also tend to be drawn from relatively advantaged social strata (Bangham, 2019). As these trends have been paralleled by growth in the proportion of households with no property wealth, it seems clear that housing asset trajectories are becoming increasingly unequal and that this compounds labour market inequalities.

Using housing wealth

Until recently, housing was considered a rather illiquid form of wealth that was only really accessible at death or when moving (Ong et al, 2013). Yet innovations in housing equity withdrawal products mean that housing assets can increasingly be tapped in situ and this raises questions about how, when and why people draw down on their equity stocks. Research suggests that two life course concepts can help us to better understand these processes: timed events and solidarities.

Timed events

In their longitudinal analysis of the pre-GFC period, Ong and colleagues (2013) showed that each year around a fifth of UK homeowners extracted equity, overwhelmingly through in situ borrowing. They estimate this injected between £37–63 billion per year into the British economy. Crucially, housing equity withdrawal does not appear to fund additional consumption but rather acts as a welfare resource that people use to cope with life events or pressures such as separation or the costs of childrearing (Wood et al, 2013). Equity withdrawal also appears to be something people do repeatedly and mostly out of necessity (Ong et al, 2013). Taken together, this evidence fits with the idea that state retreat from collective service provision (for instance in providing social care) is creating a system of 'asset-based welfare' where individuals must draw on their own resources in times of need (Lowe et al, 2012).

The use of housing equity as a safety net contrasts starkly with how affluent landlords draw on their property investments. Bangham (2019) shows that 44 per cent of landlords use their rental investments to fund retirement despite often having large pension pots and owning their own home outright. In a general sense, these disparities in how housing wealth is accumulated and used fit with Forrest and Hirayama's (2018) idea that housing wealth is increasingly stratified, as some families are amassing property portfolios while others have nothing or are dissipating their limited wealth gains just to get by. These processes can only be fully understood by considering housing careers alongside events and processes occurring across other domains of life as well as in the broader political-economic context.

Solidarities

Housing wealth is increasingly a familial as well as a personal resource. Until the 1990s, most work on intergenerational housing wealth transmissions concentrated on inequalities in inheritance. However, high rates of owner-occupation among older cohorts – coupled with their increased longevity and younger cohorts' difficulties accessing owner-occupation – have raised the prospect that *inter vivos* intergenerational transmissions of extracted housing wealth are growing as children rely on (grand)parental transfers when buying their first home (Lowe et al, 2012).

Unfortunately, robust empirical evidence specifically about the extraction and intergenerational transmissions of housing wealth (rather than wealth per se) is scarce and should be a priority for future research. If housing wealth is indeed increasingly viewed as a familial resource, then this indicates that some families may face tough decisions about how to balance the competing pressures of using wealth for personal (for example care costs) as opposed to family needs (for instance helping younger members enter the housing market). This again reminds us that the use of housing wealth is not simply an individual decision, but rather depends on the interconnected, multidimensional linked lives of family members (see Chapter 6).

Summary

Research and debate about the connections between labour market and housing processes typically focuses on broad national or cross-national trends. Yet these aggregate patterns are ultimately driven by the decisions and experiences of large numbers of individuals as they move through life. This chapter sought to foreground these life course processes by examining how employment and housing careers are today intertwined in unequal ways.

Although the chapter has ranged widely, three key points underpin much of the discussion. First, there is no straightforward single causal pathway linking labour market to housing processes. Both careers influence one another in ways that are often complex and which vary from person to person and across time and space. Second, the life course principle of time and place is perhaps particularly significant for labour market and housing career processes. How people engage in paid work and move between homes and neighbourhoods over the life course are both strongly conditioned by the contextual economic conditions they encounter.

Finally, the evidence reviewed in this chapter indicates that inequalities in the labour market tend to be compounded by housing career processes (and vice versa). In essence, those with an advantaged position in the labour market are best placed to develop their own housing career and also to use housing as a vehicle for further accumulation. This amplification process has intensified over time as labour markets have become more polarised, collective welfare provision has been scaled back and housing has become a key arena for asset accumulation. Equally, those with an advantageous housing position are best placed to gain from the labour market as moving to opportunities, coordinating home and work or starting one's own business are all generally easier for those with abundant housing resources. Overall, we can conceptualise the labour market and the housing system as twin interconnected engines of 21st-century economic inequalities.

6

Health, well-being and care

How housing is thought to relate to health has long influenced urban policy and the COVID-19 pandemic provided a powerful reminder of just how important these connections still are in the 21st century. Recent research shows that housing conditions directly influenced health through the pandemic as patterns of physical vulnerability and viral transmission were influenced by household structures, dwelling characteristics and neighbourhood attributes such as population density (Tinson and Clair, 2020). COVID-19 lockdowns also threw into sharp relief the more indirect ways housing shapes well-being as having space to work or study at home, access to outdoor space and supportive relationships with neighbours, all became important psychological resources. The pandemic's wake thus seems a timely moment to take a fresh look at how housing and health are interwoven across contemporary life courses.

Housing, public health and the life course

Recognition that housing is a health issue in need of significant government attention can be traced back to the British state's first systematic public health interventions in the mid-1800s (Lund, 2017). In the early Victorian era, many social reformers and paternalistic industrialists sought to publicise and tackle the squalor and disease they saw in the unplanned areas of dense, poorly built housing that had sprung up in Britain's growing industrial cities. Often their concern for the health of the working-classes was not simply altruistic as many believed that poor living conditions undermined the nation's spiritual well-being[1] and the population's fitness for hard work and imperial service. In response, a succession of parliamentary Acts were passed from the 1840s to gradually improve working-class housing conditions through municipal sanitation, regulation of dwelling standards and, later, through clearance programmes and public housing provision. Growing acceptance that housing is a health issue thus catalysed the development of housing policy and helped shape Britain's emerging welfare state and system of local governance (Lund, 2017).

Today, the relevance of housing to health is seen in a more nuanced light. Shaw (2004) argues this is partly because the links between these domains change as societies develop and progress through the *epidemiological transition*.

Hallmarks of progression through the epidemiological transition include major declines in infant mortality and increased life expectancy as improved medical care, mass vaccination, better working and living conditions, enhanced nutrition and other public health measures mean that degenerative diseases (such as cardiovascular conditions, dementia or cancers) come to replace infections as the leading causes of death.

Shaw (2004) contends that as societies pass through the epidemiological transition, the health effects of the 'hard' physical dimensions of housing (such as thermal comfort or crowding) are joined by 'softer' issues related to how effectively dwellings function as secure homes. In essence, as affluence rises and most people's basic housing needs are fulfilled, what comes to matter for public health is more how well dwellings satisfy higher order needs (for instance for safety, identity and belonging). This implies that the social meaning of housing and not just its physical characteristics are important determinants of health in today's ageing Global North societies. Research thus needs to consider how more perceptual and social dimensions of housing such as the affordability, security and desirability of homes support or undermine health (Bentley et al, 2016).

However, Baker and colleagues (2013) caution that unpicking how these different facets of housing influence health is surprisingly difficult. Key challenges include issues relating to:

- *Causality*: Due to data limitations, comparatively few studies of housing and health can move beyond documenting associations to robustly identify causal relationships.
- *Confounding*: People do not randomly allocate themselves to housing as differences in preferences, resources and so on channel particular sorts of people into particular types of dwelling in particular places. Often these sorting mechanisms are very difficult to measure and so cross-sectional correlations between housing and health – even those estimated from statistical models which control for observed confounders – may be biased by unmeasured differences between people.
- *Bidirectionality*: Although most studies explore how housing affects health, there is also good evidence that health has impacts on the types of housing people need and prefer, as well as the sorts of homes they can afford. The causal processes producing any observed correlation between housing and health may thus run in both directions.
- *Context-dependence*: Housing's relevance to health varies across space and time with the social and institutional setting (Bentley et al, 2016).
- *Bundling*: Housing is a complex bundle of attributes and each of these could affect health in different ways that may counterbalance or interact with each other (Tinson and Clair, 2020).

The life course perspective with its emphasis on the contextually embedded development of human lives provides a useful framework for addressing these complexities. The rest of this chapter thus applies Chapter 2's life course toolbox to synthesise what we know about how housing interacts with three crucial and interwoven domains of health careers: (1) physical health and disability, (2) mental health and psychological well-being, and (3) health-related caring practices.[2]

Although much of the public discussion of health and housing concentrates on how these careers interact in later life, this chapter argues that biological age is not by itself a very useful predictor of housing-related health events or care needs (Grenier, 2015). This is partly because there is mounting evidence that housing and health careers interact over the entire life course. In addition, processes of societal ageing are going hand in hand with increasingly diverse later-life trajectories and this diversification means we can also no longer assume that health considerations dominate or even play a major role in residential decision-making at older ages. While many older people do struggle with health problems and caring demands that may interact with their housing career, most of us will also know people in their eighties and nineties who are enjoying healthy, busy and fulfilling lives that belie traditional stereotypes of older age as a time of dependence and frailty. Such diversity of later-life careers is partly due to differences in accumulated experiences and so housing and health career processes can only be fully understood when set within a longer-term life span context (Grenier, 2015).

Physical health and disabilities

Public health research often divides the factors influencing health into downstream and upstream determinants (Gibson et al, 2011). Downstream determinants such as biology are often fairly easy to identify while upstream determinants comprise the less visible social structures which shape exposure to risk, behaviours and both physical and mental resilience. Housing is one such upstream determinant and enhanced housing precarity over recent decades might help explain why Global North health inequalities are deepening (McKee et al, 2017c). Indeed, at the population level, there are clear statistical associations between a range of housing variables and health outcomes (see Figure 6.1 for examples) and so housing measures are often incorporated into multidimensional indices of area advantage like the UK Indices of Multiple Deprivation.

Evidence that housing and health outcomes are correlated does not prove that housing causes health to vary. As Baker and colleagues (2013) point out, such bivariate associations are often produced by the non-random selection

Figure 6.1: Local house prices are positively correlated with life expectancy at birth across England and Wales

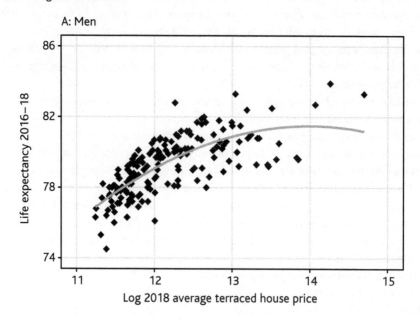

A: Men

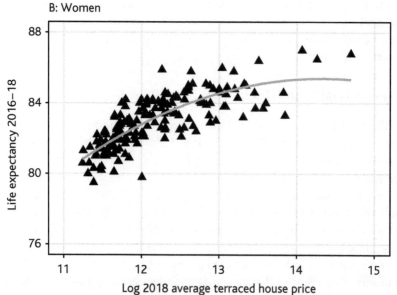

B: Women

Source: Based on data from HM Land Registry (2021) and ONS (2019a). Contains HM Land Registry data © Crown copyright and database right 2020. Contains public sector information licensed under the Open Government Licence v3.0.

of people with particular health profiles into particular types of housing. For example, those living in places with higher housing prices are likely to also have higher qualifications and incomes than those living in lower cost areas, and it may be that these confounding characteristics are what actually boosts longevity.

However, existing research indicates that four material and meaningful aspects of dwelling conditions have some form of causal impact on physical health. The first is accommodation type. In many countries, housing tenure is associated with health as homeowners have better physical outcomes and greater longevity than public tenants (Baker et al, 2013). At first glance this appears to be a compositional selection effect produced by people in poor health having difficulties in the labour market and thus lacking the resources to enter or sustain owner-occupation. Moreover, in countries with dualist rental systems like the UK, social housing providers usually also actively prioritise accommodating people with health-related problems.

However, Baker et al (2013) note that homeowners' feelings of prestige, security and pride may combine with the greater average comfort of owned dwellings to boost the health of owner-occupiers over that of tenants. Work by Clair and Hughes (2019) supports this thesis as they found that blood concentrations of C-reactive protein (CRP) – a biomarker of inflammation associated with infection and stress – were *ceteris paribus* higher for UK private tenants than for homeowners. CRP levels were also found to be lower for people living in detached homes. Although the magnitude of these effects was modest and the study is observational, Clair and Hughes' (2019) research does suggest that housing tenure and dwelling type may directly influence physical health.

Second, most people spend a good deal of time at home and so housing conditions influence their exposure to health hazards. These include the likelihood of accidents as well as exposure to harmful substances such as radon, carbon monoxide, lead from pipes or paintwork and asbestos released from damaged ceilings, walls and so on. The 2017 Grenfell Tower disaster has led to particular public concern about domestic fire safety, especially in cladded high-rise accommodation. However, overall, trends such as improved electrical standards, reductions in arson and the more widespread use of smoke alarms mean that domestic fire safety has actually improved markedly this century. Between 1997–98 and 2019–20 the annual number of house fires in England roughly halved while the number of fire-related fatalities fell by more than 50 per cent despite significant population growth (Home Office, 2022).

Dwelling quality and thermal comfort are the third and perhaps the best documented housing-related determinants of physical health. Evidence strongly suggests that cold, damp and mouldy housing conditions cause or aggravate a range of health problems including high blood pressure and raised cholesterol, respiratory conditions, asthma, inflammations, headaches and neurological problems (Shaw, 2004; Clapham, 2005). Poor quality homes and inadequate heating are normally a by-product of poverty and meta-analysis demonstrates that housing interventions to boost thermal comfort significantly improve the health of low-income households (Gibson et al, 2011). Fortunately, the quality of English dwellings has improved considerably over time. Since 2006, the share of homes officially classed as non-decent has roughly halved, while the proportion with damp problems fell from 12.8 per cent in 1996 to 3.4 per cent in 2019 (MHCLG, 2020a). However, the massive escalation of fuel prices and the general cost of living squeeze that began in 2022 now threaten to undermine these gains as it becomes far more expensive for lower-income households to heat their homes through the winter months.

Finally, housing affordability and security have been shown to impact on physical health. Difficulties keeping up with housing-related payments and a perceived lack of residential security create stress and anxiety that predominantly affect lower-income private tenants with short lettings contracts (Tinson and Clair, 2020). While the psychological impacts of housing precarity will be explored later, for now it is important to note that stress and anxiety have physical implications by weakening the immune system and making it difficult for people to keep up with healthy behaviours like eating well, exercising, getting enough sleep and enjoying fulfilling social interactions. The health effects of affordability may also be channelled through overcrowding if people opt to live in larger households in order to meet housing costs.

The evidence reviewed thus far indicates that various dimensions of housing can shape physical health. However, Clapham (2005) cautions that the evidence that objective housing conditions influence health is often weaker than we might expect. He argues that this is because health is not just determined by objective dwelling characteristics, but also by how people actually perceive and use their homes. In Clapham's (2005, p 123) view:

> So-called objective standards of housing quality are social constructs that reflect the views of professionals and politicians who derive and implement them, but are not necessarily superior to the views of residents themselves. These universal standards are unable to reflect the meaning that houses have for households which are at the core of satisfaction. This is likely to vary between different households.

Clapham (2005, p 120) is not arguing for a totally relativist position as he notes that 'it is difficult to disagree with the concept of minimum standards of house conditions and amenities'. Instead, his point is more that once a baseline of standards are met, what matters for health is more how well dwellings satisfy the diverse subjective needs and preferences of individuals as these evolve over the life span. This argument implies that a longitudinal life course perspective provides a good framework for exploring how housing relates to physical health in varied and dynamic ways. We now turn to examine these issues using three collections of the life course conceptual tools sketched in Chapter 2: biographical timing and trajectories, cohort processes and geographical context-dependence.

Biographical timing and trajectories

The cross-sectional design of most research means that relatively little is known about the long-term impacts that perceived or actual housing conditions have on physical health. This is problematic as the impacts of housing conditions probably depends on the biographical timing of exposure as levels of vulnerability and resilience tend to vary over the life course. One area of particular concern is that poor housing conditions may be especially damaging if these are experienced in the womb or during the first years of life. According to a 2019 report by the House of Commons Health and Social Care Select Committee:

> The first 1000 days, from a child's conception to age 2, is a critical period. During this time of heightened vulnerability, the foundations of a child's health and development (physical, cognitive, social and emotional, and behavioural development) are laid and a trajectory is established.

Housing conditions during this crucial early phase may thus directly affect lifetime health trajectories and, indeed, research shows that early exposure to cold and damp living conditions is associated with subsequent respiratory problems (Shaw, 2004). The long-term effects of childhood housing conditions may also operate more indirectly if perceptions that housing is poor quality or insecure create stress, damage parents' relationships with each other and undermine their capacity to nurture their children. As one respondent to the 2019 Select Committee inquiry explained:

> We had to move into rented accommodation when my first daughter was small. I had had no idea how unsecure [sic] rented accommodation was, especially for those who are not well off. We've negotiated and worked ourselves into a better position now, but many can't, or haven't, yet. Unsecure housing [sic] is such a stress for parents and children suffer as a result.

In addition, longer durations of exposure to housing problems are more damaging for health than shorter periods spent in inadequate dwellings.

Shaw (2004) argues that the fact that poor housing appears to have a dose-dependent association with poor health indicates that this is a causal relationship. The impacts of duration are further likely to be dynamic with adverse housing events (such as becoming homeless) functioning as turning points that have long-lasting consequences for physical and psychological well-being.

The cohort effects of global heating

The UK's cool maritime climate means that cold and damp dwellings have traditionally been the primary target for housing-related health interventions. However, global heating means that these will not be the only or perhaps the main housing-related health risk facing cohorts living through the rest of the 21st century. Current modelling indicates that even if global greenhouse gas emissions are cut quickly and dramatically, existing atmospheric concentrations will still lock in enough extra heat to ensure the UK experiences far more regular and severe summer heatwaves (like that experienced across Europe in 2022), more extreme drought and rainfall events, and serious problems of coastal erosion and flooding from storms, watercourses and the sea. The 2021 UK Climate Change Committee's third Risk Assesssment (CCRA3) thus identified 'risks to human health, wellbeing and productivity from increased exposure to heat in homes and other buildings' as a top priority for urgent government action to adapt to our changing climate.

CCRA3 also lays bare how little is being systematically done to prepare the UK's housing stock for the more extreme and less predictable climate that is emerging. This constitutes a serious dereliction of duty by recent generations of housing policymakers and is also a false economy as immediate actions – for example investment to heat- and flood-proof existing stock (targeted to low-income households) and enforcement of far higher standards for newbuilds – would be much cheaper than retrofitting. In the absence of government action, CCRA3 predicts that heat-related deaths per annum will more than triple above 2020 baselines by 2050. Although this increase will to some extent be counterbalanced by reduced cold weather mortality, this type of zero-sum accounting is not a moral justification for inaction, as reducing overall mortality is usually the espoused policy objective. Moreover, the risk of exposure to excessive heat and flooding will be greatest for the least advantaged households living in the worst housing conditions. For example, evidence from the 1995 Chicago and 2003 Paris heatwaves suggested that heat-related deaths were concentrated among the poor, the socially isolated and those living in poorly built flats and older dwellings (Braubach and Fairburn, 2010).

Geographical determinants

Thus far this chapter has focused on the health implications of dwelling attributes. Yet there is strong evidence that where homes are located – sometimes termed the residential context – has powerful implications for health (Braubach and Fairburn, 2010). Residential contexts influence health through several mechanisms, the first of which is exposure to social and physical hazards. In terms of social hazards, the perceived risk of falling victim to crime may directly influence levels of stress and anxiety as well as one's willingness to undertake health-promoting activities like regular exercise, socialising or participating in community activities.

The two logistic regression models shown in Table 6.1 demonstrate that fear of crime varies systematically across residential contexts in Great Britain. Living in a neighbourhood classed as within the most deprived 20 per cent (as opposed to living in a neighbourhood with an average level of deprivation) increases the probability of worrying about being a victim of crime by an average of 7.8 percentage points and the probability of feeling unsafe after dark by an average of 11.4 percentage points. Living in the least deprived 20 per cent of neighbourhoods meanwhile reduces the probability of feeling unsafe by 5.2 percentage points. Table 6.1 also shows that housing circumstances predict perceived social risks as living in the parental home reduces worries about crime while renters (especially social tenants) are more likely to feel unsafe than homeowners. This echoes evidence from US housing voucher experiments which showed that improved perceptions of neighbourhood

Table 6.1: Average marginal effects of housing tenure and neighbourhood deprivation on worrying about crime and feeling unsafe after dark

Variable	1. Worry about crime	2. Feel unsafe after dark
Housing tenure (ref = homeowner)		
Parental home	−0.044** (−0.076, −0.013)	0.006 (−0.019, 0.032)
Private tenant	−0.009 (−0.034, 0.015)	0.027** (0.008, 0.048)
Social tenant	−0.020 (−0.042, 0.001)	0.066*** (0.050, 0.086)
Deprivation quintile (ref = middle 60%)		
Least deprived 20%	−0.014 (−0.030, 0.003)	−0.052*** (−0.066, −0.041)
Most deprived 20%	0.078*** (0.058, 0.100)	0.114*** (0.099, 0.135)
Unweighted N	33,185	33,185

Notes: * $p<0.05$, ** $p<0.01$, *** $p<0.001$ with 95% confidence intervals in parentheses. Models control for age, sex, ethnicity, partnership status, children and income.

Source: Own analysis of weighted UKHLS data enriched with Indices of Multiple Deprivation.

safety were one reason why residents of poor neighbourhoods experienced better health after relocating to more prosperous areas (Gibson et al, 2011).

Physical hazards are also an important place-based health determinant. Braubach and Fairburn (2010) describe how a lack of resources channels poor households into cheaper neighbourhoods with higher levels of pollutants and proximity to hazardous sites such as waste incinerators or industrial plants. The UK legal system is gradually coming to accept this view that health is shaped by where you live as a coroner ruled in late 2020 that the death of 9-year-old Ella Adoo-Kissi-Debrah was attributable to exposure to air pollution around her Lewisham home.

Differential access to shops, services and public resources is a second way in which places shape health. A long history of research into 'food deserts' has shown that access to healthy food is often lower in less advantaged neighbourhoods. These locations also tend to be more heavily served by the fast-food outlets, betting shops and alcohol stores that can undermine healthy behaviours. In addition, the quality of health-promoting public services are often lower in poorer neighbourhoods than in more affluent places. Finally, access to safe and high quality outdoor public environments such as parks, playing fields, woodlands and other natural spaces varies greatly across space and according to whether people have access to a car.

The two mechanisms discussed thus far concern how the built environment to some degree influences health. However, norms and patterns of behaviour provide a third more social mechanism through which places can promote or undermine health (Shaw, 2004). A huge range of local behavioural norms and patterns may be relevant here, including those related to:

- diet and exercise;
- consumption of alcohol and other drugs, including tobacco;
- engagement with health services;
- social interactions and support; and
- participation in health promoting activities such as community events and sports.

As yet, difficulties disentangling the effects of behaviours from the characteristics of the people who engage in them means that relatively little is known about the ways in which behaviour mediates or directly influences spatial patterns of health.

Disabilities

The life course insights reviewed in the previous section provide a useful lens for assessing how disabilities impact on housing careers. As Beer and Faulkner (2011) note, disabilities are not innate biophysical states, but rather are produced by society's failure to accommodate particular impairments. In this vein, the Equality Act 2010's definition of disability as a 'physical or mental impairment that has a "substantial" and "long-term" negative effect on your ability to do normal daily activities' provides a useful (albeit crude) instrument for evaluating housing inequalities between those with and without such impairments.

Data from the Annual Population Survey (APS) (ONS, 2019b) indicate that UK homeownership levels among working-age adults are much lower among those with a disability (42 per cent in 2018–19) than for those with no such impairment (53 per cent). Adults with a disability are conversely much more likely to live in social housing (25 per cent) than those without an impairment (8 per cent). However, as Beer and Faulkner (2011) note, these types of cross-sectional comparison hide considerable variation in the longitudinal experiences of people with disabilities. These authors argue that a nuanced life course perspective on disability needs to recognise how the type, severity and timing of disabilities all influence how impairments impact on housing careers.

Viewing disabilities as dynamic and varied allows us to understand how these can influence housing careers in multiple ways:

- Disabilities that limit one's ability to sustain paid employment often reduce resources and make it more difficult to live apart from family members who can provide unpaid care. People with significant impairments are thus disproportionately reliant on supported and social housing, while the onset of serious health problems can trigger exits from owner-occupation (Wood et al, 2017).
- Survey data show that residential preferences vary with disability status as many Australians with disabilities value living near to services more highly than other population groups (Beer and Faulkner, 2011).
- Lower incomes together with a dearth of disability-friendly housing vacancies mean that disability can reduce people's propensity to move home (Beer and Faulkner, 2011).
- Greater dependence on benefits means that the housing careers of those with disabilities are often particularly strongly shaped by social security policy.
- Disabilities can have ripple effects on the housing careers of family members who are providing unpaid care. Some studies indicate that carers often live in suboptimal housing as they prioritise the needs of the person they are supporting over their own interests (Beer and Faulkner, 2011).

The APS data allow us to evaluate how the housing disparities associated with disabilities also vary with life course position. The panels of Figure 6.2 compare the housing tenure status of UK adults aged 25–64 by age and

Figure 6.2: Housing tenure by age varies with disability status, 2018–19

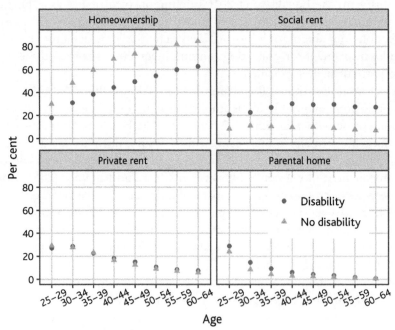

Source: Based on APS data from ONS (2019b).

whether or not they have a disability. A key pattern is that as age increases, those with disabilities become less likely to own their home than those without impairments. This gap widens from a 12 percentage point disparity among 25–29-year-olds to more than 20 percentage points after age 45. The reverse is true for social housing as over a quarter of adults with disabilities aged 35–64 are social tenants as compared with under 10 per cent of those without a disability.

The large APS sample also makes it feasible to disaggregate housing circumstances by impairment type. The data show that those with problems related to personal mobility, sight and hearing have the highest homeownership rates (ONS, 2019b). By contrast, over two thirds of adults with learning difficulties or autism disorders live in parental homes. This evidence matches Beer and Faulkner's (2011) results from Australia and shows just how important it is to distinguish between different types of impairment.

Psychological health and well-being

Psychological well-being is increasingly viewed as a fundamental component of health careers. As a result, in Britain the ONS now monitors a range of well-being measures – including estimates of the population's short-term affective feelings (such as anxiety) and longer-term evaluative sentiments (like overall life satisfaction) – alongside conventional population and economic indicators. The case for public interventions to improve mental health is usually made through the language of economic efficiency, with, for example, the Organisation for Economic Co-operation and Development (OECD) (2018) estimating that mental health problems shaved 4.1 per cent off 2015 UK GDP through direct treatment costs and reduced productivity. While valuable, this approach overlooks the fact that psychological well-being is also an equity issue. Although around 17 per cent of the population is experiencing some form of psychological illness at any one point in time, women and lower-income groups are much more likely to report these problems than men and those with higher incomes (OECD, 2018).

The meaningful dimensions of housing are increasingly recognised to be upstream determinants of psychological as well as physical health. The basic idea is that housing matters for psychological well-being as it forms an important prerequisite for human flourishing. Flourishing can be defined broadly as being able to live a life that is happy, healthy, meaningful and fulfilling. In this view economic security, access to opportunities, the ability to enjoy meaningful social relations and to construct a desired identity in a secure, controllable and private home space are all housing-related determinants of well-being and so ultimately one's capacity for flourishing (Hoolachan et al, 2017).

While there is a growing interest in analysing how housing matters for psychological health, this literature is scattered and largely empirical with little integration or synthesis. This creates two problems. First, studies often draw comparisons across research examining a huge variety of outcome measures, each of which might have different relations to housing. These outcomes range from single survey questions on life satisfaction through to multi-item self-assessment questionnaires and administrative data on diagnoses or hospital admissions. Second, the laudable concern for social justice evident in many studies means that more emphasis is typically placed on the ways housing undermines rather than supports or enhances psychological health and well-being. However, juxtaposing work on inadequate or precarious housing with studies of volitional residential events is essential for creating a more holistic understanding of the varied ways in which housing career processes shape psychological well-being. We now turn to examine how three sets of life course principles and conceptual tools – agency and construction, notions of turning points and ordering, and finally changing times and places – can together help us build a better understanding of how housing matters for psychological health and well-being.

Agency and construction

The degree of agency people have in housing decisions has two impacts on well-being. First, Clapham (2005) argues that simply feeling one has agency in major decisions boosts one's sense of personal efficacy and well-being. The basic idea here is that feeling in control of important life decisions and believing that these are not threatened are vital prerequisites of good psychological health. Crucially, it seems that it is perceptions rather than the actual level of agency and threat that are the most relevant for well-being. For instance, Hoolachan et al (2017) show that short contracts and limited protections mean that many UK private tenants feel insecure despite only 7 per cent of private rented moves actually being initiated by landlords (Lupton, 2016). Overall, it seems that perceptions of housing threat and a perceived lack of agency create a sense of precariousness among private tenants which, regardless of how closely it matches reality, undermines ontological security and through this mental well-being.

Second, the degree to which people can actively construct their housing career indirectly shapes well-being by influencing whether they can adjust their housing consumption to satisfy their changing demands. While having the resources and opportunities to exercise agency and make 'advantaging moves' is likely to improve well-being, the opposite is more likely to be true for those restricted or constrained to either make 'disadvantaging moves' or stay in places they want to leave (Lupton, 2016). Recent longitudinal studies provide evidence for this by demonstrating that satisfaction with housing, and to a lesser extent other areas of life, improves with residential moves (Nowok et al, 2018). Crucially, the degree of agency involved in residential mobility configures the extent to which moves boost satisfaction as improvements in housing satisfaction are larger and last longer when moves are desired (Nowok et al, 2018). In contrast, being unable to act on a desire to move or making an unwanted move is likely to damage well-being by preventing people from living in housing they desire (Coulter and van Ham, 2013). There is likely to be a normative dimension to these processes as an inability to enter homeownership in line with the age-graded social scripts laid down by previous generations appears to be harming the well-being of younger cohorts of less affluent Britons (Hoolachan et al, 2017).

Turning points and ordering

Literature on the determinants of psychological well-being highlights how affective sentiments of happiness and anxiety, evaluative assessments of life satisfaction and levels of mental health all vary dynamically over the life course as people experience life events and transitions. Crucially, meta-analysis by Luhmann and colleagues (2012) shows that the psychological effects of life events vary depending on the type of event and the outcome measure being considered. The authors note that longitudinal data are essential for analysing these dynamics as well-being often changes systematically in the years leading up to and then following an event. For example, notions of a 'hedonic treadmill' posit that the positive or negative psychological effects of life events are both transient as people usually adapt psychologically to their new circumstances and revert back to their baseline level of well-being.

Taking a longitudinal view of the relationships between housing events and psychological well-being is useful for assessing whether housing events have long-lasting (as in notions of turning points) or short-term (more in line with hedonic adaptation) implications for well-being. This has been the subject of a growing literature on the mental health implications of housing affordability problems. UK studies show that psychological health deteriorates when housing becomes unaffordable, even after controlling for general levels of hardship (Taylor et al, 2007). The impact of housing affordability also appears to be gendered as payment problems and arrears trigger a major rise in male psychological distress while longer-term affordability problems are more damaging for women (Taylor et al, 2007). Importantly, this type of individual-level analysis is likely to underestimate the cumulative psychological impacts of housing events as the reduced well-being of one individual may have ripple effects on the well-being of those they are 'linked' to through family ties. Moreover, behavioural changes made as a result of affordability problems – ranging from increasing household size to boost income through to experiencing money conflicts in intimate relationships – are likely to exacerbate poor mental health.

Longitudinal analysis provides the only robust way to disentangle whether psychological health changes occur before and/or after housing events. This is crucial if we are to understand the direction of causality. Understanding the causal links between ordered events is perhaps especially important for research into homelessness. Here, an understandable dependence on cross-sectional data means that it is often difficult to tell whether psychological illness caused the loss of a home, was a consequence of this traumatic housing event, or some combination of the two (Shaw, 2004). All are plausible scenarios but formulating policies to prevent homelessness and support those who experience it requires some appreciation of causality.

One example of longitudinal data that enable a deeper understanding of the temporal ordering of housing- and health-related events are the London Combined Homelessness and Information Network records of outreach workers' contacts with rough sleepers in the capital. The longitudinal nature of these data enables different rough sleeping pathways to be distinguished. For example, longitudinal research showed that in 2009–10 around 61 per cent of rough sleepers in London were sleeping rough for the first time, 27 per cent were long-term rough sleepers and 13 per cent were returning to rough sleeping after not having been seen on the streets for a year (Broadway Homelessness and Support, 2010). This type of longitudinal information is vital for designing and evaluating support interventions.

Changing times and places

The life course principle of time and place reminds us that the links between housing and health depend on contextual circumstances. Two issues are relevant here. First, the housing attributes that people consider to be acceptable and desirable are not static but rather shift over time with changes *inter alia* in demography, affluence, culture and technology (Clapham, 2005). For instance, since the 19th century an indoor toilet has gone from being a luxury to a standard facility to a feature that many households have in abundance. What matters for residential preferences and assessments of how well these are being satisfied is thus how one's housing consumption is perceived to measure up to the standards of the day.

Second, the changing policy context matters for the relationship of housing to psychological health. Here we need to consider not just the domain of housing but also the often contradictory and ill-coordinated actions of other government departments and institutions whose remit has a strong bearing on housing. In Britain these include the Treasury, the Department for Work and Pensions and the Bank of England. The way housing straddles multiple policy domains at multiple layers of governance means that its relevance to health can only be understood by considering the broader multi-scalar political-economic contexts within which people are living.

Empirical studies provide good evidence that policy variation influences how housing shapes psychological well-being. Reeves and colleagues (2016) show how coalition government cuts to housing-related benefits triggered increased psychological distress among low-income tenants equivalent to propelling 26,000 people into depression. Similarly, Bentley et al (2016) show how affordability problems and little public welfare support mean that tenants in Australia are more vulnerable to poor mental health triggered by housing affordability problems than their more insulated UK counterparts. Taken together, these studies illustrate how post-2008 austerity in governments' housing-related expenditure has delivered a mental health double whammy to poor households. Austerity has not only increased poor households' exposure to affordability problems but has also increased their psychological vulnerability as only a more threadbare and stigmatised social safety-net is left to fall back on in hard times. Housing thus needs to be viewed as an integral part of the social infrastructure supporting or undermining psychological health, well-being and ultimately human flourishing.

Health-related care

All too often research and policy reduce health to the presence or absence of measurable events and conditions or the occurrence of some kind of spell or state (for instance reporting a long-term limiting illness). This approach has the virtue of simplicity, but it does tend to oversimplify health down to a discrete categorical outcome – for example you do/do not have cancer or feel in poor/fair/good health. To create a richer view, it is useful to take the life course perspective and reconceptualise health as a continuously evolving career which can change slowly and gradually or suddenly and dramatically over the entire life span. In essence, this involves thinking of health as both an unfolding process as well as a career that can be punctuated by events. One consequence of considering health in this way is that this draws our attention towards the often long-term and deeply relational caring practices that sustain the health and well-being of many people in the ageing societies of the Global North.

Housing is fundamentally important for health-related care as a large proportion of care work takes place in domestic spaces. Tasks such as helping with dressing, washing, cooking, cleaning, gardening, laundry and household management all involve the home and so are shaped by the care recipient's household type, dwelling characteristics and location. Moreover, the practice of caring, in turn, changes the meaning of home and how housing is perceived (both in an abstract generalised sense as well as in terms of the characteristics of the current dwelling), both for the person receiving care as well as for the carers and institutions involved in its provision. For example, Reid (2021) shows how the adoption of smart technologies to support caring has altered how Scottish recipients and providers perceive and respond to a variety of risks ranging from falls through to reputational damage.

Traditional approaches to studying housing and health run into two problems when applied to understand housing and health-related caring. These problems relate to:

1. *Individual-level focus*: While much research looks at how housing is related to health within the lives of individuals, care by definition involves relationships and interactions: either between individuals (who may or may not live together) or between people and institutional actors. This means that analyses of housing and care dynamics need to place linked lives centre-stage by exploring how individuals are connected to and interact with others within their household and others living in other places. Crucially, these relational webs of connection and interaction are not static, but are themselves changed by the demand for, supply and receipt of care. For example, long hours spent caring for someone else in one's household or having to travel a long way to care could change the

relationship one has with the care recipient and also have consequences for one's own well-being.

2. *Meanings of home*: caring radically disrupts the conventional assumption that home is a private space where people live an autonomous life free from surveillance and interference. Both face-to-face and technologically mediated forms of care involve other people either coming into or being able to monitor and, if necessary, intervene in one's home life (Reid, 2021). Understanding how this affects residential satisfaction, preferences and demands thus requires analysing specific caring practices and not just where care providers and recipients live or how much support they exchange.

Two blocks of conceptual tools derived from life course frameworks – timed events (blending notions of biography, sequencing, cohort and period with the life course principle of timing in a more general sense) and family solidarities – can help us to better understand these issues. Purely for brevity, the rest of this chapter focuses mostly on caring practices provided in later life rather than those provided to people earlier in the life course, for instance to those with physical or cognitive impairments.[3]

Timed events

Litwak and Longino (1987) were among the first to create a simple framework for understanding how health and care influence residential behaviour in later life. They argued that later-life moves can be divided into three chronologically ordered types, not all of which any given individual will necessarily experience: (1) amenity-driven retirement moves, (2) moves related to the anticipated or actual onset of minor disabilities, and (3) moves in old-age driven by the serious and chronic disabilities which often carry people into institutions. In general, Litwak and Longino (1987) posited that the importance of health in shaping residential needs increases with age and across the three types of move as proximity to family members able to provide care becomes a stronger determinant of locational choice. Crucially, the authors argue that these patterns are, however, stratified by resources and nativity as migrants are particularly likely to move in with relatives to form multigenerational households when they need later-life care. The backdrop to this is that the proportion of older people living in multigenerational households in Europe and North America has declined since the early 20th century as more people live alone or just with a partner through later life (Grundy, 2011).[4]

Litwak and Longino's (1987) study has informed a growing body of work on the way that anticipated and actual health events trigger residential adjustment moves and dwelling modifications in later life. Understanding the timing and sequencing of health events in relation to housing transitions is a central aim of this literature as residential adjustments are generally more effective at protecting well-being if undertaken in anticipation rather than in response to health problems. In their analysis of UK panel data, Evandrou et al (2010) found that poor health is to some extent a mobility trigger for later-life moves in Britain. However, the authors tempered this conclusion with three cautionary notes: (1) moves in later life are much rarer than we might expect; (2) age is a poor proxy for the health-related moves which occur across later life; and (3) later-life moves are more strongly associated with the same sorts of life event and socio-demographic factors (such as partnership changes and housing tenure) as moves in the general population. This evidence casts doubt on the utility of age-specific models by showing that health must always be considered as a potential driver of housing career processes at any stage in the life span. Greater diversity in later-life health trajectories is also delinking health-related housing needs from age as individuals experience biological ageing in increasingly varied ways (Grenier, 2015).

In Britain, the timing of health-related residential adjustments in later life has been heavily influenced by the housing market and the policy environment in at least two ways. The first is that mobility rates among older adults are low partly because there are few opportunities or financial incentives to move and in particular to downsize. In many parts of the country, a lack of suitable dwellings (in particular bungalows or dwellings adapted to universal design principles) impedes people from downsizing. Furthermore, Stamp Duty transaction tax makes it expensive to move, while a regressive council tax system means that it is relatively cheap to over-consume housing space.

Second, policies governing social care and in particular the provision and accessibility of residential care settings impact on the relationship between health and residential behaviours in later life. Grundy's (2011) analysis showed that older adults' rate of entry into institutional care settings accelerated through the 1980s as multigenerational living declined, before subsequently slowing and became more selective of individuals in poorer health through the 1990s. She attributes this trend to policy shifts, which, in the early 1990s, pared back state spending on residential care and introduced means-testing to restrict these settings to only the most vulnerable. A similar tendency for people to only enter institutional care settings very late in life when experiencing severe health issues and when life expectancy is low has been reported in other datasets (Robards et al, 2014). This is perhaps hardly surprising given that social care policy in many countries encourages ageing in place.

In addition to shaping the timing of health-related relocations, social care policies also impact on the selectivity of housing adjustments in later life.

In Britain, housing tenure has been found to significantly influence not only health but also the likelihood of moving into a residential care setting. McCann and colleagues' (2012) analysis showed that owner-occupiers in Northern Ireland were less likely than tenants to move into care settings after 2001. After testing several potential explanations, the authors determined that the means-tested requirement for those with sizeable assets to contribute towards the costs of care means that families try hard to avoid the sale of older adults' homes by, for instance, increasing their informal support or by paying for a private carer to keep their older relative at home. Such a desire is only likely to increase as safeguarding dynastic housing assets becomes an increasingly critical issue for family members.

Family solidarities

The previous discussion highlights how solidarity between family members infuses the connections between care and housing dynamics. Most care in Britain is provided informally within the family with 12.7 per cent of 35–74-year-olds providing up to 20 hours and 5.4 per cent more than 20 hours of care per week at the time of the 2001 census (Ramsay et al, 2013). Although much caring takes place within households (for example between partners) and care outside the household is increasingly mediated by technology, the physicality of much care work and the fact that virtual oversight must always be able to trigger a physical intervention means that geographical proximity to non-resident kin is an important resource that may motivate the locational choices of family members. In essence, the anticipated or actual provision and receipt of care may alter locational needs and preferences or restrict the spatial choice set available to people at various stages of the life course.

Unpicking how the geography of non-resident kin influences the moving behaviour of older people and their adult children has become an important strand of work within a broader literature exploring how family ties matter for migration (Mulder, 2018). The paucity of UK data sources means that much of this work has been conducted in countries like the Netherlands and Sweden that maintain administrative population registers. In Sweden, Artamonova et al (2021) show that living with or near to children reduces the likelihood that parents move into institutional care. The fact this effect is more pronounced for those in worse health indicates that informal care support among family members living with or near to each other explains these patterns. More generally, work by Petterson and Malmberg (2009) indicates that moves made by people in families with an elderly member tend to increase intergenerational proximity, although it was not clear from this study if care or a desire for contact is the main motivation for these patterns.

This points to two problems with the literature on family geographies of care. First, a largely data-driven focus on proximity and moving behaviour (rather than caring practices) forces many studies into either drawing essentially speculative conclusions about the motives for residential behaviour or eschewing causal interpretation entirely. This is understandable but not particularly helpful for developing our knowledge of how housing and care dynamics are interconnected over the life course. Second, even those longitudinal studies that track the moving behaviour of family members typically only do so for a few years. This is not really long enough to adequately pick up anticipative behaviour as it seems likely that future health-related care needs are at least at the back of the minds of many parents and children for long periods of the life course. Overcoming this issue requires a more biographical approach to understanding how family solidarity impacts on residential needs, preferences and decisions over the life span.

Summary

This chapter has used the life course tools developed in Chapter 2 to take a fresh look at how housing and health are interrelated. Three main lines of argument have been advanced. The first is that the links between housing and health are far more complex, multifaceted and delinked from biological age than is often assumed. Part of the reason for this complexity is that the connections between housing and health are often bidirectional, confounded and difficult to disentangle. In addition, the ways housing and health interlink are strongly shaped by the demographic, economic, cultural, political and technological circumstances of a particular time and place. Indeed, one consistent theme of this chapter is that policies across a range of domains have had significant impacts on how housing and health interact over the life course. Sometimes this has been beneficial (for example when interventions have driven improvements in physical dwelling standards) but significant damage to health has also been inflicted by housing-related policy, most recently through austerity cuts (McKee et al, 2017c).

The chapter's second contention is that the connections between health and housing can only be grasped by adopting a more holistic view of health. This partly involves conceptualising health as encompassing both physical and psychological well-being, but it also more fundamentally means viewing health not just as an ordered sequence of events and states but also as a gradually evolving process. This means that caring needs to assume much greater prominence in housing analysis than has hitherto been usual. The chapter's third argument flows on from this: research into housing and health needs to move beyond the conventional focus on individuals and households to also consider their relations. This approach involves exploring the connections between people who may not live together, as well as the connections and interactions between people and the norms and institutions they encounter as they pass through life.

Changing places

The previous chapters have examined how events and processes in the housing career interact with those in other domains of life. In keeping with most life course scholarship, these chapters have focused primarily on the dynamics of lives and the ways these are shaped by a variety of contextual forces. While this micro-level approach is clearly essential for understanding residential behaviour, one limitation is that places are often conceptualised as external containers within which life course processes unfold. Yet geographical research has long shown that the ways people selectively stay in or leave places over the life course actively alters the population composition and social fabric of neighbourhoods and localities. There is thus a two-way relationship between the dynamics of life courses and places: when places change, lives change and when lives change, places change.

This chapter begins by sketching how life course perspectives can be applied to understand local processes of population change. It shows how patterns of residential behaviour – specifically the ways people make decisions to stay in, leave, enter or avoid particular residential locations – mediate how changes in life courses have aggregate impacts on the demographic and socio-economic composition of neighbourhoods and localities. The chapter's remaining sections then unpack how the sorts of life course dynamics explored in previous chapters reshape local populations by altering (1) residential preferences and aspirations, (2) resources and restrictions, (3) life events and transitions, and (4) opportunities and constraints. Examples of each mechanism are explored in turn although in reality all four will always matter for local processes of population change.

Understanding local population dynamics

Defining what neighbourhoods are is a vital but surprisingly difficult first step for any study of local population change. For Galster (2012, p 85), neighbourhoods are 'the bundle of spatially based attributes associated with clusters of residences, sometimes in conjunction with other land uses'. This definition highlights that neighbourhoods are compact residential spaces which often have distinctive physical attributes (types of buildings, infrastructure, environmental attributes and so forth) and social characteristics that derive from their residents (for instance their demographic and socio-economic mix). The fact that neighbourhood characteristics derive in part from the people living there implies that any changes within residents' lives or in who lives in a particular place will alter the area's aggregate characteristics.

The existence of commercial geodemographics highlights the applied value of understanding the socio-demographic characteristics of neighbourhoods. The basic idea of a geodemographic classification is to use a large number of input variables to statistically categorise small areas into a set of mutually exclusive groups, whose populations each have distinctive types of characteristics. When done well, knowing the geodemographic group a given neighbourhood belongs to provides a highly effective way to predict the views and behaviours of its residents.

Tracking how the geodemographic classifications of neighbourhoods changes over time can provide a broad overview of local population dynamics. Figure 7.1 provides an example by showing how the Temporal Output Area Classification of neighbourhoods in the east London borough of Barking and Dagenham changed between the 2001 and 2011 censuses

Figure 7.1: The spread of ethnic diversity in Barking and Dagenham, 2001–11

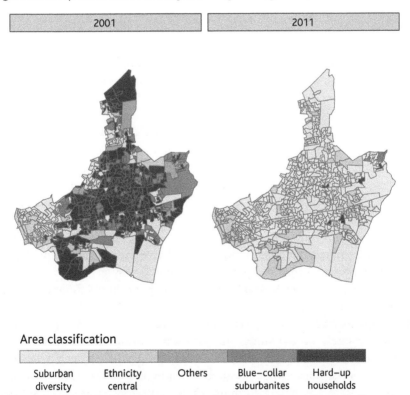

Source: Adapted from CDRC (2021). Boundary data from Office for National Statistics licensed under the Open Government Licence v3.0. Contains OS data © Crown copyright and database right [2022].

(Singleton et al, 2016). The map panels show how formerly ethnically White working-class neighbourhoods (classified in Figure 7.1 as blue-collar suburbanites and hard-up households) changed into areas of ethnic diversity over this period as minority populations grew and diffused out of inner London.

While studies of neighbourhood dynamics stretch back at least a century, interest has burgeoned in recent years as cities have become more unequal, ethnically diverse and often polycentric. This growing interest in neighbourhood change has been accompanied by intellectual fragmentation as separate subfields have emerged to look at particular processes. While 20th-century scholarship was dominated by work into the geography of class and race, research has since become more specialised as analyses of these concerns have spun-off into distinct subfields and been joined by largely separate literatures on other dynamics such as studentification. This specialisation has generated new insights but also a degree of intellectual balkanisation as few studies attempt synthesis or explore interlinkages between processes (Malmberg and Clark, 2021).

Life course insights

Engagement with life course perspectives provides one way in which to develop a stronger overarching framework to understand how residential decisions help drive a wide variety of aggregate changes in local populations. Viewing processes of residential selection and their consequences for neighbourhoods through a life course lens has several benefits:

1. *A stronger focus on process and mechanism*: much work on neighbourhood change examines the distribution of groups (Piekut, 2021). Yet concentrating on how populations are distributed does not answer the critical question of why people live in particular places. This focus on pattern over process makes it difficult to assess the need for policy interventions and decide what form these should take in countries which uphold citizens' freedom of movement. As we shall see, analysing the life course processes that lead people to selectively stay in or move between places provides deeper insight into the forces driving different forms of residential sorting.[1]

2. *Recognition that neighbourhood change is multidimensional*: neighbourhood change rarely occurs along only one axis and different dimensions of change may interact in ways that are missed when focusing on only one process. For example, Malmberg and Clark (2021) show that high immigration has reduced ethnic residential segregation across Sweden while the economic polarisation of neighbourhoods has grown. They argue that growth in the minority populations of gateway cities has

triggered more intense income sorting as poor migrants cluster in cheap neighbourhoods and this motivates out-moves among better-off members of the ethnic majority. The life course perspective's framing of lives as comprised of multiple intersecting careers overlain onto identities reminds us that people staying in, leaving and entering neighbourhoods are defined not simply by one attribute, but by their intersections.

3. *Attention to multiple dimensions of time*: time is, by definition, essential for neighbourhood change. However, examining aggregate patterns at particular snapshots makes it difficult to separate out different temporal processes. For example, biographical processes – such as desires to construct a particular lifestyle or to live in a place familiar from childhood – influence residential behaviour, while period effects like influxes of migrants also shape how local populations change. Moreover, neighbourhood change is a cohort process as the times people grow up in and live through shape their subsequent paths through the residential mosaic. Longitudinal data and methods are essential for empirically disentangling these sorts of varied temporal processes.

Conceptualising neighbourhood change

Figure 7.2 sketches a conceptual framework for understanding how life course dynamics help change the socio-demographic makeup of neighbourhoods and localities.[2] The right-hand side of Figure 7.2 develops Bailey's (2012) insight that two processes drive shifts in the socio-demographic composition of neighbourhoods: *in-situ changes in population composition and in residents' lives* (for example births, income changes, health events and deaths) and *changes created by people selectively moving in and out*. The left-hand side of Figure 7.2 indicates that life course dynamics play a key role in driving these twin motors of neighbourhood change. These patterns of life course dynamics are themselves produced by: (1) the changing composition of the population (its age structure, immigration and emigration rates, fertility and mortality, employment patterns and so forth) as well as (2) changing attitudes and behaviours (originating in the family, health, education, housing and employment careers covered in previous chapters). Both compositional and behavioural change can thus alter life courses which, over time, combine to reconfigure neighbourhood populations.

Crucially, the middle part of Figure 7.2 shows that the impact of life course dynamics on neighbourhoods is mediated by residential behaviours. How changes within lives affect neighbourhood populations depends heavily on whether people with specific attributes or those experiencing a given process decide to stay in their current dwelling – perhaps adapting it or changing their behaviour in situ– or instead opt to relocate. If they relocate, where they go and who, if anyone, replaces them becomes the crucial question.

Figure 7.2: Life course processes of neighbourhood change

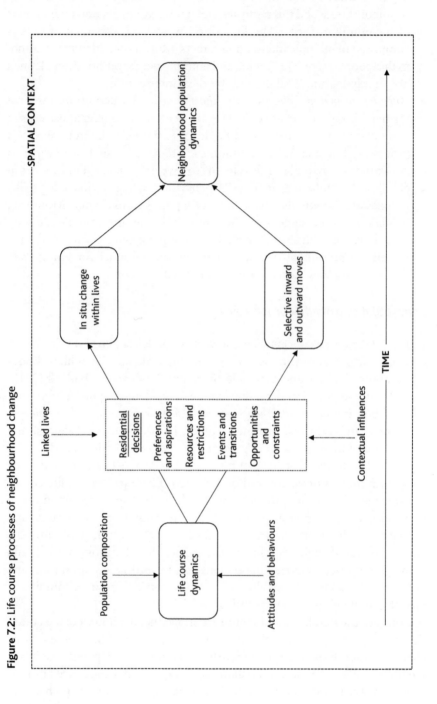

Understanding how life course dynamics change neighbourhoods thus requires a focus on residential decisions and the ways these are shaped by the four sets of factors listed in the central rectangle of Figure 7.2: preferences and aspirations, resources and restrictions, events and transitions, and opportunities and constraints (Mulder and Hooimeijer, 1999). The rest of this chapter now explores each of these in turn.

Preferences and aspirations

Variations in short-term residential preferences and longer-term aspirations have important consequences for mobility behaviour and thus for local population structures. As previous chapters have explained, changes within people's lives can gradually alter residential preferences as dissatisfaction with one's current home rises past a personal tolerance threshold to trigger housing search. New preferences can also emerge rapidly, for example when life events create an urgent need to move. The net result is that residential demands vary across the population and over the life span in ways that motivate people with particular attributes (for example age, ethnicity or family status) to seek residential spaces that they anticipate will fulfil their specific constellation of needs. Shared types of housing preference and aspiration thus play important roles in sorting people with particular types of attribute into particular types of neighbourhoods and geographical locations.

Locational preferences and sorting

Locational preferences can be conceptualised as having three dimensions. The first dimension is the preference for staying in or leaving one's current location. In Britain, around a quarter to a third of adults typically report wanting to move – frequently due to dissatisfaction with housing and neighbourhood conditions – although far fewer subsequently act on these desires (Coulter et al, 2011).

If relocation is desired then people will usually identify a general area within which they want, can and/or need to live. This size of this space will vary and it forms the second dimension of residential preferences (see Chapter 5). Life course position is a crucial determinant of these broad locational preferences as variations in housing desires and demands for access and amenities mean people in different life stages and with different attributes tend to sort themselves into specific parts of cities (for example the inner core versus the suburban fringe) and particular places in the settlement hierarchy (for instance major conurbations versus smaller towns). These processes of city- and regional-scale population sorting have been likened to a life course conveyor (Damhuis et al, 2019). The conveyor metaphor is useful as it emphasises that changes in residential demands over the life course systematically pull people in particular life phases to move towards places that will satisfy their new needs.

Migration research provides ample evidence of life course conveyors in action. In the US, Plane and colleagues (2005) show that young adults, the highly educated and singles tend to flow up the urban hierarchy to large cities while older families and retirees typically move down the conveyor to less densely populated areas. A similar conveyor has been documented in Britain where London gains international migrants and young people but exports older adults who often flow to less densely populated areas (Lomax and Stillwell, 2018). Flows of affluent retirees from cities to rural and coastal towns further validate the conveyor idea.

Crucially, the direction and speed of these life course conveyors can shift over time with changes in the residential preferences associated with particular social groups and life phases. For example, while middle-class families generally abandoned urban cores for the suburbs during the late 20th century, Damhuis et al (2019) and Lomax and Stillwell (2018) show that this process slowed during the early 2000s in both the Netherlands and Britain. Butler and Hamnett (2012) argue that this is because middle-class families' residential preferences have bifurcated in recent decades as some continue to prioritise dwelling space in lower density areas (urban fleeing) while others now seek cosmopolitan, gentrified and amenity-rich inner-city neighbourhoods (urban seeking). They argue that for those with resources, this bifurcation indicates that tastes and lifestyles have emerged as important aspects of residential preference alongside more traditional concerns for dwelling space, lower-density neighbourhoods and homeownership.

Once people have settled on the broad area within which they want to live, they then need to winnow the dwelling choice set down to neighbourhoods that are desirable or at least acceptable (Clark, 2021). This is where the third dimension of residential preferences, preferences for neighbourhood attributes, comes into play. The significance of neighbourhood-level factors for residential preferences varies greatly with such factors typically being more relevant for people who:

- spend more time in the local area, for example older adults or young families;
- rely heavily on local social networks, for example those with limiting health conditions or recent immigrants;
- intend to stay in the neighbourhood, for example older in-movers rather than more transient young adults;
- are more invested in the neighbourhood, for example through homeownership.

Neighbourhood preferences have both a physical and a social aspect and the weight attached to each varies with life course position. On the physical side, the accessibility of workplaces and other amenities as well as the type, cost and tenure of the housing stock are important determinants of neighbourhood preferences. On the social side, perceptions about the composition of people living in an area and their behaviours (which need not match reality), as well as the local area's perceived reputation, influence where people want to live. While people with few resources and those reliant on social housing have little scope to choose their neighbourhood, the existence of gated communities and the way different strands of the middle-classes sort into different kinds of neighbourhood to display their varied collective identities (for example as cultural-capital rich cosmopolitans versus prosperous suburban families) attest to the way neighbourhood preferences are both socially determined and highly influential (Butler and Hamnett, 2012).

Residential segregation

The role preferences play in determining where people from different ethnic or racial groups live (often referred to as patterns of segregation, although this term is heavily contested) is perhaps the most politicised question confronting researchers working on neighbourhood dynamics. One reason this topic is so contentious is that much of the existing evidence about ethnic residential preferences has been inferred from assessments of how groups are distributed across neighbourhoods (Finney et al, 2015). While data limitations mean this is understandable, privileging the analysis of residential patterns over the processes that generate them has helped to create a number of flashpoints in the literature that have unhelpfully spilled out to confuse public debates. These flashpoints include clashes over:

1. *How segregation is defined* and whether the term is ever useful, *which segregation indices to use,* and *what dimensions of segregation* should be measured (for example how evenly groups are distributed, the exposure of one group to others, group isolation, overall diversity and so on).
2. *The scale and domain of analysis* given that different sorting processes may operate at different scales, segregation may occur in domains other than the residential environment (for example workplaces or schools) and that how spatial zones are drawn affects estimates of segregation levels (Piekut, 2021).
3. *The underlying data* and in particular *how groups are constructed and compared.* For example, Cantle and Kaufmann (2016) assert that overall mixing among all ethnic groups has increased in Britain as super-diverse urban neighbourhoods have emerged. However, they argue that comparing

minorities as a whole against the White British population paints a contrasting picture of increased ethnic majority isolation.

4. *The stability of patterns.*
5. *The extent to which residential segregation determines group integration*, what integration means, whether it is desirable, and thus whether high levels of residential segregation are a policy problem for societies which espouse freedom of movement. This most critical of issues involves normative judgements about what makes for a thriving society and so cannot be overcome with technical fixes like measuring segregation across multiple areas of life or using ever-more granular data to track who people meet during the day.

The inevitably partial nature of quantitative analyses of segregation means that multiple interpretations of the same data are often possible. Perhaps the most notorious cautionary tale here comes from 2005 when the then chair of the Commission for Racial Equality, Trevor Phillips, provocatively suggested Britain was 'sleepwalking' towards pernicious levels of segregation. This claim was partially based on his reading of census data as well as some academic studies looking at where different ethnic groups lived. However, Phillips's thesis was subsequently challenged by other analyses of the same 1991 and 2001 censuses (joined later by 2011 data) which suggested that ethnic segregation was, in general, declining 'via the somewhat benign processes of births and deaths, and internal migration from urban clusters' (Catney, 2016, pp 1691–2). Overall, the Phillips controversy illustrates just how important it is to look behind residence patterns at the life course processes and the preferences and moving behaviours that help drive changes in the composition of local populations.[3] It is to this we now turn.

Ethnicity and residential preferences

We have a surprisingly poor understanding of how strongly residential preferences are informed by desires to live with neighbours of a similar ethnic or cultural background and/or to avoid those perceived as being different. In the US, stated preference experiments suggest that most groups prefer living with a modest level of diversity tempered by a strong degree of co-ethnic presence (Clark, 2021). However, the reasons for this are unclear and Clark (2021) explains that multiple factors (including negative stereotyping and a more neutral desire for familiarity) are all plausible contributors. Kaufmann (2018) develops this theme of complexity by arguing that in Anglophone countries some members of White majorities 'flee' diversity by isolating themselves into mono-ethnic areas while others actively 'join' the mixing process (most notably by forming mixed-ethnic partnerships). Focusing on averages may thus obscure the way preferences to live with or to avoid residential mixing vary within as well as between ethnic groups with factors such as age, cohort and education.

Evidence for even small average differences in who people from different groups would prefer to live with is often viewed as a key motor of segregation. This argument derives from simulations by Schelling which indicated that diversity is unstable and that extreme inter-group segregation could emerge even when people have only a very mild preference to live among similar others (Malmberg and Clark, 2021). Schelling's ideas informed 20th-century debates about 'White flight', ethnic avoidance and the neighbourhood 'tipping points' that may trigger the onset of these processes. The basic hypothesis underpinning these notions is that an influx of minorities past a particular threshold reduces the appeal of a neighbourhood to the White ethnic majority. This causes White people living elsewhere to avoid moving in (avoidance) while encouraging White residents to move out (flight) to places with fewer minorities (Malmberg and Clark, 2021). The reduced appeal of living among a growing number of minority or immigrant neighbours could have many causes, including overt prejudice, a tendency for people to seek similarity (homophily), fears about social cohesion, or a desire to avoid the problems (for example crime, transience and worse schools) and declining property values that are sometimes perceived to accompany an influx of poorer migrants.[4] Regardless of the underlying reasons, these models all posit that preferences for co-ethnic neighbours are one mechanism through which large-scale immigration to gateway cities stimulates new patterns of residential preference which gradually helps transform these places into majority–minority spaces.

British evidence for ethnically distinct residential preferences is more limited than in the US. However, the idea that some minorities (in particular South Asian Muslims) deliberately self-segregate into ethnically homogenous neighbourhoods where they can lead 'parallel lives' disconnected from the mainstream has gained political traction in recent decades (Phillips, 2007). Through the 2000s, this strand of thinking prompted debates about the failure of multicultural tolerance and the need for greater social integration of immigrants – to be delivered partly through pro-mixing housing policies – in order to boost community cohesion and counter extremism (Robinson, 2005). These ideas have retained their currency with the 2016 Casey Review identifying residential separation to be undermining cohesion, trust and equality in some parts of the country (MHCLG, 2016). Kaufmann (2018) has reoriented this debate towards the White British majority by arguing that it mainly this group that is becoming more ethnically isolated outside of the largest cities. He argues this is in part due to some White Britons' preference to avoid diversity but that this is complicated by other factors including ethnically varied rates of natural increase, White British avoidance of unaffordable urban housing and some White Britons seeking out diverse metropolitan areas. The inferred housing preferences of different groups have thus become a contested battleground for broad and often polarised debates about 21st-century British identities.

Life course insights

Finney and colleagues (2015) suggest that a longitudinal life course perspective can help us to better understand how residential preferences influence local patterns of ethnic change. The idea here is that longitudinal methods allow us to directly model how life course dynamics, stated preferences and self-reported assessments of neighbourhood desirability shape where people from different groups want and opt to live. Crucially, longitudinal analysis also provides information about the life course dynamics of stayers and in particular their in situ fertility, mortality and social mobility. These in situ changes have significant implications for local population dynamics and may even drive a large proportion of neighbourhood-level change (Catney, 2016).

Enriching the study of ethnic residential preferences with longitudinal life course insights can help tackle four gaps in what we know about the forces driving local patterns of (de)segregation.

Geographical variations

Stockdale and Catney (2014) have called for scholars to build greater sensitivity to the demographic, economic, cultural and institutional setting into life course analyses of local population change. This point is particularly apposite for work on ethnic residential geographies, which has been heavily shaped by US research. Theories and evidence from the US may not, however, be particularly useful for explaining the ethnic residential dynamics of European countries with very different population structures and migration histories, lower economic inequality and more active welfare states.

In Britain, cross-sectional analysis of residential patterns and longitudinal analyses of residential behaviour both provide little evidence of strong self-segregating preferences across ethnic groups. Census research shows that neighbourhood-level diversity and mixing have increased as minority populations have spread out from the cores of gateway cities to suburban areas and gradually down the settlement hierarchy (Catney, 2016). Finney and colleagues (2015, p 38) observe that these 'movements out of cities are often a result of counterurbanisation, with housing motivations common to all ethnic groups. While preferences for co-ethnic residence exist, these sit alongside aspirations for mixed, rather than ethnically exclusive, neighbourhoods'. In essence, it appears that residential preferences have multiple dimensions as many people want to better their housing conditions but would also prefer to live in places where at least some neighbours are from a similar background.

It is likely to be difficult to find an affordable location that perfectly satisfies all these demands and so most moving decisions will usually involve making complex trade-offs about dwelling and neighbourhood attributes.

Cantle and Kaufmann (2016) temper this largely positive narrative by arguing that the process of increasing ethnic diversity is, however, rather slow. They further contend that greater neighbourhood-level diversity does not necessarily translate into greater residential mixing between White Britons and minorities as immigration and high natural increase refuel the minority populations of large cities (Catney, 2016). Moreover, diverse and densely populated urban spaces predominantly attract younger White Britons who often stay for a relatively short sojourn before moving away to less diverse neighbourhoods (in either less densely populated areas or more affluent parts of the city) later in life when forming families. These complexities indicate that no analysis of ethnic residential preferences is complete without some consideration of how geographical life course conveyors may operate differently for different ethnic groups. Housing market forces and the historic patterns of group settlement that determine origin neighbourhoods are also important additional considerations.

The argument that shared housing demands underpin the residential preferences of all ethnic groups is broadly supported by longitudinal studies. These show that all groups tend to move to less ethnically concentrated and less deprived neighbourhoods when they move – albeit to a greater extent for White Britons than for most minority groups – and that all groups use education and higher incomes to buy into more advantaged places with larger ethnic majority populations (Coulter and Clark, 2019). Studies also provide little evidence for large-scale White flight from diversity: 'White British are no more likely to leave diverse wards than other ethnic groups. Indeed, all ethnic groups tend to leave wards with high concentrations of minority groups' (Kaufmann and Harris, 2015, p 1577). Similarly, Clark and Coulter (2015) confirm that ethnicity and levels of neighbourhood ethnic change are far weaker predictors of moving preferences than most other demographic and socio-economic variables. Overall, it appears that life course dynamics and the preferences they generate play a crucial role in determining moving behaviours, regardless of personal ethnic background.

The role of events and transitions

Many people move neighbourhood in response to life events and so ethnic differences in how strongly such events act as moving triggers, how frequently trigger events are experienced and variations in their biographical timing could all produce ethnically patterned residential preferences (Finney, 2011). For example, delayed home-leaving by South Asians as compared with earlier education-related exits among White Britons (see Chapter 4) is likely to mean the two groups have very different residential needs through early adulthood. Similarly, group variation in fertility rates may have a bearing on housing preferences. Unfortunately, relatively little is known about the way that differences in the anticipated and actual biographical timing of life events influences the housing preferences of different groups.

The importance of services and solidarities

Most scholars agree that a completely even spatial distribution of ethnic groups is neither feasible nor desirable. As Peach (1996) explained, residential clustering has a positive side in that people may prefer to live among similar neighbours in order to benefit from the specific services and opportunities for solidarity these areas provide. For instance, people living in areas with many co-ethnic or co-religionist neighbours may:

- benefit from specialist services that need a population of local users to be viable, for example religious centres or food shops;
- develop a strong sense of local community and belonging while maintaining their cultural heritage;
- profit from established social and kin networks and the support these provide;
- avoid racism and harassment from other groups;
- feel freer to visibly practise specific cultural or religious behaviours.

These factors suggests that preferences for clustering are likely to be more potent for disadvantaged minorities, groups that are more culturally distinct and more recent migrants. Some of the aforementioned benefits of clustering are also likely to be relevant for members of the ethnic majority and mean they too have some degree of desire to live together. Although spatial assimilation models hold that over time minorities accumulate resources and seek to move away from gateway cities, this is clearly not always the case as can be seen in the long-term persistence of culturally distinctive but affluent parts of many cities.

Variation with duration and cohort

Spatial assimilation models highlight that duration and cohort may be important factors in the neighbourhood preferences of minority groups. Darlington-Pollock and colleagues (2019) show that first- and second-generation status, as well as time spent in the UK, influence the moving propensity of ethnic minorities (which are generally lower than for comparable White Britons). Evidence that second-generation minorities tend to move to less White British neighbourhoods than White Britons is also unsurprising if we recognise that (1) most people from all groups relocate over short distances to places with fairly similar populations and that (2) most second-generation minorities grow up in much more diverse neighbourhoods in (3) more diverse cities than their White British peers. In essence, these points indicate even if people from all groups had identical preferences and moving behaviours, differences in the starting locations of the different groups means that we would expect the historic patterns of minority settlement and local ethnic diversity to be quite 'sticky' over time (Coulter and Clark, 2019).

Preferences for co-ethnic neighbours and for diversity may be further shaped by the context experienced during childhood socialisation. This implies that preferences for different configurations of neighbours may vary across cohorts and places depending on when and where people grew up. In their analysis of London, Sturgis et al (2014, p 1304) find evidence 'that growing up in a multicultural society in which ethnic minorities play a visible and positive role serves to shift the attitudes and behaviours of younger ethnic majority cohorts in prosocial directions'. The residential preferences of White Britons growing up in more multicultural times and places may thus be more pro-diversity (or at least less anti-diversity) than those of previous generations and their peers growing up in less diverse spaces. This again highlights the need to set changes in (de)segregation in the broader context of longer-term changes in life course dynamics.

Resources and restrictions

Acting on residential preferences requires resources and this means cities are divided by income and class as people sort into areas with housing they can afford. This socio-economic sorting works to the detriment of many ethnic minority groups as their lower average incomes mean they are disproportionately channelled into cheaper rental housing in more deprived neighbourhoods. This can be seen in Table 7.1 which shows that groups with the smallest proportion of low-income members (White British, White Other and Indian) have low rates of residence in deprived areas. In contrast, ethnic groups with higher proportions of low-income members (Black, Bangladeshi and Pakistani) are much more concentrated in the least advantaged neighbourhoods.

However, Table 7.1 shows that socio-economic sorting cannot fully explain why some ethnic groups are more exposed to deprivation. For example, the Chinese and Black groups have a similar proportion of low-income members but nearly twice the proportion of Black individuals live in deprived neighbourhoods. These types of complexities have led some to argue that differences in group composition (for example age structure and historic settlement patterns) as well as preferences, resources and constraints

Table 7.1: Low household income and neighbourhood deprivation by ethnicity

Ethnicity	Per cent in lowest 20% of household incomes (2016–19)	Per cent in most deprived 10% of neighbourhoods (2019)[†]
White British	18	9
White Other	19	8
Indian	21	8
Chinese	30	8
Black	31	15
Bangladeshi	37	19
Pakistani	47	31

[†]Data for England.

Source: Based on data from Race Disparity Unit (2020; 2021). Contains public sector information licensed under the Open Government Licence v3.0.

intersect to create complex patterns of 'eth–class segregation' in 21st-century cities (Tammaru et al, 2021).

Socio-economic sorting

The way cities are divided into areas of wealth and poverty has attracted attention since Charles Booth's street-level survey of occupations and incomes in late Victorian London. Much of this early work was descriptive but by the mid-20th century scholars began to develop explanatory economic models to explain geographical patterns of urban housing and land use (Butler and Hamnett, 2012). Although these now seem simplistic, their basic insight that people sort into parts of the city they can afford remains as potent as ever.

Studies conducted across the Global North show that people with more economic resources and security are more likely to live in and move to less deprived neighbourhoods than those with fewer resources (Clark and Morrison, 2012). This is partly because housing costs are higher in more desirable neighbourhoods, but such patterns also emerge because these areas tend to have a larger proportion of owner-occupied stock that is inaccessible to the poor. Yet there are two reasons why socio-economic sorting and its impact on neighbourhood populations is perhaps less straightforward than it might at first appear. First, in some contexts, like the US, there is evidence for place stratification whereby ethnic minorities are prevented from using higher incomes to buy access to desirable neighbourhoods (Pais et al, 2012). There is, however, little UK evidence for place stratification as economic disadvantage and a tendency to originate in more deprived spaces broadly explain why ethnic minority movers tend to relocate to less advantaged neighbourhoods than their White British peers (Coulter and Clark, 2019). However, it does appear that neighbourhood characteristics are particularly 'sticky' for those people living in the most deprived neighbourhoods who are the least likely to move 'up' the neighbourhood hierarchy when they do relocate (Clark et al, 2014).

Second, Bailey's (2012) evidence suggests that selective moves are not necessarily the principal driver of local socio-economic dynamics. His results indicate that migration is weakly selective by occupational status as other life course dynamics complicate the economic sorting process. For example, young adults leaving home often have low incomes and move to less advantaged city neighbourhoods than they came from and this – coupled with frequent changes in address, living arrangements and jobs during early adulthood – means young people have complex patterns of neighbourhood transition that do not just reflect economic sorting.

In line with this argument, different sorts of less advantaged areas appear to play different functional roles within urban life course conveyors. Robson et al's (2008) analysis differentiated 'isolate' areas where residents are trapped in deprivation from deprived transit, escalator and improver areas which exchange population with less disadvantaged neighbourhoods. The higher connectivity of the latter three types of deprived area suggests they play valuable life course functions within urban systems, for example by providing cheap starter housing for migrants and younger households. Robson and colleagues' (2008) work further shows that the local context influences how deprived neighbourhoods function within life course conveyors as Liverpool and Manchester had relatively more isolate areas than London.

Bailey's (2012) evidence also suggests that in situ processes of ageing, mortality and social mobility help drive aggregate changes in neighbourhood socio-economic characteristics. This is perhaps unsurprising as the high costs, disruption and uncertainty of moving are likely to deter people (in particular those who are worse off) from quickly adjusting their housing consumption in response to changes in household finances.[5] This friction helps to explain why people often remain living in declining places even when work disappears. To fully grasp how neighbourhoods change we thus need to look beyond residential moves to also consider births, deaths, who stays in neighbourhoods and how their lives change in situ with broader processes of demographic and economic restructuring.

Context and linked lives

The life course principles of (1) time and place and (2) linked lives provide further insight into the role resources play in tying together life course and neighbourhood socio-economic dynamics. Focusing first on geographical context, Tammaru et al (2021) note that socio-economic sorting across neighbourhoods is strongest where there are higher levels of income inequality. This is because resource disparities are more extreme in unequal societies and also because inequality undermines social cohesion, leading the rich to cluster for security. Sorting is also more intense when housing is mostly allocated by the market and is lower in countries with large unitary rental sectors (Tammaru et al, 2021). Empirical support for these points comes from Australia where a marketised housing system and a weak welfare state mean those living in affordable housing tend to move to better neighbourhoods while poor households in unaffordable housing churn through disadvantaged areas (Baker et al, 2016).

Context is also about time and shifts in economic conditions can generate cohort-specific patterns of resources that reconfigure geographical life course conveyors. For example, Moos (2016) argues that recent cohorts of young adults have concentrated in dense urban neighbourhoods partly because reductions in income and job security prevent them from moving away to form families and access owner-occupation. Similarly, Butler and Hamnett (2012) stress that deindustrialisation and the professionalisation of London's workforce were important pre-conditions for the capital's gentrification. In their view, gentrification is not just the product of working-class displacement due to price pressures. Rather, gentrification also occurs through cohort replacement as older generations of working-class residents retire, move out or die and are replaced by younger cohorts who are more likely to work in the service-sector jobs that now make up a larger share of urban employment. Taken together, these arguments remind us that neighbourhood change is influenced by both the preferences and resources of successive birth cohorts as they move through life.

Over the last two decades, research has begun to demonstrate that neighbourhood attainments are not just an individual matter but are also transmitted between intergenerationally linked lives. Evidence from several countries shows that parental neighbourhood socio-economic status influences where children live through later life (Sharkey, 2008; van Ham et al, 2014). The basic finding is that even after controlling for personal attainments, children from poor neighbourhoods are more likely to live in poor neighbourhoods through later life than those who grew up in less deprived spaces. Sharkey (2008) terms this the intergenerational transmission of context and argues that it forms a critical mechanism through which inequality passes down the generations. Worryingly, both Sharkey (2008) and van Ham and colleagues (2014) find that this intergenerational transmission is especially potent for ethnic minorities. Much more research is needed here to identify the precise mechanisms that transmit spatial disadvantage across generations in uneven ways.

Policy responses

British policy responses to socio-economic sorting have two parallels with responses to ethnic segregation. First, both issues tend only to be viewed as policy problems when they produce what are perceived to be problematic residential clusters. In Britain, elite views that something must be done about clusters of poverty have historically been driven by a changing blend of concerns encompassing paternalistic altruism as well as fears that problems generated in areas of concentrated poverty (such as disease, criminality or social unrest) will spill out into wider society (Lund, 2017). Second, the clustering of both the ethnic majority and the affluent – as well as the sorting processes which lead these groups to live together – are not viewed as policy issues. Instead, it is the residential clustering of minorities and the poor that are viewed as the cause of urban problems.

In Britain, the post-war decades probably marked the high-water mark of state interventions that dampened socio-economic sorting. On the demand side, the Keynesian consensus drove down income inequality through full employment, strong wage growth and redistributive taxation while on the supply side the mass production of public housing provided affordable accommodation for a broad cross-section of the working- and lower middle-classes (Lund, 2017). These approaches began to disintegrate from the 1970s and in recent decades state retreat from both economic affairs and housing provision means policy interventions have become more limited and targeted towards areas of high deprivation, for example through New Labour's 2001– 10 New Deal for Communities. While even this focus disappeared during the laissez-faire 2010s, the current Conservative government's nebulous levelling up agenda suggests that area-based policy has once again become politically acceptable.

Events and transitions

Each of the previous chapters explored how events and transitions in life course careers often motivate people to adjust their housing consumption. This evidence implies that at the aggregate level, any shifts in the types or biographical timing of the events people experience – as well as the extent to which these trigger relocations – can alter how geographical life course conveyors operate and thus shape the social composition of the neighbourhoods and localities people move between. Table 7.2 provides some examples of broad macro-level processes that can have these types of effects across various timescales. While it is possible to conceive of many forms of geographical change brought about by changing patterns of life events, the next section shines a spotlight on two particularly important

Table 7.2: Examples of processes driving changes in the types and timings of life events

Timescale	Example driving forces	Examples of life events
Immediate or short-term	External societal shocks; major changes in local or national policies	Spike in US foreclosures after the GFC; delayed home-leaving and increased boomeranging during the COVID-19 pandemic
Medium-term	Fluctuations across business cycles	Variation in the risk of unemployment over economic cycles
Long-term	Gradual changes in population structure and behaviours under the Second Demographic Transition	Delayed fertility; increased risk of partnership dissolution

dynamics: (1) educational events and the way these intersect with the geography of population ageing, and (2) the more localised impacts of policy-driven residential mobility.

Education and ageing

At first glance it appears odd to consider educational events and ageing together but both, in fact, intersect to shape local patterns of demographic change. Like the rest of the Global North, the UK population is ageing with the median age rising by 2.5 years from 37.9 in 2001 to 40.4 in 2020 (ONS, 2021c). This ageing is predicted to continue and will dramatically alter the types of life events experienced by the population. In general, ageing is likely to lead to many neighbourhoods having fewer economically active residents, while strong growth in the oldest-old population will increase pressure on local health and social care services. Ageing neighbourhoods may also become more stable places as older people and outright homeowners tend to move infrequently.

However, the pace of ageing varies substantially across Britain. Table 7.3 shows the ten UK local authority districts estimated to have experienced the greatest changes in median age between mid-2001 and mid-2020. Most of the districts where median age fell significantly during this period are cities home to university campuses while more peripheral rural areas dominate the places where ageing has been the most pronounced. These patterns suggest that the expansion of HE has disrupted the national ageing trend as university towns and cities pull in large numbers of young adults from elsewhere in Britain and from abroad. Greater HE participation has also had neighbourhood-level impacts within university towns and cities as distinctive local geographies of studentification emerge.

Table 7.3: Local authorities with the largest absolute changes in median age, 2001–20

Local authority	Mid-2001 median age	Change to mid-2020
Greatest declines		
Newcastle upon Tyne	36.2	-4.1
Coventry	35.1	-3.1
Nottingham	32.7	-3.0
Bristol	35.0	-2.6
Exeter	36.0	-2.6
Lincoln	35.6	-2.5
Oxford	31.0	-2.4
Welwyn Hatfield	38.1	-2.3
Norwich	35.4	-2.1
Salford	36.8	-2.1
Greatest increases		
Harrogate	40.3	+7.4
Powys	43.1	+7.5
Dumfries and Galloway	42.5	+7.5
Rutland	40.3	+7.6
Melton	40.2	+7.7
Derbyshire Dales	43.7	+7.8
Argyll and Bute	42.0	+8.1
Hambleton	42.0	+8.3
Eden	42.7	+8.5
Maldon	40.6	+8.8

Source: Adapted from ONS (2021c). Contains public sector information licensed under the Open Government Licence v3.0.

Policy-induced mobility

Encouraging or forcing people living in particular spaces to move is one of the most direct ways in which policymakers manipulate life events in order to alter life courses and change places. In the US, policy efforts have included supporting families to move away from disadvantaged public housing estates in programmes such as the Moving to Opportunity experiment. Sometimes this focus on mobility has been coupled with demolition and restructuring to create more mixed-income communities, as in the HOPE VI programme (Goetz, 2013). The basic idea underpinning these mobility-promoting interventions is that providing assistance to help households move to non-poor areas (for example by providing rental discount vouchers) will allow them to better their lives, as moving should improve their safety, educational opportunities, health and job prospects. On an aggregate level this should then help to both deconcentrate and reduce poverty. However, evaluations of these programmes typically report an unexpectedly complex pattern of effects with variations by age, city, duration and across different life course domains (Goetz, 2013; Clark, 2021).

In Europe, policymakers have tended to focus more on restructuring disadvantaged neighbourhoods in order to improve their physical fabric. Again, this has often involved also trying to create mixed-incomes spaces. Living in a neighbourhood that undergoes this type of restructuring is a major life event with far-reaching consequences. While much of the academic focus has been on those displaced to new areas, Kleinhans and Kearns (2013) argue that displacement is only part of the story as the effects of being relocated are duration-dependent and highly varied. They note that this means that longitudinally tracking people over time as well as the types of places they move between can help policymakers assess the impacts of restructuring initiatives.

Opportunities and constraints

Contextual opportunities and constraints profoundly influence residential behaviour and thus how neighbourhood populations change. These effects work in two ways. First, who moves or stays in response to life course processes is determined partly by the opportunities and constraints to moving. Second, contextual factors influence where people move when they do relocate and how much choice they have in selecting a new neighbourhood. While everyone has some kind of residential preference, the extent to which these can be acted upon depends not just on resources but also on broader constraints that may prevent choice being exercised. Although many types of opportunity and constraint matter for neighbourhood change, the rest of this section concentrates on two sets of housing-related factor: (1) the objective distribution and affordability of dwellings, and (2) more institutional housing access constraints.

Dwelling stock and affordability

Housing generally lasts a long time and this means that the current geography of dwelling types and tenures is determined by historic patterns of housing production modified by subsequent adjustments (for instance densification through breaking large houses into flats) and tenure transfers. Broadly speaking, this means that anyone seeking a particular type of dwelling will only be able to move to the subset of neighbourhoods where those types of housing are found. Meanwhile, when looked at from a neighbourhood perspective, the local stock composition and its costs determine who flows in and out of any area. Demographic conveyors and socio-economic sorting will thus work differently in different times and places depending on stock composition and societal patterns of housing affordability.

In Britain, low rates of social housing construction in recent decades mean that past geographies of production exert a particularly strong constraining influence on social tenants. In essence, those entering or moving within the socially rented sector typically have a much more restricted neighbourhood choice set than those in private markets (Butler and Hamnett, 2012). Meanwhile, the fact that access to the dwindling stock of social housing has, over time, become more stringently restricted means that disadvantaged populations are continually being channelled into the tenure. This 'residualisation' is exacerbated by discounted Right to Buy sales to sitting tenants, which tend to lead better-off households in the most desirable stock to transfer their homes into the owner-occupied sector (Murie, 2016). When taken together, these sorting dynamics mean that areas with lots of post-war social housing (especially flats) are prone to becoming areas of concentrated disadvantage.

For most people social housing is not an option and so the dynamics of housing markets play a critical role in reconfiguring neighbourhood populations. Areas with a large proportion of owner-occupied stock are generally fairly stable with a large share of neighbourhood change driven by in situ life course processes and ageing. Access to these sorts of areas is primarily governed by ability to pay and so housing market movements shape local populations. Meanwhile, the growth of the UK private rented sector since the late 1990s has been driven by a cocktail of factors that includes greater demand from both traditional sources (students, migrants, young professionals and so on) as well as new constituencies (for example low-income households and younger families) unable to afford the increased costs of homeownership and yet excluded from social housing (Kemp, 2015). This growing heterogeneity of demand – with some groups renting out of choice and others due to constraint – has had geographical consequences, as diversifying rental submarkets have transformed urban neighbourhood dynamics.

Two broad geographical trends in rental markets are particularly evident. On the one hand, the private rented sector has expanded in the suburbs and on the fringes of UK cities to cater to lower-income households priced out of central areas (Zhang and Pryce, 2020). Some of this stock has come directly from privately built homes but some has also leaked out of the social sector via Right to Buy sales (Murie, 2016). On the other hand, Paccoud (2017) argues that buy-to-let investment has created new gentrification frontiers within cities. He argues that investor landlords have bought up cheap housing in neighbourhoods overlooked by traditional owner–gentrifiers who are usually looking for a long-term home and thus are unwilling to buy into more disadvantaged spaces. By contrast, students and young adults are often transient and so letting to these groups allows private landlords to exploit emerging rent-gaps in more disadvantaged parts of the city (Paccoud, 2017). These two trends have been documented in other contexts such as Amsterdam where affordability problems and rental deregulation have displaced poorer young renters to the periphery (Howard et al, 2021). Escalating problems of housing affordability appear to also be driving greater age segregation across UK neighbourhoods as recent cohorts are unable to move to high-cost areas with lots of owner-occupied stock (Sabater et al, 2018).

While most of the analysis of these trends has been conducted at the aggregate level, it is crucial to recognise that behind these changes are patterns of lived experiences with a strong cohort dimension. Ultimately, it is people who experience neighbourhoods changing around them, are displaced, undertake and profit from gentrification, or are unable to buy into neighbourhoods. Much more qualitative work needs to be done to understand these lived life course dynamics of housing-related neighbourhood change and their long-term biographical consequences.

Access and institutions

Residential opportunities and constraints are also socially determined. Through the late 20th century, much attention was devoted to the way overt discrimination in housing markets limited the residential options of minorities. Discriminatory practices included lenders turning down mortgage applications by minority households, refusing to lend to those buying in areas with large minority populations (redlining) and landlords or agents either rejecting tenancy applications on the basis of a person's perceived origin or steering some groups towards less desirable locations (Phillips, 2007). While this sort of overt discrimination has long been illegal in Britain, from time to time media exposés highlight continued problems of racial discrimination or, at best, unconscious bias in private rental markets. It is also likely that some groups have internalised expectations that discrimination will occur and this, like fears of racist harassment or worries about feeling out of place, limits their housing searches to only those neighbourhoods that are perceived to be safe spaces (Robinson, 2005).

Opportunities to access housing are generally more socially constrained for poorer groups. In the US, research indicates that suburban landlords are often unwilling to let to low-income households using housing vouchers to cover part of their rent (Clark, 2021). This channels poor renters into more disadvantaged inner-city neighbourhoods where landlords are less selective. In Britain, rental adverts frequently stipulate 'professionals' and 'no children', and commonly used to specify 'no DSS' (shorthand for the Department for Social Security, which formerly administered housing benefits).[6] While the latter has become less common after a 2020 court ruling that it contravenes equalities legislation, it is extremely hard to tell how unexpressed prejudices factor into lettings decisions. Similar sorts of power-laden issues have been documented in the social housing sector where Clapham (2005) describes how housing officers' views on what constitutes a good neighbour influenced how they interacted with tenants. Taken together, these points indicate that residential behaviour and neighbourhood processes are influenced by social as well as by more objective housing-related constraints.

Summary

This chapter has demonstrated how changes in the population composition of neighbourhoods can be better understood by setting these within a life course framework. In essence, life course dynamics in the aggregate change places and the way these processes unfold varies over time and space. Crucially, it is not simply the case that mobility is the only engine of change in the neighbourhood mosaic. Births, deaths and in situ shifts in people's lives also matter and thus the key question is how and why do people move or stay in different places as their lives unfold in different ways. Moving and staying need to be seen not as discrete events but rather as related biographical processes which are both important and inseparable drivers of neighbourhood change.

The chapter has consistently stressed that local population change is often uneven, frequently multidimensional, and that it is carried out and experienced by people moving along life course conveyors. Preferences and aspirations, resources and restrictions, events and transitions, and opportunities and constraints all influence how people move between and stay in neighbourhoods over time as their lives change. Understanding how these processes work therefore requires looking behind aggregate level changes in local populations by using longitudinal data to track residential decisions and behaviours over the life course.

8

Understanding housing and life course dynamics

There is now a growing consensus that much of the Global North is in the grips of a housing crisis. Although the precise form this crisis takes varies from place to place, one common feature is that housing problems are always tightly bound up with wider issues of social inequality. Inequalities along multiple axes spanning many areas of life are both causes and outcomes of contemporary housing problems and so need to be placed centre-stage within housing-related research and debate.

This book sought to provide a fresh perspective on these issues by showing how who we are matters for our housing and how housing helps make us into who we are. This focus on how housing is embedded into the dynamics of 21st-century life courses enriches research and debate in two ways. First, the book has shown that residential decisions and behaviours are deeply intertwined with events and processes across the other domains of people's lives, as well as in the lives of their significant others. The way housing careers unfold also varies geographically with shifts in housing behaviour helping to drive changes in local populations and in the social fabric of places. Taken together, these insights remind us that housing is not a discrete field of enquiry which can be boxed off and either theorised about or analysed on its own. Instead, aggregate trends in housing careers must be related to broad processes occurring elsewhere in modern societies, for instance shifts in their demographic structures, education systems, labour markets, cultures and public policies. Housing careers are closely intertwined with processes in other areas of life and ultimately it is these interactions which structure the overarching course of people's lives in ways which reshape places and societies.

Second, the book's focus on residential careers helps enrich our understanding of how housing systems function. Figure 8.1 depicts how housing systems can be viewed as constructed from three pillars: housing provision (how housing is supplied, exchanged, financed, regulated and so forth), the residential careers examined throughout this book, and the social meanings housing has for individuals (Clapham, 2005). While the provision pillar normally attracts the lion's share of the research and policy attention, provision-centric approaches often view people simply as passive respondents to market or state forces rather than diverse agents with their own life experiences, aspirations and preferences, goals, and ties to others

Figure 8.1: Three pillars of housing systems

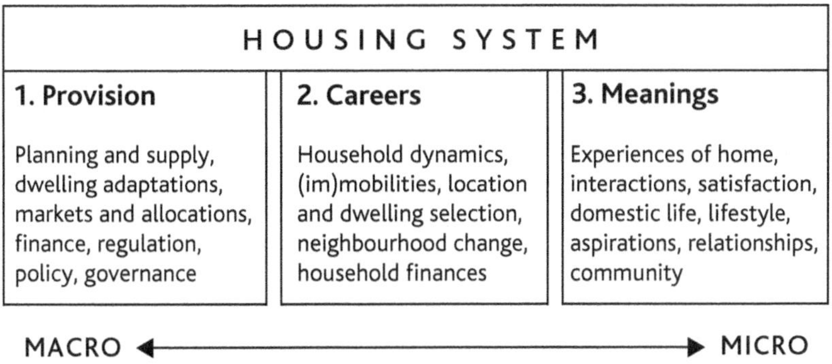

HOUSING SYSTEM		
1. Provision	**2. Careers**	**3. Meanings**
Planning and supply, dwelling adaptations, markets and allocations, finance, regulation, policy, governance	Household dynamics, (im)mobilities, location and dwelling selection, neighbourhood change, household finances	Experiences of home, interactions, satisfaction, domestic life, lifestyle, aspirations, relationships, community

MACRO ⟵——————————————————⟶ MICRO

(Clapham, 2005). Privileging the provision pillar over the others in this way is therefore risky as it can lead to overly simplistic assumptions being made about housing demands or how people will respond to particular policy interventions. Addressing this by devoting greater research effort towards the careers and meaning pillars is therefore not only intellectually important but could also aid with policy formulation, evaluation and critique. Figure 8.1 places housing careers as the central pillar of housing systems as it is arguably by shaping people's residential circumstances that patterns of provision come to influence the subjective meanings housing holds for individuals (and vice versa as demands in turn influence provision). In essence, residential careers mediate how housing provision interacts with the social meanings of housing.

This chapter summarises how the book's life course framework can be used to further our understanding of contemporary housing career patterns and processes and their links to changing lives, places and inequalities. The chapter starts by recapping the key features of modern life course perspectives. It then reviews how the life course conceptual tools developed in Chapter 2 can be applied in customisable ways to integrate and synthesise what we know about housing and life course dynamics. Future applications of the twelve tools are then sketched before the chapter concludes with ten general guidelines about how best to apply life course insights to research, policy deliberations and simply when thinking about or discussing housing. This concluding section is designed to be useful to anyone interested in understanding the social dimension of contemporary housing issues.

Housing and life course dynamics

This book's central contention is that the life course perspective provides a useful conceptual framework for understanding 21st-century residential behaviours, patterns and processes. Drawing on life course frameworks to understand residential behaviour is not, in itself, a major innovation – population and housing scholarship have been using these approaches since at least the late 1980s (Feijten, 2005) and at the time of writing a Google Scholar search keyed on 'housing' and 'life course' returns several million hits.

However, there are two problems with the way life course insights are currently applied to housing questions. First, existing research is scattered across the social sciences and is usually published as short empirical articles concentrating on one particular phenomenon. Second, the classic texts that exist on housing and the life course are now rather dated, as theory, data, methods and the structure of societies have all changed considerably since they were published. Taken together, these issues mean that life course research on housing is fragmented and rarely synthesised into a coherent and modern perspective. The field of life course infused housing scholarship is thus like an immense jigsaw which has been split into multiple sections whose pieces have then each been distributed to teams working in separate rooms. While those in each room are carefully fitting together their small section of the puzzle, the fragmented division of labour makes it difficult to see how all the sections fit together to form a complete picture.

Integration and synthesis

Chapters 1–2 responded to these challenges by outlining a modern life course framework for understanding residential decisions, behaviours and careers. Chapters 3–7 then used this framework to synthesise what we know about the dynamics of 21st-century housing careers and their implications for people, places and inequalities. The crux of the book's life course approach is that lives are comprised of multiple parallel careers which are interdependent and constantly unfolding in context-dependent and socially embedded ways (Bernardi et al, 2019). Housing is just one of these careers and, indeed, one of the life course perspective's strengths is its multidimensionality. This guides housing researchers to look far beyond housing to the ways that events and processes in other domains both impact on and are reshaped by residential processes. Housing careers are thus just one part of the life course which is characterised by diversity, dynamism and interconnection within and between lives, as well as with changing contextual settings.

One particularly useful feature of the life course framework is that this helps adapt the much-maligned concept of housing careers to make it better suited to 21st-century realities. While notions of housing careers have long been criticised for unrealistically assuming that people generally move up the 'housing ladder' (Clapham, 2005; Beer and Faulkner, 2011), the pathways and transitions frameworks these authors have proposed as correctives both have their own weaknesses. By contrast, in the life course perspective the term career is normally used flexibly to describe the diverse, dynamic and non-linear routes people follow in different domains of life. People thus have educational, employment, family and health careers that interact with each other and with their housing career. Viewing housing careers in this more nuanced and interwoven fashion casts them as more closely akin to careers in professional sports which vary from person to person, are always changing, and often encompass both ups and downs as well as shocks and periods of stability and change. This more flexible conceptualisation of housing careers as one career among many provides a powerful way to think about today's destandardised residential behaviours.

Another valuable feature of the life course framework is that this explicitly distinguishes the macro-structural from the proximate determinants of housing career events and processes (Bernard et al, 2016). Chapter 1 argued that aggregate patterns of housing behaviour are ultimately driven by four constellations of intersecting macro-level factors: economic processes, demography, public policies and culture. Changes in any of these areas can have major impacts on the structure of housing careers, although these impacts usually vary depending on the institutions and technological development of a given society. Crucially, however, macro-structural forces do not themselves directly change micro-level residential behaviours and Chapter 1 identified four sets of intervening mechanisms through which broad changes in society come to shape people's decisions and behaviours (Mulder and Hooimeijer, 1999). These mechanisms are changes in:

• preferences and aspirations
• resources and restrictions
• events and transitions
• opportunities and constraints

These four mechanisms can be thought of as the proximate determinants of housing behaviour as it is by altering them that macro-level social changes have consequences for how people actually move through the housing system (Bernard et al, 2016). Examples of how each of these mechanisms work have been discussed throughout this book.

Using life course frameworks

Before proceeding any further, it is useful to note some general points about how the book's life course framework should and should not be used. While life course ideas are sometimes labelled as theories or models, this book's framework is not designed to function as either a predictive theory or a grand explanatory model of housing-related behaviour. Instead, the book's life course approach is designed as an organising framework or perspective with some common guiding principles that can help suggest housing-related questions and also assist with devising research, interpreting evidence and suggesting improvements to policy and practice. These common principles and the twelve conceptual tools derived from them can be used flexibly in different ways that can be customised, adapted, fused and tailored to different research topics and contexts.

The fact that the life course approach does not deal directly with causal models and explanation does, however, mean that it alone will rarely provide sufficient conceptual apparatus for any research project. Formulating hypotheses and attempting to explain phenomena will normally require supplementing the life course framework with middle-range theories relating to the particular processes of interest. To understand what this means it is helpful to consider a hypothetical example. Let us imagine a researcher wants to understand why some people move into more disadvantaged neighbourhoods than they start out living in. Adopting a life course perspective would guide the researcher to look for event and status predictors across multiple life careers: for example separation in the family career, the onset of a disability in the health career and/or unemployment in the employment career. Life course principles would also suggest that the timing of moves needs to be considered (perhaps low-income young adults leaving home temporarily move to these sorts of areas) along with the influence of biographies and linked lives (perhaps elderly parents' needs draw people back to deprived origins) as well as contextual settings (perhaps such moves are more common in recessions or in cities with depressed labour markets). This example shows how life course ideas can provide a useful overarching framework to hone research questions and guide project design.

However, the life course approach does not, by itself, provide any explanatory clues about causality or which variables will matter for an outcome. Generating hypotheses will thus require middle-range theories and detailed knowledge regarding the process in question: in this case what factors might lead people to move into more disadvantaged places (for instance economic precarity, family disruption and/or ethno-racial discrimination). Similarly, an overarching life course framework might need to be supplemented with social theory of the type used in the pathways framework if the goal is not just to understand aggregate patterns of behaviour or outcomes but also to elucidate the subjective meanings of housing (Clapham, 2005). Sound research design will often therefore require using the life course perspective *in conjunction* with other theories and possibly also other conceptual approaches.

Importantly, the flexibility of life course perspectives means they can be harnessed by research approaching housing questions from many philosophical and methodological standpoints. In general, quantitative approaches aiming to build up a population-level picture of patterns and processes currently dominate life course housing scholarship. These are essential for understanding material inequalities and for formulating sound policy, which practically always deals with aggregates. Crucially, however, Chapter 2 explained that contemporary life course research on housing issues is neither positivist nor antithetical to qualitative methods. The research reviewed throughout this book shows that very few of today's life course studies seek to build universal laws, uncritically accept constructed social categories or assume behaviour is totally rational and detached from subjectivity. Instead, contemporary life course housing scholarship tends to search for nuanced contingent causalities, aims to understand unfolding interactions between people and contexts, is sensitive to social construction and often seeks to describe and explain differences of experience, process and outcome. Contemporary life course research thus draws far more on postpositivist scientific approaches than on positivism (Johnston et al, 2014). Indeed, there is no *prima facie* reason why the general principles of the life course approach cannot be incorporated into more interpretivist research and in studies using qualitative methods to unpack how people exercise bounded agency and attach meanings to housing (for example Bailey et al, 2021). None of the twelve life course conceptual tools outlined in Chapter 2 are methodologically proscriptive, although some probably do lend themselves more strongly to particular forms of research over others.

Twelve conceptual tools

A conceptual framework is only useful if it can actually be used to help understand something. To help grasp how the life course perspective can be applied to better understand housing careers, this book returned to Elder's five classic life course principles of life span development, timed events, linked lives, agency, and historical time and geographic place (Elder et al, 2003). Twelve conceptual tools were then derived from these five principles to provide a flexible toolbox of concepts that can be drawn on when studying residential processes. These conceptual tools can be used to design research and interpret empirical findings, or simply to help synthesise existing evidence in the manner adopted by this book.

Like the contents of any good toolbox, each of this book's twelve conceptual tools is customisable and multipurpose in that they can all be used in many different ways in lots of situations. Many examples of how each tool can be used have been discussed across the previous chapters and some of the most significant examples of housing career insights gained from using each conceptual tool are shown in Table 8.1. Readers interested in the full details about each of the tabulated examples are advised to revisit the chapters listed in parentheses in the right-hand column.

It is important to reiterate that these tools are not intended to form a definitive list to be applied in a certain way in every project. No single study

Table 8.1: Insights about housing careers obtained by using life course conceptual tools

Principle	Tool	Example insights (chapter numbers)
1. Life span	Biography	Past experiences of housesharing at university can shape future household structures (C4)
	Cumulation	Housing wealth gains disproportionately accrue to the most economically advantaged (C5)
2. Timing	Order and sequence	Couples' housing transitions often anticipate fertility (C3) Employment and housing transitions occur in varied orders (C5)
	Duration	Location-specific capital accumulates at university (C4) Longer exposures to bad housing worsen health (C6)
	Transitions and turning points	Separation has prolonged impacts on housing careers (C3) Onset of severe illness can reshape housing trajectories (C6)
	Timetables and scripts	Cultural norms affect age at leaving home and tenure choice (C3) Higher education systems influence migration patterns (C4/7)
3. Linked lives	Synchronisation and ripples	Boomerang moves to the parental home affect family relations (C3) Care needs can motivate moves to reduce distance to kin (C6)
	Solidarities	Parental transfers support child homeownership entry (C3) The geography of co-ethnic networks can influence mobility (C7)
	Household relations	Dual-career partners' spatially constrained job access constrains where skilled couples can live (C5)
4. Agency	Construction	Parental housing choices aim to get children into good schools (C4) Identity informs middle-class neighbourhood selection (C7)
5. Time and place	Cohort and period	Cohorts' varied educational experiences shape housing careers (C4) Recent cohorts' ownership entry was disrupted by the GFC (C5)
	Changing places	Pathways out of the parental home vary spatially (C3) Neighbourhood change is a life course process (C7)

can do everything effectively and so the selection of which tools to draw on and how to use, fuse and adapt them needs to be dictated by the research questions, knowledge of the topic and context, and by the other theories and conceptual frameworks that are being deployed. For example, the concept of biographies can be used to investigate how tenure sequences over the life span covary with partnership and fertility careers (Spallek et al, 2014), or, in a completely different fashion, to understand immigrants' interwoven job and housing precarity in a new society (Bailey et al, 2021). Researchers thus need to exercise judgement and pick which tools are most useful for their particular topic and questions. Although it is neither necessary nor possible for any single study to make detailed use of all twelve conceptual tools, it will nevertheless be helpful to always bear them all in mind when designing research and interpreting findings. The latter is perhaps particularly important as reflecting carefully on which aspects of the life course perspective have not or could not be explored can help researchers draw more sensitive and nuanced conclusions.

One example of how each of the twelve life course conceptual tools could be applied to develop our understanding of an important housing career process is shown in Table 8.2. This table shows how different strands of research could use each conceptual tool to improve our understanding of how homeownership fits into Global North life courses. The table is designed to illustrate one possible topical application and similar tables could be developed for many other housing career events or processes. Overall, the varied nature of the applications shown in Table 8.2 highlights how research using all the tools can – if the evidence is effectively integrated, synthesised and in some cases considered alongside deeper insights about subjectivities gained from pathways infused research – help us to build up a rich picture of contemporary residential career dynamics and their implications for social inequalities.

Ten guidelines

The life course conceptual toolbox can further our knowledge of housing careers by providing a shared research framework and vocabulary. This framework and vocabulary are still in their infancy and honing them is a priority for future work. Yet even so, the book's chapters collectively can still offer some much broader lessons for research, policy and public debates about housing and inequality. These wider points can be distilled into a series of ten straightforward guidelines that everyone can usefully keep in mind when conducting housing research or when engaging with debates and evidence about housing. Each of these ten guidelines is now briefly described in turn using one or two brief examples drawn from across the preceding chapters.

1. Two-way causality

Much of this book has focused on how housing careers are shaped firstly by processes in the careers of family, education, work and health and secondly

Table 8.2: Applying life course conceptual tools to homeownership-related questions

Tool	Example research strands
Biography	Multichannel sequence analysis of housing tenure and other careers (Spallek et al, 2014) or interviews about the place of homeownership goals in life plans
Cumulation	Longitudinal modelling to uncover how the type, timing and place of first home purchase influences subsequent housing wealth trajectories
Order and sequence	Survival analysis of how staying in the parental home versus moving out early to rent affect the timing of homeownership entry (Bayrakdar et al, 2019)
Duration	Survival analysis of the duration new homeowners spend in the tenure and why some subsequently exit owner-occupation (Wood et al, 2017)
Transitions and turning points	Longitudinal analysis of how timed events in other careers (for example unemployment, separation or fertility) affect ownership entry (Feijten, 2005)
Timetables and scripts	Narrative interviews exploring the age-grading of tenure preferences or quantitative analysis of when parents provide gifts to support homebuying
Synchronisation and ripples	Quantitative or qualitative analysis of the adjustments to labour force participation and family care partners make in order to afford homeownership
Solidarities	Modelling the receipt and tenure impacts of family transfers (Suh, 2020) and qualitative work to unpack how these are interpreted
Household relations	Analysis of how tenure impacts on partnership stability (Coulter and Thomas, 2019) or partners' labour force participation over the life span
Construction	Interviews exploring how tenures are stigmatised/valorised and related to perceived social status, class identities and family-related norms
Cohort and period	Modelling to examine which life course, economic and housing factors explain how age-graded homeownership rates have changed across birth cohorts
Changing places	Small-area analysis of how shifts in local tenure mix and housing affordability affect population composition and migration flows (Paccoud, 2017)

by the structure of the social and spatial environment. However, each chapter also shows that causality never flows in only one direction, as housing career processes always have some influence on these other domains (Mulder, 2006). For example, Chapter 5 showed that employment events and job opportunities shape residential behaviours but that housing career processes in turn impact on labour markets (for example by influencing self-employment practices). Similarly, Chapter 6 stressed that health and care dynamics influence residential behaviour but that housing also helps to determine health.

It is therefore important to recognise that *housing and other life course dynamics always influence each other.* Changes anywhere in the life course can thus have knock-on consequences for housing careers and vice versa.

2. Intersections

The concept of intersectionality captures how combinations of characteristics (for example of gender, education, ethnicity and/or sexuality categories) matter for social privilege and disadvantage. The basic idea is that each characteristic does not have a simple one-to-one relationship to (dis)advantage as what matters more is how the categories overlap and interact. This is a useful insight for understanding housing and life course dynamics as all chapters of this book show how various combinations of characteristics stratify residential processes in ways that are missed when looking only at one category at a time. For example, Chapter 3 discussed how local opportunity structures shape the home-leaving options of working-class youth more than their middle-class counterparts. Meanwhile, Chapter 5 emphasised that age, time and place of home purchases intersect to govern subsequent asset accumulation trajectories.

This discussion shows that it is always necessary to consider how *interactions and combinations of life course attributes matter for housing career processes*.

3. Diversity

Agency is a core principle of the life course perspective and this agency – along with the fact that lives are often unpredictable and shaped by external events – means that a diversity of process and outcome are always to be expected within housing careers. However, neither quantitative nor qualitative approaches currently provide a rich understanding of housing career diversity. On the quantitative side, the use of global regression models estimating one coefficient per variable or a limited number of interaction terms does not allow much diversity in process or outcome to be uncovered. By contrast, qualitative studies can provide rich detail on individuals' housing career processes but, for obvious reasons, can say less about the general prevalence or patterning of particular processes across the entire population. Overall, it seems that multiple methods often need to be brought to bear to effectively describe and also explain diversity in both objective and subjective housing careers (Clapham et al, 2014).

The key point that emerges from this is that *diversity in housing and life course dynamics are to be expected and should be treated as something to be described and explained*.

4. Stability and change

Housing careers are comprised of spells in states divided by transitions. Yet although spells and transitions are both constitutive elements of the housing career, it is the latter which usually attracts most of the attention. This imbalance is problematic for several reasons. First, residential stability is often a desired and valued aspect of housing careers, for example among parents whose children are attending school (Chapters 3–4). Spells spent in a particular dwelling are often very meaningful and can form a crucial part of personal identity. Second, many people do not move in response to changes elsewhere in the life course and Chapter 7 shows that the balance of who moves and who stays as lives change is an important driver of local population dynamics. Third, Chapters 3, 5 and 7 showed that remaining in the parental home or in a well-known locality is a strategy that less advantaged groups use to help navigate an insecure labour market and to avoid spaces perceived as hostile. This implies that periods of stability are not just an absence of movement but can be an active strategy people use to achieve particular ends (Preece, 2018). Subjectivities and housing-related practices may also change during periods of residential stability (Clapham, 2005).

This discussion indicates that *periods of 'stability' are as important for housing careers as moments of change.*

5. Multiple dimensions of time

This book has consistently stressed that time can be understood to have multiple dimensions which all have a bearing on housing careers. These multiple dimensions of time include:

1. processes linked to biographical *ageing* such as changes in health (Chapter 6) or the accumulation of wealth (Chapter 5);
2. differences in the size of birth *cohorts* and in the constellations of opportunities and constraints each cohort experiences as its members enter and move through a housing system in shared chronological time;
3. *period effects* at particular historical moments (for example the GFC), which may have uneven or age-graded impacts;
4. the *absolute timing* and *relative ordering* of events within life course biographies as well as the *duration* of states; and
5. the *timing of housing events relative to social timetables and scripts* such as the normative age for leaving the parental home (Chapter 3).

While no single study can ever fully unpack all of these, when interpreting evidence about residential behaviours it is very important to be aware that *multiple dimensions of time and temporal process are always relevant for housing career processes and outcomes.*

6. Placing housing careers

All of the book's chapters have demonstrated that local, regional and national settings shape residential processes and how they interact with other life course dynamics. This might seem a basic point, but it is one that is often missed amid the prevailing tendency to conduct country-level analysis. Chapter 3 showed that for some processes geographical patterning is very influential (for example there are major differences in the age at which young people leave home across Europe), whereas for others it is surprisingly small (for instance separation seems to affect housing mobility in a fairly consistent way across contexts). The reasons for levels of spatial patterning in housing processes as well as the magnitude, direction and scale at which geographical settings influence housing careers are thus important empirical questions. Moreover, Chapter 7 reminds us that housing career processes themselves change the social composition of places as people with different attributes selectively make decisions to move or stay as their lives change. Geographical processes like segregation or gentrification are therefore not abstract phenomena but rather are driven by the residential behaviours of individuals and households over the life course. Housing careers are thus one way in which changes in lives, places and society constantly influence each other.

Overall, the key point to bear in mind is that *housing careers are shaped by geographic settings, while residential behaviour also reshapes places.*

7. Connected lives

Housing research has traditionally viewed households as the main actors in the housing system. However, several limitations of this approach emerge when housing careers are viewed through a life course lens. First, the life course perspective reminds us that households are not stable units but rather form, disband and experience compositional changes over time through births, deaths, split-off exits, joining moves and outright dissolutions. Second, households are not unified units as they are often comprised of separate individuals who have their own biographies, preferences, needs and goals. Individual agency may pull household members who want to live together in different directions and so household-level housing decisions often involve tricky and power-laden interpersonal processes of bargaining and negotiation. Third, housing careers are often shaped by the life course dynamics of non-resident others whom household members are linked to through social or kin bonds. For example, Chapter 3 described how intergenerational assistance enables some contemporary young adults to enter owner-occupation, while Chapter 7 argued that rich local social networks and support exchanges can motivate some migrants and ethnic minorities to value living in residential clusters. Taken together, these three points imply that housing careers should be conceptualised at the level of individuals and not households. These individual housing careers do not, however, unfold in an atomised fashion, as the careers of different individuals often interact and may run together for long periods (for example when in a committed partnership).

This discussion indicates that *individuals have housing careers, but these often intersect and are shaped by relationships to other people both inside and outside the household.*

8. Transformative connections

Recent scholarship emphasises that housing careers are not simply influenced in a passive fashion by the lives of significant others. Instead, lives are relational as the connections between people, their identities and, in some cases, the wider trajectory of their life courses are all actively and constantly transformed by the interactions between individuals' decisions and behaviours. For example, Chapter 3 discussed how boomerang moves by adult children not only transform the housing pathways of parents and their offspring but can also reshape their intergenerational relations. Parental help for children's housing purchases (Chapter 3) or intergenerational childcare or later-life care exchanges (Chapters 3 and 6) are further examples of housing-related practices that actively transform the pre-existing relationships linking lives together. Housing careers are therefore a site where linked lives are refashioned over the life course (Holdsworth, 2013).

The take-home message here is that *housing career processes can reshape social relationships, perhaps especially within families.*

9. Beyond housing policy

Chapter 1 argued that residential behaviours are influenced by current and historic public policies. However, while it is tempting to concentrate on the impacts of housing policy, such an approach is inevitably partial as it is often policies related to other life course domains that most strongly influence the structure of housing careers (Lupton, 2016). Essentially, housing is a domain that spans government departments and so policies across a whole range of areas need to be factored into all housing analysis. All chapters of this book have therefore attempted to show how policy interventions across a diverse range of fields, including labour markets, immigration, education, taxation and social security, have impacted on housing careers in ways that have often been unequal and sometimes unforeseen. This complexity makes it very difficult to conduct large cross-national comparisons as deep local knowledge of institutional developments, policies, definitions (for example of tenure or affordability) and political-economic history is essential for fully grasping how each country's housing system works (Lowe, 2011). One empirical solution is to move away from large multi-country comparisons towards more targeted comparative analysis of a much smaller number of better-known contexts (Thomas and Mulder, 2016).

To sum up, *policies across the whole range of government domains influence housing careers in complex and sometimes contradictory and unforeseen ways.* Many housing-related problems thus cannot be solved purely through housing interventions.

10. Longitudinal methods

This final guideline is neither complex nor especially novel. All chapters of this book have repeatedly stressed that longitudinal approaches where people's life courses are tracked through time provide the most powerful window into residential career processes. Longitudinal analysis is more powerful than analysis of snapshots of time as many life course concepts such as cumulation or event timing are almost impossible to explore using cross-sectional data. Moreover, knowing when events happen and in what order allows causality to be more deeply assessed (and in some cases tested) than is possible with cross-sectional snapshots. While longitudinal research is certainly becoming common within the housing field, it is more technically complex than cross-sectional work and it also requires richer data resources. Fortunately, a growing number of longitudinal housing-related datasets are now available, ranging from cohort and panel surveys, administrative population registers and longitudinally linked census data through to repurposed consumer registers. Researchers are also increasingly experimenting with qualitative longitudinal approaches such as repeat interviews.

Overall, *longitudinal data where the same individuals are followed through time provide a particularly rich resource for empirically examining housing and life course dynamics.*

Summary

This book has developed a modern life course approach to conceptualise and analyse residential decision-making and behaviour and the implications these have for other aspects of people's lives, for places and for social inequalities. This life course approach was sketched early in the book before later chapters then applied Chapter 2's conceptual toolbox to integrate and synthesise what we know about housing and life course dynamics (with a particular focus on Britain). This final chapter has drawn the book to a close by revisiting the life course perspective and demonstrating how the twelve conceptual tools can offer a powerful framework for future housing-related scholarship. The chapter has also derived ten broad guidelines that scholars, policymakers and anyone interested in housing issues can reflect on when conducting research or engaging in housing-related debates.

Housing constitutes one of the most important public policy challenges of the coming decades and solving contemporary housing problems in ways which also help us address the 21st century's other significant challenges – in particular mitigating and adapting to the climate crisis while reducing social inequalities – will require looking beyond provision towards how people move through housing systems as their lives change. This book contributes to this agenda by bringing people and their lives to the forefront of 21st-century research and debates about housing.

Notes

Chapter 1

[1] Unemployment rates are, however, considerably higher for younger Britons.

[2] The extent to which migrants cluster in these types of location does vary significantly across groups. For instance, many Eastern European migrants arriving since 2004 initially moved to rural areas with shortages of agricultural labour.

[3] This does not mean that age- or phase-based analysis – for example examining housing in later life – is always inappropriate. Such studies are very valuable if they aim to better understand the diversity of residential processes and outcomes people experience at similar biological ages or the ways these change over time.

Chapter 2

[1] Ideas of housing histories and biographies have also been used sporadically (Forrest, 1987).

[2] Mulder and Hooimeijer's (1999) model says little about the role biographical context plays in residential decisions.

[3] This 'strong' model of residential biographies resonates with Clapham's (2005) pathways approach.

Chapter 3

[1] This book concentrates on the adult life course as adults are the main actors in residential decision-making. Housing is, of course, also a crucial domain in children's lives and one which has been significantly understudied.

[2] Even with deposit support, most prospective first-time buyers will still need to demonstrate to a lender that they have a sufficient income and job security to meet their mortgage repayments.

Chapter 4

[1] These authors estimate that 75 per cent of all UK moves are made by those aged 17–35.

[2] One obvious difference is that student lettings markets tend to run to seasonal timetables aligned to local HEI term dates.

[3] Children from lower-income families are generally much more likely to go to their local school than children from more affluent families (Piekut, 2021). This means that policies to promote school choice often favour middle-class parents with the resources to pay for children's travel.

Chapter 5

[1] Rossi's focus on family life cycle drivers is understandable given that his study examined local moves within Philadelphia.

[2] It is usually easiest for policies or businesses to alter protections, support or entitlements through a process of 'cohort layering' (Kemp, 2015). Layering involves bringing in new terms and conditions for new entrants while leaving insiders on the pre-existing framework.

[3] Right to Buy was an experimental privatisation but not a total rupture as Murie (2016, p 26) estimates that around 288,000 council homes were sold between 1960 and 1979.

[4] Housing assets and low living costs associated with outright ownership could have conflictual effects if they encourage early retirement. Surprisingly little is known about this.

Chapter 6

[1] Key to this was the assumption that living in cramped high-density housing fosters social and spiritual ills ranging from drinking, incest, promiscuity and family breakdown through to reduced churchgoing.

[2] It is important to note that this division is artificial as there are many overlaps, interactions and blurred boundaries between the three domains.

[3] Many of the points raised here are nonetheless valid to care provision at other life stages.

[4] Grundy (2011) notes that this should largely be seen as a positive trend as higher incomes, better health and improvements in technologies within the home, in transport and in communications enable older people to live independently for longer. Nonetheless, she also observes that individualism and longer working hours (particularly among women) may have reduced family members' ability and inclination to care for older relatives.

Chapter 7

[1] Heated debate about terminology, and whether a particular process is pernicious or benign, is a feature of most subfields of neighbourhoods research.

[2] To keep the diagram legible, the arrows in Figure 7.2 show only the most important lines of causality.

[3] This episode also illustrates the danger of using value-laden terms such as enclave or ghetto. Although Phillips later apologised for 'mangling' some of the evidence, he has strongly defended his conclusions and has developed them further in subsequent media appearances.

[4] This is sometimes termed the racial proxy hypothesis as the race or ethnicity of incomers acts as a visible proxy for perceived social problems.

[5] Bailey (2012) also observes that the social security system to some extent insulates people from having to move in response to economic shocks.

[6] Early evaluation of the coalition government's housing benefit cuts suggested this had led some landlords in high-demand areas to cease offering tenancies to claimants (Beatty et al, 2014).

References

Abraham, M., Auspurg, K. and Hinz, T. (2010) 'Migration decisions within dual-earner partnerships: a test of bargaining theory', *Journal of Marriage and Family*, 72(4): 876–92.

Andrew, M. (2012) 'The changing route to owner-occupation: the impact of borrowing constraints on young adult homeownership transitions in Britain in the 1990s', *Urban Studies*, 49(8): 1659–78.

Arnett, J.J. (2000) 'Emerging adulthood: a theory of development from the late teens through the twenties', *American Psychologist*, 55(5): 469–80.

Artamonova, A., Brandén, M., Gillespie, B.J. and Mulder, C.H. (2021) 'Adult children's gender, number and proximity and older parents' moves to institutions: evidence from Sweden', *Ageing and Society*, (2): 342–72.

Arundel, R. (2017) 'Equity inequity: housing wealth inequality, inter and intra-generational divergences, and the rise of private landlordism', *Housing, Theory and Society*, 34(2): 176–200.

Arundel, R. and Doling, J. (2017) 'The end of mass homeownership? Changes in labour markets and housing tenure opportunities across Europe', *Journal of Housing and the Built Environment*, 32(4): 649–72.

Arundel, R. and Lennartz, C. (2017) 'Returning to the parental home: boomerang moves of younger adults and the welfare regime context', *Journal of European Social Policy*, 27(3): 276–94.

Arundel, R. and Ronald, R. (2016) 'Parental co-residence, shared living and emerging adulthood in Europe: semi-dependent housing across welfare regime and housing system contexts', *Journal of Youth Studies*, 19(7): 885–905.

Arundel, R. and Ronald, R. (2021) 'The false promise of homeownership: homeowner societies in an era of declining access and rising inequality', *Urban Studies*, 58(6): 1120–40.

Atkinson, R. and Jacobs, K. (2016) *House, Home and Society*, London: Palgrave.

Bailey, A.J. (2009) 'Population geography: lifecourse matters', *Progress in Human Geography*, 33(3): 407–18.

Bailey, A.J., Ng, R.W.Y., Hankins, K. and De Beer, S. (2021) 'Migration, precariousness, and the linked lives of newcomers in Hong Kong', *Population, Space and Place*, 27: e2400.

Bailey, N. (2012) 'How spatial segregation changes over time: sorting out the sorting processes', *Environment and Planning A*, 44(3): 705–22.

Baker, E., Bentley, R., Lester, L. and Beer, A. (2016) 'Housing affordability and residential mobility as drivers of locational inequality', *Applied Geography*, 72: 65–75.

Baker, E., Bentley, R. and Mason, K. (2013) 'The mental health effects of housing tenure: causal or compositional?', *Urban Studies*, 50(2): 426–42.

Bangham, G. (2019) *Game of Homes: The Rise of Multiple Property Ownership in Great Britain*, London: Resolution Foundation. Available from: https://www.resolutionfoundation.org/publications/game-of-homes-the-rise-of-multiple-property-ownership-in-great-britain/

Battu, H., Ma, A. and Phimister, E. (2008) 'Housing tenure, job mobility and unemployment in the UK', *The Economic Journal*, 118(527): 311–28.

Bayrakdar, S. and Coulter, R. (2018) 'Parents, local house prices, and leaving home in Britain', *Population, Space and Place*, 24(2): e2087.

Bayrakdar, S., Coulter R., Lersch, P. and Vidal, S. (2019) 'Family formation, parental background and young adults' first entry into homeownership in Britain and Germany', *Housing Studies*, 34(6): 974–96.

Beatty, C., Cole, I., Powell, R., Kemp, P., Brewer, M., Browne, J. et al (2014) *The Impact of Recent Reforms to Local Housing Allowances: Summary of Key Findings*, London: DWP. Available from: https://www.gov.uk/government/publications/local-housing-allowance-monitoring-the-impact-of-changes

Beer, A. and Faulkner, D. with Paris, C. and Clower, T. (2011) *Housing Transitions through the Life Course: Aspirations, Needs and Policy*, Bristol: Policy Press.

Bentley, R.J., Pevalin, D., Baker, E., Mason, K., Reeves, A. and Beer, A. (2016) 'Housing affordability, tenure and mental health in Australia and the United Kingdom: a comparative panel analysis', *Housing Studies*, 31(2): 208–22.

Bernard, A., Bell, M. and Charles-Edwards, E. (2016) 'Internal migration age patterns and the transition to adulthood: Australia and Great Britain compared', *Journal of Population Research*, 33(2): 123–46.

Bernardi, L., Huinink, J. and Settersten, R.A. (2019) 'The life course cube: a tool for studying lives', *Advances in Life Course Research*, 41: 100258.

Berngruber, A. (2016) 'Leaving the parental home as a transition marker to adulthood', in A. Furlong (ed) *Routledge Handbook of Youth and Young Adulthood* (2nd edn), Abingdon: Routledge, pp 193–8.

Berrington, A. and Murphy, M. (1994) 'Changes in the living arrangements of young adults in Britain during the 1980s', *European Sociological Review*, 10(3): 235–57.

Berrington, A. and Simpson, L. (2016) 'Household composition and housing need', in T. Champion and J. Falkingham (eds) *Population Change in the United Kingdom*, London: Rowman & Littlefield International, pp 105–24.

Berrington, A. and Stone, J. (2014) 'Young adults' transitions to residential independence in the UK: the role of social and housing policy', in L. Antonucci, M. Hamilton and S. Roberts (eds) *Young People and Social Policy in Europe: Dealing with Risk, Inequality and Precarity in Times of Crisis*, Basingstoke: Palgrave Macmillan, pp 210–35.

Berrington, A., Duta, A. and Wakeling, P. (2017) 'Youth social citizenship and class inequalities in transitions to adulthood in the UK', CPC Working Paper 81, Southampton: CPC. Available from: http://www.cpc.ac.uk/publications/cpc_working_papers/pdf/2017_WP81_Youth_social_citiz enship_Berrington_et_al.pdf

Blanchflower, D. and Oswald, A. (2013) *The Danger of High Home Ownership: Greater Unemployment*, London: CAGE/Chatham House. Available from: https://www.chathamhouse.org/sites/default/files/pub lic/Research/International%20Economics/1013bp_homeownership.pdf

Böheim, R. and Taylor, M.P. (2002) 'Tied down or room to move? Investigating the relationships between housing tenure, employment status and residential mobility in Britain', *Scottish Journal of Political Economy*, 49(4): 369–92.

Borg, I. and Brandén, M. (2018) 'Do high levels of home-ownership create unemployment? Introducing the missing link between housing tenure and unemployment', *Housing Studies*, 33(4): 501–24.

Bowie, D. (2017) *Radical Solutions to the Housing Supply Crisis*, Bristol: Policy Press.

Braubach, M. and Fairburn, J. (2010) 'Social inequities in environmental risks associated with housing and residential location: a review of evidence', *The European Journal of Public Health*, 20(1): 36–42.

Brewer, M. and Nandi, A. (2014) 'Partnership dissolution: how does it affect income, employment and well-being?', ISER Working Paper 2014–30, Colchester: ISER. Available from: https://www.iser.essex.ac.uk/research/publications/working-papers/iser/2014-30

Broadway Homelessness and Support (2010) *Street to Home: Bulletin, 2009/10*, London: Broadway. Available from: https://www.mungos.org/app/uploads/2017/07/chain_street_to_home_bulletin_2009-10.pdf

Brown, T. and King, P. (2005) 'The power to choose: effective choice and housing policy', *European Journal of Housing Policy*, 5(1): 59–75.

Butler, T. and Hamnett, C. (2012) 'Social geographic interpretations of housing spaces', in D. Clapham, W.A.V. Clark and K. Gibb (eds) *The SAGE Handbook of Housing Studies*, London: SAGE, pp 147–62.

Cantle, T. and Kaufmann, E. (2016) 'Is segregation on the increase in the UK?', *openDemocracy*, [online], Available from: https://www.opendemocr acy.net/en/is-segregation-on-increase-in-uk/

Catney, G. (2016) 'Exploring a decade of small area ethnic (de-)segregation in England and Wales', *Urban Studies*, 53(8): 1691–709.

CDRC (2021) 'Temporal OAC', [online], Available from: https://data.cdrc.ac.uk/dataset/temporal-oac

Champion, T. (2012) 'Testing the return migration element of the "escalator region" model: an analysis of migration into and out of south-east England, 1966–2001', *Cambridge Journal of Regions, Economy and Society*, 5(2): 255–70.

Champion, T. and Shuttleworth, I. (2017) 'Is longer-distance migration slowing? An analysis of the annual record for England and Wales since the 1970s', *Population, Space and Place*, 23(3): e2024.

Champion, T., Coombes, M. and Gordon, I. (2014) 'How far do England's second-order cities emulate London as human-capital "escalators"?', *Population, Space and Place*, 20(5): 421–33.

Chen, Y. and Rosenthal, S.S. (2008) 'Local amenities and life-cycle migration: do people move for jobs or fun?', *Journal of Urban Economics*, 64(3): 519–37.

Cho, Y. and Whitehead, C. (2013) 'The immobility of social tenants: is it true? Does it matter?', *Journal of Housing and the Built Environment*, 28(4): 705–26.

Christophers, B. (2018) 'Intergenerational inequality? Labour, capital, and housing through the ages', *Antipode*, 50(1): 101–21.

Christophers, B. (2019) 'The rentierization of the United Kingdom economy', *Environment and Planning A*, doi: 10.1177/0308518X19873007.

Clair, A. and Hughes, A. (2019) 'Housing and health: new evidence using biomarker data', *Journal of Epidemiology and Community Health*, 73(3): 256–62.

Clapham, D. (2005) *The Meaning of Housing: A Pathways Approach*, Bristol: Policy Press.

Clapham, D., Mackie, P., Orford, S., Thomas, I. and Buckley, K. (2014) 'The housing pathways of young people in the UK', *Environment and Planning A*, 46(8): 2016–31.

Clark, A. (2009) 'Moving through deprived neighbourhoods', *Population, Space and Place*, 15(5): 523–33.

Clark, W.A.V. (2012) 'Do women delay family formation in expensive housing markets?', *Demographic Research*, 27(1): 1–24.

Clark, W.A.V. (2013a) 'The aftermath of the general financial crisis for the ownership society: what happened to low-income homeowners in the US?', *International Journal of Housing Policy*, 13(3): 227–46.

Clark, W.A.V. (2013b) 'Life course events and residential change: unpacking age effects on the probability of moving', *Journal of Population Research*, 30(4): 319–34.

Clark, W.A.V. (2021) *Advanced Introduction to Housing Studies*, Cheltenham: Edward Elgar.

Clark, W.A.V. and Coulter, R. (2015) 'Who wants to move? The role of neighbourhood change', *Environment and Planning A*, 47(12): 2683–709.

Clark, W.A.V. and Davies Withers, S. (1999) 'Changing jobs and changing houses: mobility outcomes of employment transitions', *Journal of Regional Science*, 39(4): 653–73.

Clark, W.A.V. and Dieleman F. (1996) *Households and Housing: Choice and Outcomes in the Housing Market*, New Brunswick, NJ: Center for Urban Policy Research.

Clark, W.A.V. and Lisowski, W. (2017) 'Prospect theory and the decision to move or stay', *Proceedings of the National Academy of Sciences*, 114(36): E7432–E7440.

Clark, W.A.V. and Morrison, P.S. (2012) 'Socio-spatial mobility and residential sorting: evidence from a large-scale survey', *Urban Studies*, 49(15): 3253–70.

Clark, W.A.V., Deurloo, M. and Dieleman, F. (2003) 'Housing careers in the United States, 1968–93: modelling the sequencing of housing states', *Urban Studies*, 40(1): 143–60.

Clark, W.A.V., van Ham, M. and Coulter, R. (2014) 'Spatial mobility and social outcomes', *Journal of Housing and the Built Environment*, 29(4): 699–727.

Climate Change Committee (2021) 'Independent Assessment of UK Climate Risk: Advice to Government for the UK's Third Climate Risk Assessment (CCRA3)', 16 June 2021, [online], Available from: https://www.theccc.org.uk/publication/independent-assessment-of-uk-climate-risk/

Cooke, T.J. (2008) 'Gender role beliefs and family migration', *Population, Space and Place*, 14(2): 163–75.

Cooke, T.J., Mulder, C.H. and Thomas, M. (2016) 'Union dissolution and migration', *Demographic Research*, 34(26): 741–60.

Core Cities (2019) *Understanding the Growth in Private Rented Housing*, Manchester: Core Cities. Available from: https://www.corecities.com/publications

Corlett, A. and Judge, L. (2017) *Home Affront: Housing across the Generations*, London: Resolution Foundation. Available from: http://www.resolutionfoundation.org/publications/home-affront-housing-across-the-generations/

Coulter, R. (2017) 'Local house prices, parental background and young adults' homeownership in England and Wales', *Urban Studies*, 54(14): 3360–79.

Coulter, R. (2018) 'Parental background and housing outcomes in young adulthood', *Housing Studies*, 33(2): 201–23.

Coulter, R. and Clark, W.A.V. (2019) 'Ethnic disparities in neighbourhood selection: understanding the role of income', *International Journal of Urban and Regional Research*, 43(5): 947–62.

Coulter, R. and Hu, Y. (2017) 'Living apart together and cohabitation intentions in Great Britain', *Journal of Family Issues*, 38(12): 1701–29.

Coulter, R. and Thomas, M. (2019) 'A new look at the housing antecedents of separation', *Demographic Research*, 40(26): 725–60.

Coulter, R. and van Ham, M. (2013) 'Following people through time: an analysis of individual residential mobility biographies', *Housing Studies*, 28(7): 1037–55.

Coulter, R., van Ham, M. and Feijten, P. (2011) 'A longitudinal analysis of moving desires, expectations and actual moving behaviour', *Environment and Planning A*, 43(11): 2742–60.

Coulter, R., van Ham, M. and Findlay, A.M. (2016) 'Re-thinking residential mobility: linking lives through time and space', *Progress in Human Geography*, 40(3): 352–74.

Crawford, J. and McKee, K. (2018) 'Hysteresis: understanding the housing aspirations gap', *Sociology*, 52(1): 182–97.

Damhuis, R., van Gent, W., Hochstenbach, C. and Musterd, S. (2019) 'The regional and local dynamics of life course and housing', in M. Moos (ed) *A Research Agenda for Housing*, Cheltenham: Edward Elgar, pp 165–81.

Darlington-Pollock, F., Lomax, N. and Norman, P. (2019) 'Ethnic internal migration: the importance of age and migrant status', *The Geographical Journal*, 185(1): 68–81.

DCLG (2017) *Fixing Our Broken Housing Market*, London: DCLG.

De Groot, C., Mulder, C.H., Das, M. and Manting, D. (2011) 'Life events and the gap between intention to move and actual mobility', *Environment and Planning A*, 43(1): 48–66.

De Jong, G.F. and Fawcett, J.T. (1981) 'Motivations for migration: an assessment and a value-expectancy research model', in G.F. De Jong and R.W. Gardner (eds) *Migration Decision Making: Multidisciplinary Approaches to Microlevel Studies in Developed and Developing Countries*, Oxford: Pergamon, pp 13–58.

DfE (2019a) *Childcare and Early Years Survey of Parents in England, 2019*, London: DfE. Available from: https://assets.publishing.service.gov.uk/government/uploads/system/uploads/attachment_data/file/853358/CEYSP_2019_Report.pdf

DfE (2019b) *Independent Panel Report to the Review of Post-18 Education and Funding*, London: DfE.

DfE (2020) 'Academic year 2018/19: progression to higher education or training', [online], Available from: https://explore-education-statistics.service.gov.uk/find-statistics/progression-to-higher-education-or-training/2018-19

DLUHC (2021) *Housing supply: net additional dwellings, England: 2020 to 2021*, [online], Available from: https://www.gov.uk/government/statistics/housing-supply-net-additional-dwellings-england-2020-to-2021

Druta, O. and Ronald, R. (2017) 'Young adults' pathways into homeownership and the negotiation of intra-family support: a home, the ideal gift', *Sociology*, 51(4): 783–99.

Duncan, S., Carter, J., Phillips, M., Roseneil, S. and Stoilova, M. (2013) 'Why do people live apart together?', *Families, Relationships and Societies*, 2(3): 323–38.

DWP (2019) 'Benefit caseload and expenditure tables 2019', [online], Available from: https://www.gov.uk/government/publications/benefit-expenditure-and-caseload-tables-2019

Elder, G.H. and George, L.K. (2016) 'Age, cohorts and the life course' in M.J. Shanahan, J.T. Mortimer and M. Kirkpatrick Johnson (eds) (2016) *Handbook of the Life Course: Volume II*, Cham, Switzerland: Springer, pp 59–85.

Elder, G.H., Johnson, M.K. and Crosnoe, R. (2003) 'The emergence and development of life course theory', in J.T. Mortimer and M.J. Shanahan (eds) *Handbook of the Life Course*, Boston, MA: Kluwer Academic/Plenum Publishers, pp 3–19.

Ermisch, J. (1999) 'Prices, parents, and young people's household formation', *Journal of Urban Economics*, 45(1): 47–71.

Ermisch, J. and Jenkins, S.P. (1999) 'Retirement and housing adjustment in later life: evidence from the British Household Panel Survey', *Labour Economics*, 6(2): 311–33.

Ermisch, J. and Washbrook, E. (2012) 'Residential mobility: wealth, demographic and housing market effects', *Scottish Journal of Political Economy*, 59(5): 483–99.

Evandrou, M., Falkingham, J., Qin, M. and Vlachtoni, A. (2020) 'Changing living arrangements, family dynamics and stress during lockdown: evidence from four birth cohorts in the UK', *SocArXiv*, [online], Available from: https://osf.io/preprints/socarxiv/kv8dg/

Evandrou, M., Falkingham, J. and Green, M. (2010) 'Migration in later life: evidence from the British Household Panel Study', *Population Trends*, 141: 74–91.

Faggian, A. and McCann, P. (2009) 'Universities, agglomerations and graduate human capital mobility', *Tijdschrift voor Economische en Sociale Geografie*, 100(2): 210–22.

Falkingham, J., Sage, J., Stone, J. and Vlachantoni, A. (2016) 'Residential mobility across the life course: continuity and change across three cohorts in Britain', *Advances in Life Course Research*, 30: 111–23.

FCA (2021) 'Mortgage lending statistics', [online], Available from: https://www.fca.org.uk/data/mortgage-lending-statistics

Feijten, P. (2005) *Life Events and the Housing Career: A Retrospective Analysis of Timed Effects*, Delft: Eburon.

Feijten, P. and Mulder, C.H. (2002) 'The timing of household events and housing events in the Netherlands: a longitudinal perspective', *Housing Studies*, 17(5): 773–92.

Feijten, P. and van Ham, M. (2010) 'The impact of splitting up and divorce on housing careers in the UK', *Housing Studies*, 25(4): 483–507.

Feijten, P., Hooimeijer, P. and Mulder, C.H. (2008) 'Residential experience and residential environment choice over the life-course', *Urban Studies*, 45(1): 141–62.

Felstead, A. and Reuschke, D. (2021) 'A flash in the pan or a permanent change? The growth of homeworking during the pandemic and its effect on employee productivity in the UK', *Information Technology & People*, doi: 10.1108/ITP-11-2020-0758.

Ferreira, F., Gyourko, J. and Tracy, J. (2010) 'Housing busts and household mobility', *Journal of Urban Economics*, 68(1): 34–45.

Fielding, A. (1992) 'Migration and social mobility: South East England as an escalator region', *Regional Studies*, 26(1): 1–15.

Finney, N. (2011) 'Understanding ethnic differences in the migration of young adults within Britain from a lifecourse perspective', *Transactions of the Institute of British Geographers*, 36(3): 455–70.

Finney, N., Catney G. and Phillips, D. (2015) 'Ethnicity and internal migration', in D. Smith, N. Finney, K. Halfacree and N. Walford (eds) *Internal Migration: Geographical Perspectives and Processes*, Farnham: Ashgate, pp 31–46.

Flowerdew, R. and Al-Hamad, A. (2004) 'The relationship between marriage, divorce and migration in a British data set', *Journal of Ethnic and Migration Studies*, 30(2): 339–51.

Ford, J., Rugg, J. and Burrows, R. (2002) 'Conceptualising the contemporary role of housing in the transition to adult life in England', *Urban Studies*, 39(13): 2455–67.

Forrest, R. (1987) 'Spatial mobility, tenure mobility, and emerging social divisions in the UK housing market', *Environment and Planning A*, 19(12): 1611–30.

Forrest, R. and Hirayama, Y. (2018) 'Late home ownership and social re-stratification', *Economy and Society*, 47(2): 257–79.

Galster, G. (2012) 'Neighborhoods and their role in creating and changing housing', in D. Clapham, K. Gibb and W.A.V. Clark (eds) *The SAGE Handbook of Housing Studies*, London: SAGE, pp 84–106.

Galster, G. and Wessel, T. (2019) 'Reproduction of social inequality through housing: a three-generational study from Norway', *Social Science Research*, 78: 119–36.

Gamsu, S., Donnelly, M. and Harris, R. (2019) 'The spatial dynamics of race in the transition to university: diverse cities and White campuses in UK higher education', *Population, Space and Place*, 25(5): e2222.

Gibb, K. (2012) 'Institutional economics', in D. Clapham, W.A.V. Clark and K. Gibb (eds) *The SAGE Handbook of Housing Studies*, London: SAGE, pp 131–46.

Gibson, M., Petticrew, M., Bambra, C., Sowden, A.J., Wright, K.E. and Whitehead, M. (2011) 'Housing and health inequalities: a synthesis of systematic reviews of interventions aimed at different pathways linking housing and health', *Health & Place*, 17(1): 175–84.

Goetz, E.G. (2013) 'Too good to be true? The variable and contingent benefits of displacement and relocation among low-income public housing residents', *Housing Studies*, 28(2): 235–52.

Gordon, I., Champion, T. and Coombes, M. (2015) 'Urban escalators and interregional elevators: the difference that location, mobility, and sectoral specialisation make to occupational progression', *Environment and Planning A*, 47(3): 588–606.

Gram-Hanssen, K. and Bech-Danielsen, C. (2008) 'Home dissolution: what happens after separation?', *Housing Studies*, 23(3): 507–22.

Green, A. (2017) *The Crisis for Young People: Generational Inequalities in Education, Work, Housing and Welfare*, London: Palgrave Macmillan.

Green, A.E. (2018) 'Understanding the drivers of internal migration', in T. Champion, T. Cooke and I. Shuttleworth (eds) *Internal Migration in the Developed World: Are We Becoming Less Mobile?*, London: Routledge, pp 31–55.

Grenier, A. (2015) 'Transitions, time and later life', in J. Twigg and W. Martin (eds) *Routledge Handbook of Cultural Gerontology*, London: Routledge, pp 404–10.

Grundy, E. (2011) 'Household transitions and subsequent mortality among older people in England and Wales: trends over three decades', *Journal of Epidemiology and Community Health*, 65(4): 353–9.

Halfacree, K.H. and Boyle, P.J. (1993) 'The challenge facing migration research: the case for a biographical approach', *Progress in Human Geography*, 17(3): 333–48.

Hamnett, C. (1999) *Winners and Losers: Home Ownership in Modern Britain*, London: UCL Press.

Hamnett, C. and Reades, J. (2019) 'Mind the gap: implications of overseas investment for regional house price divergence in Britain', *Housing Studies*, 34(3): 388–406.

Heath, S. and Calvert, E. (2013) 'Gifts, loans and intergenerational support for young adults', *Sociology*, 47(6): 1120–35.

Hedman, L. (2013) 'Moving near family? The influence of extended family on neighbourhood choice in an intra-urban context', *Population, Space and Place*, 19(1): 32–45.

Herbers, D.J., Mulder, C.H. and Mòdenes, J.A. (2014) 'Moving out of home ownership in later life: the influence of the family and housing careers', *Housing Studies*, 29(7): 910–36.

HESA (2022) 'Who's studying in HE', [online], Available from: https://www.hesa.ac.uk/data-and-analysis/students/whos-in-he#numbers

HM Land Registry (2021) 'UK house price index: data downloads September 2021', 17 November, [online], Available from: https://www.gov.uk/government/statistical-data-sets/uk-house-price-index-data-downloads-september-2021

Hoare, A. and Corver, M. (2010) 'The regional geography of new young graduate labour in the UK', *Regional Studies*, 44(4): 477–94.

Holdsworth, C. (2009) '"Going away to uni": mobility, modernity, and independence of English higher education students', *Environment and Planning A*, 41(8): 1849–64.

Holdsworth, C. (2013) *Family and Intimate Mobilities*, Basingstoke: Palgrave Macmillan.

Home Office (2022) 'Fire statistics data tables', [online], Available from: https://www.gov.uk/government/statistical-data-sets/fire-statistics-data-tables

Hoolachan, J., McKee, K., Moore, T. and Soaita, A. (2017) '"Generation rent" and the ability to "settle down": economic and geographical variation in young people's housing transitions', *Journal of Youth Studies*, 20(1): 63–78.

House of Commons Health and Social Care Select Committee (2019) *First 1000 Days of Life*, London: House of Commons. Available from: https://publications.parliament.uk/pa/cm201719/cmselect/cmhealth/1496/149605.htm#_idTextAnchor002

Howard, A., Hochstenbach, C. and Ronald, R. (2021) 'Rental sector liberalization and the housing outcomes for young urban adults', Centre for Urban Studies Working Paper 55, Amsterdam: Centre for Urban Studies. Available from: https://urbanstudies.uva.nl/content/working-paper-series/working-paper-series-no.55.html

Hubers, C., Dewilde, C. and de Graaf, P.M. (2018) 'Parental marital dissolution and the intergenerational transmission of homeownership', *Housing Studies*, 33(2): 247–83.

Iacovou, M. (2010) 'Leaving home: independence, togetherness and income', *Advances in Life Course Research*, 15(4): 147–60.

IFS (2021) 'Education', *Inequality: The IFS Deaton Review*, [online], Available from: https://ifs.org.uk/inequality/themes/education/

Imeraj, L., Willaert, D., Finney, N. and Gadeyne, S. (2018) 'Cities' attraction and retention of graduates: a more-than-economic approach', *Regional Studies*, 52(8): 1086–97.

Jamieson, L. and Simpson, R. (2013) *Living Alone: Globalization, Identity and Belonging*, Basingstoke: Palgrave Macmillan.

Jessop, C. and Humphrey, A. (2014) *The Reality of Generation Rent: Perceptions of the First-time Buyer Market*, London: NatCen. Available from: http://www.natcen.ac.uk/our-research/research/the-reality-of-generation-rent/

Johnston, R., Harris, R., Jones, K., Manley, D., Sabel, C. and Wang, W. (2014) 'Mutual misunderstanding and avoidance, misrepresentations and disciplinary politics: spatial science and quantitative analysis in (United Kingdom) geographical curricula', *Dialogues in Human Geography*, 4(1): 3–25.

Judge, L. (2019) *Moving Matters*, London: Resolution Foundation. Available from: https://www.resolutionfoundation.org/publications/moving-matt ers-housing-costs-and-labour-market-mobility/

Kain, J.F. (2004) 'A pioneer's perspective on the spatial mismatch literature', *Urban Studies*, 41(1): 7–32.

Kaufmann, E. (2018) *Whiteshift: Populism, Immigration and the Future of White Majorities*, London: Allen Lane.

Kaufmann, E. and Harris, G. (2015) '"White flight" or positive contact? Local diversity and attitudes to immigration in Britain', *Comparative Political Studies*, 48(12): 1563–90.

Kemp, P.A. (2015) 'Private renting after the Global Financial Crisis', *Housing Studies*, 30(4): 601–20.

Kendig, H.L. (1984) 'Housing careers, life cycle and residential mobility: implications for the housing market', *Urban Studies*, 21(3): 271–83.

Kenyon, E. and Heath, S. (2001) 'Choosing this life: narratives of choice amongst house sharers', *Housing Studies*, 16(5): 619–35.

Khambhaita, P. and Bhopal, K. (2015) 'Home or away? The significance of ethnicity, class and attainment in the housing choices of female university students', *Race Ethnicity and Education*, 18(4): 535–66.

Kleinhans, R. and Kearns, A. (2013) 'Neighbourhood restructuring and residential relocation: towards a balanced perspective on relocation processes and outcomes', *Housing Studies*, 28(2): 163–76.

Krapf, S. and Wagner, M. (2020) 'Housing affordability, housing tenure status and household density: are housing characteristics associated with union dissolution?', *European Journal of Population*, 36: 735–64.

Kulu, H. and Steele, F. (2013) 'Interrelationships between childbearing and housing transitions in the family life course', *Demography*, 50(5): 1687–714.

Lauster, N.T. (2010) 'Housing and the proper performance of American motherhood, 1940–2005', *Housing Studies*, 25(4): 543–57.

Lennartz, C., Arundel, R. and Ronald, R. (2016) 'Younger adults and homeownership in Europe through the Global Financial Crisis', *Population, Space and Place*, 22(8): 823–35.

Lennartz, C. and Helbrecht, I. (2018) 'The housing careers of younger adults and intergenerational support in Germany's "society of renters"', *Housing Studies*, 33(2): 317–36.

Lersch, P.M. and Dewilde, C. (2015) 'Employment insecurity and first-time homeownership: evidence from twenty-two European countries', *Environment and Planning A*, 47(3): 607–24.

Lersch, P.M. and Luijkx, R. (2015) 'Intergenerational transmission of homeownership in Europe: revisiting the socialisation hypothesis', *Social Science Research*, 49: 327–42.

Lersch, P.M. and Vidal, S. (2014) 'Falling out of love and down the housing ladder: a longitudinal analysis of marital separation and home ownership', *European Sociological Review*, 30(4): 512–24.

Lesthaeghe, R. (2010) 'The unfolding story of the Second Demographic Transition', *Population and Development Review*, 36(2): 211–51.

Lewis, J., West, A., Roberts, J. and Noden, P. (2016) 'The experience of co-residence: young adults returning to the parental home after graduation in England', *Families, Relationships and Societies*, 5(2): 247–62.

Litwak, E. and Longino, C.F. (1987) 'Migration patterns among the elderly: a developmental perspective', *The Gerontologist*, 27(3): 266–72.

Lomax, N. and Stillwell, J. (2018) 'United Kingdom: temporal change in internal migration', in T. Champion, T. Cooke and I. Shuttleworth (eds) *Internal Migration in the Developed World: Are We Becoming Less Mobile?*, London: Routledge, pp 120–46.

Lowe, S. (2011) *The Housing Debate*, Bristol: Policy Press.

Lowe, S., Searle, B.A. and Smith, S.J. (2012) 'From housing wealth to mortgage debt: the emergence of Britain's asset-shaped welfare state', *Social Policy and Society*, 11(1): 105–16.

Luhmann, M., Hofmann, W., Eid, M. and Lucas, R.E. (2012) 'Subjective well-being and adaptation to life events: a meta-analysis', *Journal of Personality and Social Psychology*, 102(3): 592–615.

Lund, B. (2017) *Understanding Housing Policy* (3rd edn), Bristol: Policy Press.

Lupton, R. (2016) 'The influence(s) of housing policies on the residential moves of families with young children', *Longitudinal and Life Course Studies*, 7(3): 288–301.

McCann, M., Grundy, E. and O'Reilly, D. (2012) 'Why is housing tenure associated with a lower risk of admission to a nursing or residential home? Wealth, health and the incentive to keep "my home"', *Journal of Epidemiology and Community Health*, 66(2): 166–9.

McKee, K., Moore, T., Soaita, A. and Crawford, J. (2017a) '"Generation Rent" and the fallacy of choice', *International Journal of Urban and Regional Research*, 41(2): 318–33.

McKee, K., Muir, J. and Moore, T. (2017b) 'Housing policy in the UK: the importance of spatial nuance', *Housing Studies*, 32(1): 60–72.

McKee, M., Reeves, A., Clair, A. and Stuckler, D. (2017c) 'Living on the edge: precariousness and why it matters for health', *Archives of Public Health*, 75(13).

Malmberg, B. and Clark, W.A.V. (2021) 'Migration and neighborhood change in Sweden: the interaction of ethnic choice and income constraints, *Geographical Analysis*, 53(2): 259–82.

Mandic, S. (2008) 'Home-leaving and its structural determinants in Western and Eastern Europe: an exploratory study', *Housing Studies*, 23(4): 615–37.

Manley, D. and Johnston, R. (2014) 'School, neighbourhood and university: the geographies of educational performance and progression in England', *Applied Spatial Analysis and Policy*, 7: 259–82.

May, T. (2018) 'PM speech on making housing fairer', 5 May 2018, [online], Available from: https://www.gov.uk/government/speeches/pm-speech-on-making-housing-fairer-5-march

Meen, G. (2013) 'Homeownership for future generations in the UK', *Urban Studies*, 50(4): 637–56.

MHCLG (2016) *The Casey Review: A Review into Opportunity and Integration*, London: MHCLG.

MHCLG (2019a) 'Live Table 102', [online], Available from: www.gov.uk/government/statistical-data-sets/live-tables-on-dwelling-stock-including-vacants

MHCLG (2019b) *English Private Landlord Survey 2018: Main Report*, London: MHCLG. Available from: https://www.gov.uk/government/publications/english-private-landlord-survey-2018-main-report

MHCLG (2020a) *English Housing Survey Headline Report 2019 to 2020: Headline Report*, London: MHCLG. Available from: https://www.gov.uk/government/statistics/english-housing-survey-2019-to-2020-headline-report

MHCLG (2020b) *Planning for the Future*, London: MHCLG.

MHCLG (2021a) 'Rough sleeping snapshot in England: autumn 2020 – tables', [online], Available from: https://www.gov.uk/government/statistical-data-sets/live-tables-on-homelessness#rough-sleeping-tables

MHCLG (2021b) 'Table 100', [online], Available from: https://www.gov.uk/government/statistical-data-sets/live-tables-on-dwelling-stock-including-vacants

Michielin, F. and Mulder, C.H. (2008) 'Family events and the residential mobility of couples', *Environment and Planning A*, 40(11): 2770–90.

Michielin, F., Mulder, C.H. and Zorlu, A. (2008) 'Distance to parents and geographical mobility', *Population, Space and Place*, 14(4): 327–45.

Mikolai, J. and Kulu, H. (2018) 'Divorce, separation, and housing changes: a multiprocess analysis of longitudinal data from England and Wales', *Demography*, 55(1): 83–106.

Mikolai, J. and Kulu, H. (2019) 'Union dissolution and housing trajectories in Britain', *Demographic Research*, 41(7): 161–96.

Mikolai, J., Kulu, H. and Mulder, C.H. (2020) 'Family life transitions, residential relocations, and housing in the life course: current research and opportunities for future work', *Demographic Research*, 43(2): 35–58.

Molloy, R., Smith, C.L. and Wozniak, A. (2017) 'Job changing and the decline in long-distance migration in the United States', *Demography*, 54(2): 631–53.

Moos, M. (2016) 'From gentrification to youthification? The increasing importance of young age in delineating high-density living', *Urban Studies*, 53(14): 2903–20.

Moos, M., Revington, N., Wilkin, T. and Andrey, J. (2019) 'The knowledge economy city: gentrification, studentification and youthification, and their connections to universities', *Urban Studies*, 56(6): 1075–92.

Morris, E.W. and Winter, M. (1975) 'A theory of family housing adjustment', *Journal of Marriage and Family*, 37(1): 79–88.

Morrison, P.S. and Clark, W.A.V. (2011) 'Internal migration and employment: macro flows and micro motives', *Environment and Planning A*, 43(8): 1948–64.

Morrison, P.S. and Clark, W.A.V. (2016) 'Loss aversion and duration of residence', *Demographic Research*, 35(36): 1079–100.

Mortimer, J.T. and Moen, P. (2016) 'The changing social construction of age and the life course: precarious identity and enactment of "early" and "encore" stages of adulthood', in M.J. Shanahan, J.T. Mortimer and M. Kirkpatrick Johnson (eds) (2016) *Handbook of the Life Course: Volume II*, Cham, Switzerland: Springer, pp 111–29.

Mulder, C.H. (1996) 'Housing choice: assumptions and approaches', *Netherlands Journal of Housing and the Built Environment*, 11(3): 209–32.

Mulder, C.H. (2006) 'Population and housing: a two-sided relationship', *Demographic Research*, 15(13): 401–12.

Mulder, C.H. (2013) 'Family dynamics and housing: conceptual issues and empirical findings', *Demographic Research*, 29(14): 355–78.

Mulder, C.H. (2018) 'Putting family centre stage: ties to nonresident family, internal migration, and immobility', *Demographic Research*, 39(43): 1151–80.

Mulder, C.H. and Billari, F.C. (2010) 'Homeownership regimes and low fertility', *Housing Studies*, 25(4): 527–41.

Mulder, C.H. and Hooimeijer, P. (1999) 'Residential relocations in the life course', in L. van Wissen and P. Dykstra (eds) *Population Issues: An Interdisciplinary Focus*, New York: Kluwer Academic/Plenum Publishers, pp 159–86.

Mulder, C.H. and Malmberg, G. (2011) 'Moving related to separation: who moves and to what distance', *Environment and Planning A*, 43(11): 2589–607.

Mulder, C.H. and Wagner, M. (2010) 'Union dissolution and mobility: who moves from the family home after separation?', *Journal of Marriage and Family*, 72(5): 1263–73.

Mulder, C.H., Dewilde, C., van Duijn, M. and Smits, A. (2015) 'The association between parents' and adult children's homeownership: a comparative analysis', *European Journal of Population*, 31(5): 495–527.

Murie, A. (2016) *The Right to Buy? Selling off Public and Social Housing*, Bristol: Policy Press.

Murphy, L. (2018) *The Invisible Land: The Hidden Force Driving the UK's Unequal Economy and Broken Housing Market (IPPR Commission on Economic Justice, Discussion Paper)*, London: IPPR. Available from: https://www.ippr. org/files/2018-08/cej-land-tax-august18.pdf

Myers, D. (1999) 'Cohort longitudinal estimation of housing careers', *Housing Studies*, 14(4): 473–90.

Myers, D. and Ryu, S. (2008) 'Aging baby boomers and the generational housing bubble: foresight and mitigation of an epic transition', *Journal of the American Planning Association*, 74(1): 17–33.

Nowok, B., Findlay, A.M. and McCollum, D. (2018) 'Linking desires and behaviour of residential relocation with life domain satisfaction', *Urban Studies*, 55(4): 870–90.

OECD (2018) *Health at a Glance: Europe 2018: State of Health in the EU Cycle*, Paris/Brussels: OECD/European Union. Available from: https:// doi.org/10.1787/health_glance_eur-2018-en

Ong, R., Parkinson, S., Searle, B.A., Smith, S.J. and Wood, G.A. (2013) 'Channels from housing wealth to consumption', *Housing Studies*, 28(7): 1012–36.

ONS (2013a) '2011 census analysis: immigration patterns of non-UK born populations in England and Wales in 2011', [online], Available from: https://www.ons.gov.uk/peoplepopulationandcommunity/populat ionandmigration/internationalmigration/articles/immigrationpatternsofn onukbornpopulationsinenglandandwalesin2011/2013-12-17

ONS (2013b) 'Ethnicity and country of birth', [online], Available from: https://www.ons.gov.uk/peoplepopulationandcommunity/populat ionandmigration/populationestimates/bulletins/keystatisticsandquickstat isticsforlocalauthoritiesintheunitedkingdom/2013-10-11#ethnicity-and-country-of-birth

ONS (2014), 'Average (mean) household size', [online], Available from: https://www.ons.gov.uk/peoplepopulationandcommunity/birthsdea thsandmarriages/families/articles/householdsandhouseholdcompositionin englandandwales/2014-05-29#average-mean-household-size

ONS (2015a) 'Population estimates by marital status and living arrangements, England and Wales: 2002 to 2014', [online], Available from: https://www. ons.gov.uk/peoplepopulationandcommunity/populationandmigration/ populationestimates/bulletins/populationestimatesbymaritalstatusandliv ingarrangements/2015-07-08

ONS (2015b) 'English life tables no.17: 2010 to 2012', [online], Available from: https://www.ons.gov.uk/peoplepopulationandcommunity/birth sdeathsandmarriages/lifeexpectancies/bulletins/englishlifetablesno17/ 2015-09-01

ONS (2016) 'Travel to Work Area analysis in Great Britain: 2016', [online], Available from: https://www.ons.gov.uk/employmentandlabourmarket/peopleinwork/employmentandemployeetypes/articles/traveltoworkareaanalysisingreatbritain/2016

ONS (2017) 'Births by parents' characteristics in England and Wales: 2016', [online], Available from: https://www.ons.gov.uk/peoplepopulationandcommunity/birthsdeathsandmarriages/livebirths/bulletins/birthsbyparentscharacteristicsinenglandandwales/2016

ONS (2018a) 'Young adults living with parents, regions of England and UK constituent countries, 1996 to 2017', [online], Available from: https://www.ons.gov.uk/peoplepopulationandcommunity/birthsdeathsandmarriages/families/adhocs/008992youngadultslivingwithparentsregionsofenglandandukconstituentcountries1996to2017

ONS (2018b) 'Trends in self-employment in the UK', [online], Available from: https://www.ons.gov.uk/employmentandlabourmarket/peopleinwork/employmentandemployeetypes/articles/trendsinselfemploymentintheuk/2018-02-07

ONS (2019a) 'Life expectancy at a local level in the UK', [online], Available from: https://www.ons.gov.uk/peoplepopulationandcommunity/healthandsocialcare/healthandlifeexpectancies/bulletins/healthstatelifeexpectanciesuk/2016to2018#life-expectancy-at-a-local-level-in-the-uk

ONS (2019b) 'Disability and housing, UK: 2019', [online], Available from: https://www.ons.gov.uk/peoplepopulationandcommunity/healthandsocialcare/disability/bulletins/disabilityandhousinguk/2019

ONS (2020a) 'Marriages in England and Wales: 2017', [online], Available from: https://www.ons.gov.uk/peoplepopulationandcommunity/birthsdeathsandmarriages/marriagecohabitationandcivilpartnerships/bulletins/marriagesinenglandandwalesprovisional/2017

ONS (2020b) 'Divorces in England and Wales: 2019', [online], Available from: https://www.ons.gov.uk/peoplepopulationandcommunity/birthsdeathsandmarriages/divorce/bulletins/divorcesinenglandandwales/2019

ONS (2021a) 'Births in England and Wales: summary tables', [online], Available from: https://www.ons.gov.uk/peoplepopulationandcommunity/birthsdeathsandmarriages/livebirths/datasets/birthsummarytables

ONS (2021b) 'Young adults living with their parents', [online], Available from: https://www.ons.gov.uk/peoplepopulationandcommunity/birthsdeathsandmarriages/families/datasets/youngadultslivingwiththeirparents

ONS (2021c) 'Estimates of the population for the UK, England and Wales, Scotland and Northern Ireland', [online], Available from: https://www.ons.gov.uk/peoplepopulationandcommunity/populationandmigration/populationestimates/datasets/populationestimatesforukenglandandwalesscotlandandnorthernireland

ONS (2022a) 'Household total wealth in Great Britain: April 2018 to March 2020', [online], Available from: https://www.ons.gov.uk/peoplepopulat ionandcommunity/personalandhouseholdfinances/incomeandwealth/ bulletins/totalwealthingreatbritain/april2018tomarch2020

ONS (2022b) 'Female employment rate (aged 16 to 64, seasonally adjusted): %', [online], Available from: https://www.ons.gov.uk/employ mentandlabourmarket/peopleinwork/employmentandemployeetypes/tim eseries/lf25/lms

Oswald, A. (2009) 'The housing market and Europe's unemployment: a non-technical paper', in C. van Ewijk and M. van Leuvensteijn (eds) *Homeownership and the Labour Market in Europe*, Oxford: Oxford University Press, pp 43–51.

Paccoud, A. (2017) 'Buy-to-let gentrification: extending social change through tenure shifts', *Environment and Planning A*, 49(4): 839–56.

Pais, J., South, S.J. and Crowder, K. (2012) 'Metropolitan heterogeneity and minority neighborhood attainment: spatial assimilation or place stratification?', *Social Problems*, 59(2): 258–81.

Peach, C. (1996) 'Good segregation, bad segregation', *Planning Perspectives*, 11(4): 379–98.

Pettersson, A. and Malmberg, G. (2009) 'Adult children and elderly parents as mobility attractions in Sweden', *Population, Space and Place*, 15(4): 343–57.

Phillips, D. (2007) 'Ethnic and racial segregation: a critical perspective', *Geography Compass*, 1(5): 1138–59.

Piekut, A. (2021) 'Re-theorising spatial segregation: a European perspective', in G. Pryce, Y.P. Wang, Y. Chen, J. Shan and H. Wei (eds) *Urban Inequality and Segregation in Europe and China: Towards a New Dialogue*, Cham, Switzerland: Springer, pp 13–38.

Plane, D.A., Henrie, C.J. and Perry, M.J. (2005) 'Migration up and down the urban hierarchy and across the life course', *Proceedings of the American National Academy of Sciences*, 102(43): 15313–18.

Preece, J. (2018) 'Immobility and insecure labour markets: an active response to precarious employment', *Urban Studies*, 55(8): 1783–99.

Preece, J., Crawford, J., McKee K., Flint, J. and Robinson, D. (2020) 'Understanding changing housing aspirations: a review of the evidence', *Housing Studies*, 35(1): 87–106.

Rabe, B. and Taylor, M. (2010) 'Residential mobility, quality of neighbourhood and life course events', *Journal of the Royal Statistical Society: Series A*, 173(3): 531–55.

Race Disparity Unit (2020) 'Ethnicity facts and figures', [online], Available from: https://www.ethnicity-facts-figures.service.gov.uk/

Race Disparity Unit (2021) 'Work, pay and benefits', [online], Available from: https://www.ethnicity-facts-figures.service.gov.uk/work-pay-and-benefits

Rainer, H. and Smith, I. (2010) 'Staying together for the sake of the home? House price shocks and partnership dissolution in the UK', *Journal of the Royal Statistical Society: Series A*, 173(3): 557–74.

Ramsay, S., Grundy, E. and O'Reilly, D. (2013) 'The relationship between informal caregiving and mortality: an analysis using the ONS Longitudinal Study of England and Wales', *Journal of Epidemiology and Community Health*, 67(8): 655–60.

Reeves, A., Clair, A., McKee, M. and Stuckler, D. (2016) 'Reductions in the United Kingdom's government housing benefit and symptoms of depression in low-income households', *American Journal of Epidemiology*, 184(6): 421–9.

Reid, L. (2021) 'Home as riskscape: exploring technology enabled care', *The Geographical Journal*, 187(2): 85–97.

Reuschke, D. (2016) 'The importance of housing for self-employment', *Economic Geography*, 92(4): 378–400.

Robards, J., Evandrou, M., Falkingham, J. and Vlachantoni, A. (2014) 'Mortality at older ages and moves in residential and sheltered housing: evidence from the UK', *Journal of Epidemiology and Community Health*, 68(6): 524–9.

Robinson, D. (2005) 'The search for community cohesion: key themes and dominant concepts of the public policy agenda', *Urban Studies*, 42(8): 1411–27.

Robson, B., Lymperopoulou, K. and Rae, A. (2008) 'People on the move: exploring the functional roles of deprived neighbourhoods', *Environment and Planning A*, 40(11): 2693–714.

Rodríguez-Pose, A. and Storper, M. (2020) 'Housing, urban growth and inequalities: the limits to deregulation and upzoning in reducing economic and spatial inequality', *Urban Studies*, 57(2): 223–48.

Ronald, R. (2008) *The Ideology of Home Ownership: Homeowner Societies and the Role of Housing*, Basingstoke: Palgrave Macmillan.

Ronald, R. and Kadi, J. (2018) 'The revival of private landlords in Britain's post-homeownership society', *New Political Economy*, 23(6): 786–803.

Roseman, C.C. (1971) 'Migration as a spatial and temporal process', *Annals of the Association of American Geographers*, 61(3): 589–98.

Rossi, P.H. (1955) *Why Families Move: A Study in the Social Psychology of Urban Residential Mobility*, Glencoe, IL: Free Press.

Sabater, A., Graham, E. and Finney, N. (2018) *(Un)Affordable Housing and the Residential Separation of Age Groups*, ESRC Centre for Population Change (Briefing 45, November 2018), Southampton: ESRC Centre for Population Change. Available from: http://www.cpc.ac.uk/docs/BP45_UnAffordable_housing_and_the_residential_separation_of_age_groups.pdf

Sage, J., Evandrou, M. and Falkingham, J. (2013) 'Onwards or homewards? Complex graduate migration pathways, well-being, and the "parental safety net"', *Population, Space and Place*, 19(6): 738–55.

Samuel, G. (2012) 'Islam and the family in Bangladesh and the UK: the background to our study', *Culture and Religion*, 13(2): 141–58.

Saunders, P. (1990) *A Nation of Homeowners*, London: Unwin Hyman.

Saunders, P. and Williams, P. (1988) 'The constitution of the home: towards a research agenda', *Housing Studies*, 3(2): 81–93.

Savage, M., Allen, C., Atkinson, R., Burrows, R., Méndez, M.-L., Watt, P. et al (2010) 'Focus article', *Housing, Theory and Society*, 27(2): 115–61.

Shanahan, M.J., Mortimer, J.T. and Kirkpatrick Johnson, M. (eds) (2016) *Handbook of the Life Course: Volume II*, Cham, Switzerland: Springer.

Sharkey, P. (2008) 'The intergenerational transmission of context', *American Journal of Sociology*, 113(4): 931–69.

Shaw, M. (2004) 'Housing and public health', *Annual Review of Public Health*, 25(1): 397–418.

Shiffer-Sebba, D. and Park, H. (2021) 'US baby boomers' homeownership trajectories across the life course: a Sequence Analysis approach', *Demographic Research*, 44(43): 1057–72.

Singleton, A., Pavlis, M. and Longley, P.A. (2016) 'The stability of geodemographic cluster assignments over an intercensal period', *Journal of Geographical Systems* 18(2): 97–123.

Smith, D.P. and Higley, R. (2012) 'Circuits of education, rural gentrification, and family migration from the global city', *Journal of Rural Studies*, 28(1): 49–55.

Smith, D.P. and Holt, L. (2007) 'Studentification and "apprentice" gentrifiers within Britain's provincial towns and cities: extending the meaning of gentrification', *Environment and Planning A*, 39(1): 142–61.

Smith, S.J., Searle, B.A. and Cook, N. (2009) 'Rethinking the risks of home ownership', *Journal of Social Policy*, 38(1): 83–102.

Smock, P. (1993) 'The economic costs of marital disruption for young women over the past two decades', *Demography*, 30(3): 353–71.

South, S.J. and Lei, L. (2015) 'Failures-to-launch and boomerang kids: contemporary determinants of leaving and returning to the parental home', *Social Forces*, 94(2): 863–90.

Spallek, M., Haynes, M. and Jones, A. (2014) 'Holistic housing pathways for Australian families through the childbearing years', *Longitudinal and Life Course Studies*, 5(2): 205–26.

Stockdale, A. and Catney, G. (2014) 'A life course perspective on urban–rural migration: the importance of the local context', *Population, Space and Place*, 20(1): 83–98.

Stone, J., Berrington, A. and Falkingham, J. (2011) 'The changing determinants of UK young adults' living arrangements', *Demographic Research*, 25: 629–66.

Stone, J., Berrington, A. and Falkingham, J. (2014) 'Gender, turning points, and boomerangs: returning home in young adulthood in Great Britain', *Demography*, 51(1): 257–76.

Sturgis, P., Brunton-Smith, I., Kuha, J. and Jackson, J. (2014) 'Ethnic diversity, segregation and the social cohesion of neighbourhoods in London', *Ethnic and Racial Studies*, 37(8): 1286–309.

Suh, E. (2020) 'Young British adults' homeownership circumstances and the role of intergenerational transfers', *Longitudinal and Life Course Studies*, 11(3): 383–407.

Tammaru, T., Knapp, D., Silm, S., van Ham, M. and Witlox, F. (2021) 'Spatial underpinnings of social inequalities: a vicious circles of segregation approach', *Social Inclusion*, 9(2): 65–76.

Taylor, M.P., Pevalin, D.J. and Todd, J. (2007) 'The psychological costs of unsustainable housing commitments', *Psychological Medicine*, 37(7): 1027–36.

Thomas, M.J. (2019) 'Employment, education, and family: revealing the motives behind internal migration in Great Britain', *Population, Space and Place*, 25(4): e2233.

Thomas, M.J. and Mulder, C.H. (2016) 'Partnership patterns and homeownership: a cross-country comparison of Germany, the Netherlands and the United Kingdom', *Housing Studies*, 31(8): 935–63.

Thomas, M.J., Mulder, C.H. and Cooke, T.J. (2017) 'Linked lives and constrained spatial mobility: the case of moves related to separation among families with children', *Transactions of the Institute of British Geographers*, 42(4): 597–611.

Thomas, M.J., Stillwell, J.C.H. and Gould, M.I. (2016) 'Modelling the duration of residence and plans for future residential relocation: a multilevel analysis', *Transactions of the Institute of British Geographers*, 41(3): 297–312.

Tinson, A. and Clair, A. (2020) 'Better housing is crucial for our health and the COVID-19 recovery', 28 December 2020, [online], Available from: https://www.health.org.uk/publications/long-reads/better-housing-is-crucial-for-our-health-and-the-covid-19-recovery

Tocchioni, V., Berrington, A., Vignoli, D. and Vitali, A. (2021) 'The changing association between homeownership and the transition to parenthood', *Demography*, 58(5): 1843–65.

Valuations Office Agency (2020) 'Table CT SOP 4.0', [online], Available from: https://www.gov.uk/government/statistics/council-tax-stock-of-properties-2020

van Ewijk, C. and van Leuvensteijn, M. (2009) 'Introduction and policy implications', in C. van Ewijk and M. van Leuvensteijn (eds) *Homeownership and the Labour Market in Europe*, Oxford: Oxford University Press, pp 1–11.

van Ham, M., Hedman, L., Manley, D., Coulter, R. and Östh, J. (2014) 'Intergenerational transmission of neighbourhood poverty: an analysis of neighbourhood histories of individuals', *Transactions of the Institute of British Geographers*, 39(3): 402–17.

Wagner, M., Mulder, C.H., Weiß, B. and Krapf, S. (2019) 'The transition from living apart together to a coresidential partnership', *Advances in Life Course Research*, 39(11): 77–86.

Wheaton, B. and Gotlib, I.H. (1997) 'Trajectories and turning points over the life course: concepts and themes', in I.H. Gotlib and B. Wheaton (eds) *Stress and Adversity over the Life Course: Trajectories and Turning Points*, Cambridge: Cambridge University Press, pp 1–25.

Wheaton, W.C. (1990) 'Vacancy, search, and prices in a housing market matching model', *Journal of Political Economy*, 98(6): 1270–92.

Wilkinson, E. and Ortega-Alcázar, I. (2017) 'A home of one's own? Housing welfare for "young adults" in times of austerity', *Critical Social Policy*, 37(3): 329–47.

Wilkinson, E. and Ortega-Alcázar, I. (2019) 'Stranger danger? The intersectional impacts of shared housing on young people's health and wellbeing', *Health and Place*, 60: e102191.

Wood, G., Parkinson, S., Searle, B.A. and Smith, S.J. (2013) 'Motivations for equity borrowing: a welfare-switching effect', *Urban Studies*, 50(12): 2588–607.

Wood, G., Smith, S.J., Cigdem, M. and Ong, R. (2017) 'Life on the edge: a perspective on precarious home ownership in Australia and the UK', *International Journal of Housing Policy*, 17(2): 201–26.

Zhang, M.L. and Pryce, G. (2020) 'The dynamics of poverty, employment and access to amenities in polycentric cities: measuring the decentralisation of poverty and its impacts in England and Wales', *Urban Studies*, 57(10): 2015–30.

Index

References to figures appear in *italic* type; those in **bold** type refer to tables.